Armed Forces in Deeply Divided Societies

International Comparative Social Studies

Editor-in-Chief

Mehdi P. Amineh
(*Amsterdam Institute for Social Science Research, University of Amsterdam, and International Institute for Asian Studies, Leiden University*)

Editorial Board

Shahrough Akhavi (*Columbia University*)
W.A. Arts (*University College Utrecht*)
Sjoerd Beugelsdijk (*Radboud University*)
Mark-Anthony Falzon (*University of Malta*)
Harald Fuhr (*University of Potsdam*)
Joyeeta Gupta (*University of Amsterdam*)
Xiaoming Huang (*Victoria University Wellington*)
Nilgün Önder (*University of Regina*)
Gerhard Preyer (*Goethe University Frankfurt am Main*)
Islam Qasem (*Webster University, Leiden*)
Kurt W. Radtke (*International Institute for Asian Studies, Leiden University*)
Mahmoud Sadri (*Texas Woman's University*)
Jeremy Smith (*University of Eastern Finland*)
Ngo Tak-Wing (*Leiden University*)
L.A. Visano (*York University*)

VOLUME 57

The titles published in this series are listed at *brill.com/icss*

Armed Forces in Deeply Divided Societies

Power Sharing and Militaries in Lebanon, Bosnia, Iraq and Burundi

By

Eduardo Wassim Aboultaif

BRILL

LEIDEN | BOSTON

Originally published in hardback in 2023.

Cover illustration: by Eduardo Wassim Aboultaif. Cover design: by Samer Aljawhary

The Library of Congress has cataloged the hardcover edition as follows:

Names: Aboultaif, Eduardo Wassim, author.
Title: Armed forces in deeply divided societies: Lebanon, Bosnia-Herzegovina, Iraq and Burundi : militaries in power-sharing systems / by Eduardo Wassim Aboultaif.
Description: Leiden ; Boston : Brill, [2024] | Series: International comparative social studies, 1568-4474 ; vol. 57 | Includes bibliographical references and index.
Identifiers: LCCN 2023040213 (print) | LCCN 2023040214 (ebook) | ISBN 9789004686687 (hardcover) | ISBN 9789004687080 (ebook)
Subjects: LCSH: Lebanon–Armed Forces–Case studies. | Bosnia and Herzegovina–Armed Forces–Case studies. | Iraq–Armed Forces–Case studies. | Burundi–Armed Forces–Case studies. | Civil-military relations–Lebanon–Case studies. | Civil-military relations–Bosnia and Herzegovina–Case studies. | Civil-military relations–Iraq–Case studies. | Civil-military relations–Burundi–Case studies.
Classification: LCC UA10 .A26 2024 (print) | LCC UA10 (ebook) | DDC 355–dc23/eng/20230831
LC record available at https://lccn.loc.gov/2023040213
LC ebook record available at https://lccn.loc.gov/2023040214

Typeface for the Latin, Greek, and Cyrillic scripts: "Brill". See and download: brill.com/brill-typeface.

ISSN 1568-4474
ISBN 978-90-04-72013-8 (paperback, 2024)
ISBN 978-90-04-68668-7 (hardback)
ISBN 978-90-04-68708-0 (e-book)

Copyright 2024 by Eduardo Wassim Aboultaif. Published by Koninklijke Brill NV, Leiden, The Netherlands.
Koninklijke Brill NV incorporates the imprints Brill, Brill Nijhoff, Brill Schöningh, Brill Fink, Brill mentis, Brill Wageningen Academic, Vandenhoeck & Ruprecht, Böhlau and V&R unipress.
Koninklijke Brill NV reserves the right to protect this publication against unauthorized use. Requests for re-use and/or translations must be addressed to Koninklijke Brill NV via brill.com or copyright.com.

This book is printed on acid-free paper and produced in a sustainable manner.

To Dalia
The Love of my heart, the blessing of my life

To William Harris
The Teacher, Historian, Political Scientist, Geographer, and Friend

To Nassif Hitti
The Diplomat, Scholar, Politician and Arabist

To Theodor Hanf
The Scholarly Lord with a touch of Eminence

To Fr. Talal Hachem
For his Leadership and Wisdom

To My Parents, Walid and Samira, and Sister, Jennifer
Without you, nothing would be possible

He who fears a human like him shall be his slave.
DRUZE EPISTLE

Contents

Acknowledgements XI
List of Figures and Tables XII

1 **Introduction** 1
　1　A Critical Approach to Armies in Divided Societies　1
　2　Framework and Aim of the Book　3
　3　The Significance of Armies in Divided Societies and Research Method　5
　4　Chapters　6

2 **Civil-Military Relations, SSR, DDR, and Power Sharing**　9
　1　Civil-Military Relations　9
　2　DDR and Security Sector Reform (SSR)　17
　3　Post-Conflict Power Sharing and Security Apparatuses　21
　4　Conclusion　28

3 **The Lebanese Armed Forces**　29
　1　Origins: The LAF during the Mandate Period　30
　2　The Army after Independence　32
　　2.1　*The Formation of the Lebanese Army*　33
　　2.2　*Problems and Challenges*　35
　3　Paying the Price: Disintegration during the Civil War　42
　4　Structural and Institutional Reforms of the Lebanese Armed Forces (LAF)　45
　　4.1　*Structural Reforms in the LAF*　45
　　4.2　*The Institutional Reforms*　48
　　　4.2.1　The Higher Defense Council　48
　　　4.2.2　The Military Office　49
　5　Reconstructing the LAF　52
　6　Challenges and Responses　58
　　6.1　*Military Capabilities*　58
　　6.2　*Legitimacy and National Consensus*　59
　　6.3　*Confessional-Proofing in the LAF – Preserving Neutrality*　63
　　6.4　*Gender and Human Rights*　65
　7　Conclusion　67

4 Armed Forces of Bosnia and Herzegovina   70
1   The Yugoslav People's Army (Jugoslovenska Narodna Armija, JNA)   71
2   The Making of the AFBiH   76
3   Institutional and Structural Reforms in the AFBiH   81
      3.1 *Institutional Reforms*   82
      3.2 *Structural Reforms*   86
4   Success and Setbacks   92
5   Conclusion   96

5 The Iraqi Armed Forces   98
1   Inception: The Establishment of the Iraqi Army   99
2   Bakr Sidqi and the Rise of as-Sabbagh   102
3   The Republic of Abdul-Karim Qassim   105
4   The Rise of the Baath and the Baathification of the Army   108
5   The Army and the Baath   109
6   Reconstructing the IAF after the 2003 Invasion   115
      6.1 *CPA Civil-Military Decisions*   115
7   The Reconstruction Framework of the Iraqi Army   118
      7.1 *The New IAF*   118
8   Problems and Challenges in the IAF   122
      8.1 *Professionalism*   123
      8.2 *Civil-Military Ambiguity*   126
      8.3 *Corruption*   130
9   ISIS, the PMF and the Retraining of the Iraqi Military   131
10   Conclusion   136

6 The National Defense Force of Burundi   137
1   Burundi: The Colonial Period and Independence   138
2   The Army in Power   140
      2.1 *Micombero*   140
      2.2 *Bagaza*   141
      2.3 *Buyoya*   143
3   The Hutu Response   144
4   Arusha and Pretoria   145
5   Institutional and Structural Changes in the Armed Forces   148
      5.1 *Institutional Reforms*   149
      5.2 *Structural Reforms*   150
6   From Success to Failure: CNDD-FDD Hegemony in Security Affairs   153

7	CNDD-FDD Hegemony in the Army 155	
	7.1	*FDD Preferentialism and Elimination of Opponents* 155
	7.2	*Alternative Chain of Command and the Imbonerakure* 157
	7.3	*The National Intelligence Service (SNR) and the CNDD-FDD* 159
8	The Dangers of CNDD-FDD Politicization of the Army 161	
9	Conclusion 163	

7 Armies in Consociational, Semi-Consociational, and Post-Conflict Societies: The Quest for Stability 165
1 Armies, Deeply Divided Societies and Non-Democratic Systems 165
2 CMR and Semi-Consociationalism 168
3 CMR in Full Consociations 173
4 Post-Conflict Armies and Military Power Sharing 176
    4.1 *Military Mission* 176
    4.2 *Collective Decision Making and Military Power Sharing* 178
    4.3 *Proportionality* 181
5 Anomalies in Lebanon, Iraq, and Burundi: Militias 182
6 Conclusion 187

8 Conclusion 188
1 Armies and Consociationalism 189
2 Post-Conflict Military Reconstruction 190
3 Recommendation 191

Bibliography 193
Index 214

Acknowledgements

During the process of writing I benefitted from the amble knowledge of colleagues like Reginas Ndayiragije who expanded my humble knowledge of Burundi, and Damir Kapidzic from Bosnia-Herzegovina enlightened me on the complex relationship of the ethnic groups in the country. Joanne McEvoy, Allison McCulloch and Soeren Keil have had important input on the subject matter and helped me sharpen my analysis through many conversations we had. I learned a lot from John Nagle and his wary position on power-sharing settlements.

I am also thankful to the reviewers, Brill Publishers, editors Jason Prevost, Mehdi Amineh, and assistant editor Debbie de Wit for patiently dealing with my delays and inquiries.

Last by not least, I am thankful to my wife, Dalia Aljawhary for being a beautiful soul in this life's journey, always smiling and shining, bringing life to my life. My parents have been of tremendous support, my sister Jennifer and my brother-in-law Kamal, and their two beautiful sons, Ayan and Revan make our life glamorous. I cannot forget my father-in-law and mother-in-law for their unequivocal support, in addition to Dalia's two brothers, Samer and Akram.

Figures and Tables

Figures

1   Chain of Command of the Lebanese Armed Forces   68
2   Chain of Command according to the 2003 law on defense   87
3   Chain of command according to the 2005 law on defense   88
4   Chain of Command of the Army of Burundi   164

Table

1   Ethnic composition of the AFBiH   74

CHAPTER 1

Introduction

1 A Critical Approach to Armies in Divided Societies

On 14 March 2005, rumors spread in Lebanon that the army would not allow the anti-Syria opposition to gather in the center of Beirut, Martyrs' Square, to demonstrate against Syria's military and political influence in Lebanon. Indeed, the army raised roadblocks around the Square, while hundreds of thousands of demonstrators gathered peacefully, trying to negotiate with army personnel to allow them to pass the roadblock. Hours before the demonstration, no one knew what the army will do: will it force citizens to go back home? Will it shoot them at will? Will it stand aside and let the demonstration happen? President Emile Lahoud called Army Commander Michel Suleiman, and told him that soldiers should beat the demonstrators with their rifles to prevent the gathering. However, just before noon, the army opened the roadblocks, demonstrators were allowed into the Square, citizens were seen giving roses to soldiers on the street, and then the biggest demonstration in Lebanon's history (a million and half according to some estimates) took place that day. The question that I had that day, as a teenager, was why did the army commander reject the orders of the president?

Three years later, in early May 2008, the Lebanese government took an ill decision to confiscate the private telecommunication of Hezbollah. The response was that Hezbollah on 7 May, the party laid siege to the houses of Sunni leader Saad Hariri and Druze leader Walid Joumblatt in Beirut, then moved on to control the entrance to Beirut from the south of the city, and occupied most of West Beirut within hours. On 11 May they tried to take Shwaifet, a Druze stronghold supporting Joumblatt, and attempted to occupy strategic positions in another Druze stronghold in Aley mountains (referred to locally as the triple 8 – *Tlet Itmenent*) which overlooks the southern suburbs of Beirut (Hezbollah's stronghold). They were repelled by local Druze townsmen after heavy armed clashes. That night, Hezbollah attempted to take control of the supra-strategic Niha Mountains in Shouf region. They tried to break in from the Bekaa valley, specifically from the town of Meshgara, but local Druze townsmen were already there waiting for a possible attack. The Niha Mountains are so important that they have an unobstructed view from Cyprus north-west to Syria to the east, and Israel to the south. Hezbollah's aim was to break the Joumblatt stronghold in his area, Shouf, but local townsmen successfully encircled Hezbollah's militants. A compromise was reached that night, Hezbollah would withdraw with all its equipment and men, and a truce would be announced. The result was the Doha agreement that laid the ground for reconciliation, presidential elections, the formation of a government of national unity, and elections to be followed based on a consensual electoral law. The question, again, which I asked as an undergraduate political science student, was why did the army refrain from using force against any of the groups engaged in this limited warfare?

A series of events happened elsewhere in the region with the Arab Uprisings, particularly in Yemen, Libya and Syria. Armies took sides in the uprising with or against the regime, and eventually they disintegrated. The shock, however, was in Iraq. A country rebuilt on semi-consociational principles of power sharing and a newly built army by the Americans who spent billions of dollars on the country. During the Arab Uprising, I remember seeing the Iraqi army on TV shooting peaceful demonstrators in western Iraq, by orders from prime minister Nouri al-Maliki. I read about the army attacking peaceful demonstrators on orders from al-Maliki. Then, in 2014, ISIS emerged in Syria and took over west Iraq and Mosul in the north, even threatening Baghdad. The army in Mosul looked like a leaf falling of a tree during the autumn season. Again, the question I asked at that time as a PhD student was why did the army use violence against peaceful demonstrators in Iraq and how come did it fall so quickly to ISIS?

As I began working on ethnic conflict and deeply divided societies, I encountered the problems arising in civil-military relations and the setup armed forces. I saw that armies function very differently from one place to another, and many developing countries allow the head of executive to use the army to crush rebellions. In other cases, the weakness and inefficiency of civilian authorities allowed armies to intervene for long periods in politics, examples of which are Burundi, a case study in this book, and Iraq. The philosophy of the Lebanese army to refrain from using violence against any group when the crisis is political (except in 1972 which eventually led to its disintegration), is in contrast to the Iraqi and Burundian armies. In Yugoslavia, the Serbian domination of the army gave the community an edge in domestic politics. Hence, when the Balkan war erupted in the 1990s, the army was used by nationalist Serb politicians as an instrument to subordinate other communities. Consequently, the case of the army in Bosnia-Herzegovina, a deeply divided society that emerged after massacres and genocides during the war, is important to study to see the way the post-war army is managed. Therefore, I ask a further question in this book: How do armies in deeply divided societies preserve their legitimacy and *esprit de corps* if it attacks an ethnic community that is raising its grievances against the state, or in case of civil strife between different ethnic groups? Since all the case studies show that these countries have passed through phases of civil wars that required a peace settlement. I look at armies in the post-conflict environment to see how they are produced in the context of power sharing arrangements. By linking the establishment of armies to peace settlement and the power sharing arrangement, I can see if the success or failure is related to full or semi-consociational mode that is applied and their impact on CMR.

2   Framework and Aim of the Book

The question of civil-military relations, or in other words the relationship between the armies and civilian authorities, dates back to ancient empires. Emperors, kings, and princes built armies and controlled them. Nero ordered the army to burn Rome, his Imperial capital, to satisfy what he believed to be an artistic desire to see a beautiful city in flames; Julius Caesar exploited his position as commander of the Roman army to rule the empire; Alexander the Great marched with his army through the known part of the world at his time, in a political, military, social and spiritual enterprise, something never done before or after him. These were the days of Kingdoms: armies responded to one single person, the ruler.

In the modern world we still see cases of one ruler being the supreme leader of the armed forces, mostly in non-democratic regimes: Iranian supreme leaders, the presidents of China, North Korea, Syria, and many other places. In these systems, leaders decide whether to deploy the army to crush any domestic opposition, so the relationship is very straightforward. However, the first scholar who contributed CMR by creating an independent academic paradigm was Samuel Huntington, who studied CMR in the USA and later on moved to study CMR in other democratic systems in the developed world. He wrote that armies and societies should maintain a distance, in order to prevent military intervention in politics. In response to his work, Morris Janowiwtz believed that a subjective approach is better for states, especially if they are newly created. This subjective approach calls for further integration of armed forces into society. Huntington's approach is best applied in the developed world, where a president or prime minister is a supreme commander of the army with extensive authority over the military. On the other hand, Janowitz began his work by proposing a theory of CMR for all of the newly-independent states. At a later stage did Janowitz argue for the need to move in CMR with a regional approach: dividing the world into regions by using geography, politics, and cultural criteria to analyze CMR.[1] In this book, I believe that regional approaches are not necessarily applicable in the study of armies in divided societies. The Lebanese army has more in common with BiH's army then with its Syrian neighbor, or the Israeli army for instance. The army in Burundi has nothing in common with South Africa, but it is actually closer to the Iraqi army. From this point, it is important to move beyond the regional approach and create a new dimension for the study of armed forces. Hence, it is the contention of the author that armies in divided societies – states with ethnic, tribal, linguistic or sectarian divisions – with a power sharing political system, require comparative analysis of their respective armies. The way armies are made up, function, and created in deeply divided societies are different than those in non-divided places. The example of states in the developed world cannot be applied in such cases, nor in developing countries where there are no deep divisions. Consequently, this book also asks how do armies function in divided societies? What happens when armies do not respect communal coexistence and intervene in politics, whether by their own decision or through a civilian government? How are armies created in a post-conflict environment? What are the requirements of power sharing in building armies that can promote stability? How does military power sharing help avoid disintegration and empower the legitimacy of armed forces?

I am looking at four case studies which share the central characteristic of being deeply divided: Lebanon is deeply divided according to sectarian lines, Iraq is divided by a combination of ethnic and sectarian identities, Bosnia and Herzegovina (BiH) has ethnic divisions, and finally Burundi also has ethnic divisions. In addition to these divisions, the cases at hand passed through a phase of civil war, where the army either disintegrated or was used by the dominant ethnic group to fight other communities. When the civil war in these countries was over, they implemented a power sharing arrangement that included an agreement to rebuild the armed forces. The power sharing arrangement is contextualized in a full consociational system in Lebanon and BiH, or a semi-consociational system in Burundi and Iraq. By framing the case studies in such a manner, I intend to show the differences of having armies in post-conflict divided societies with full and semi-consociational systems. This helps policymakers, practitioners, and scholars to invest more time when crafting peace arrangements to end civil wars and recreate national armies with legitimacy that can sustain domestic upheavals.

---

1   Morris Janowitz, "Introduction," in *Civil-Military Relations: Regional Perspectives*, ed. Morris Janowitz, (California: Sage Publications, 1981), 13.

3   The Significance of Armies in Divided Societies and Research Method

Security concerns and lack of trust between ethnic communities are central themes in deeply divided societies. Communities tend to compete over state resources to secure their vital interests, and an important element in this context is the security question, as it is the key to safeguard the existence of these antagonistic societies. Naturally, armed forces are a sphere of contestation between groups aiming at controlling decision making in the army, by over-representation of a community in the officer corps, ranks, and files of the military to safeguard the community's wellbeing. In Burundi, Iraq, and Lebanon, the post-colonial armies after independence were controlled by minorities, and it took decades to create communal balance at different levels. In Yugoslavia, the Serb community (which was the single largest one in the country) represented the hardcore of the army during the whole period, especially in the last decade at the level of officer corps. In BiH, only after the disintegration of Yugoslavia, the army respected proportionality in its ranks. Hence, researchers need to look at the central security questions of having national armies that represent communities and empower military power sharing.

Power sharing in armed forces is a result of political power sharing. The importance of this paradigm is that policymakers need to take into account that ethnic proportionality in the rank, files, and officer corps is not enough. Communities need to share important decisions in the army, especially regarding deployment, promotion, and molding the missions of the army. This book attempts to understand the success of military power sharing and the problems that arise in its absence by a thorough analysis of four cases. Caroline Hartzell and Matthew Hoddie have done an extraordinary work in tackling questions related to peace agreement and military power sharing through their work on a big N.[2] Hartzell and Hoddie talked about four forms of power sharing: territorial, political, military and economic.[3] The military power sharing, however, does not specify in detail the constitutional and legal provisions that defines the nature of CMR in their case studies. There is no correlation between military power sharing and the nature power sharing arrangements, contrary to the argument of this book, where the full and semi-consociational arrangement have different impact on how CMR is defined. Moreover, rather

---

2   Caroline A. Hartzell and Matthew Hoddie, *Crafting Peace: Power-Sharing Institutions and the Negotiated Settlement of Civil Wars* (Pennsylvania: Pennsylvania State University Press, 2007).
3   Caroline A. Hartzell and Matthew Hoddie, "Institutionalizing Peace: Power Sharing and Post-Civil War Conflict Management," *Journal of Political Science* 47, no. 2 (2003): 320.

than using a large *N*, a small *n*, gives the opportunity for the reader to learn in detail about the interaction of communities in full and semi-consociations within the army, the structure, the institutional reforms along with the failure and success that each army experienced in the post-conflict arrangements. This small *n* qualitative work is based on a comparative approach of the four case studies, with inductive reasoning that allows the author to theorize about CMR in post-conflict divided societies with full and semi-consociational systems. Each case study includes institutional and structural reforms after the conflict resolution and introduction of security reforms. Consequently, policymakers and researchers will be able to use these lessons to implement them in the prospective armies of Libya, Yemen, Syria, Ethiopia, Myanmar, and other cases after the crises ends and the political settlement matures into a peace agreement.

This qualitative study of small *n* begins in each case with the origins of the national armies. Then, I analyze the developments that led to the hegemonic control of a specific ethnic community over the army, and how the army's participation in civil wars led to "militialization" of national armies, that is when an army is controlled by a community or political party which leads to the loss of legitimacy and national endorsement. Consequently, I am able to refer in each case to the set of reforms within the context of full and semi-consociations and point out the success and failure in the reconstruction of their armies. This leads to a discourse-comparative analysis between the case studies to see the impact of full and semi-consociations on the reconstruction of armies in divided societies after the civil wars.

4   Chapters

After introducing the topic in this chapter, I move on to discuss the theoretical framework in chapter two. The theories related to armies in divided societies include power sharing with emphasis on consociational and semi-consociational systems, a detailed analysis of CMR, and security sector reform (SSR) in addition to demobilization, disarmament and reintegration (DRR) as I discuss post-conflict environment. Also, I explain the connection between these theories and the importance in creating the new paradigm of armies in divided societies. The reader will also encounter a thorough investigation of the structural and institutional reforms that each army underwent in its reconstruction process after the end of civil wars.

In chapter three I begin the empirical analysis with the Lebanese army. Lebanon is a unique example of a heterogeneous country with a semi-consociational arrangement after independence that was developed into a full consociation with the end of the civil war and the implementation of the Taif Agreement. The Lebanese army in the semi-consociational model came under the direct control of the president, who had the exclusive right to deploy the army for domestic purposes. However, the role of the army commander Fouad Shihab in prioritizing army cohesion and *esprit de corps* instead of blindly following the orders of presidents, who wanted to use the army to crush rebellions, opened the door for analysis with respect to supreme authority of armies in divided societies. Consequently, the disintegration of the army during the Lebanese civil war played an important role in reconstructing a national army with ethnic military power sharing.

In chapter four I talk about the army of BiH. In this case study I begin with Tito's Yugoslavia and his multiethnic army, to point out the rise of ethnic tension between communities due to misrepresentation in the armed forces. However, even with a more balanced representation in the army, the question of authority over the military was not resolved (Serbs had the upper hand in this) and consequently during the war, the army disintegrated along ethnic lines. This led to the rise of several ethnic armies, to which I am interested in the Bosnian case as one with full consociational provisions. It is the consociational safety-net and military power sharing that allowed the successful integration and preservation of three armies into one national military. It is a very rich case study with many lessons to learn of multiethnic armies in authoritarian systems that could be used to compare with the Iraqi and Burundian cases.

In chapter five, the Iraqi case is introduced with its army originating from remnants of the Great Arab Revolt of Sherif Hussein and Arab officers of the Ottoman army. These elements forged the army of the Iraqi monarchy, but it was highly politicized and strong, which led to hijacking the monarchy in political terms and then in its coup in 1958. The army then established the republic of Iraq, and was only subdued when the Baath took power in the late 1960s. Until the American invasion of Iraq in 2003, the tactics of tribalizing the military have played a coup-proofing mechanism to protect Saddam's regime. With the new army trained and equipped by the Americans, we have a rich account of armed forces in semi-consociational systems. This can explain the rise of partisanship and its impact on army professionalism, in addition to hegemonic control over the army that de-legitimized it in the eyes of the Sunni population. Eventually, this played into the hands of the Islamic State in Iraq and Syria (ISIS) that knocked down the Iraqi army, leading to its disintegration and re-creation.

The final case study is that of Burundi in chapter six. Similar to Iraq, Burundi was a monarchy-turned republic by the army. Its army was controlled by the Tutsi minority (same as Iraq and the minority-Sunni control until 2003), highly politicized, ethnicized, and tribalized by the Tutsis from Bururi region. The interesting case of the Arusha agreement – a semi consociational arrangement – which created a new army, considered ethnic representation to be the same as military power sharing. It was a mistake as events showed that in the end, power sharing in the military is required to guarantee that no group uses the army for domestic political purposes.

In chapter seven I apply comparative analysis between the four cases. This chapter provides important analysis on multiethnic armies under authoritarian systems, full and semi-consociations. The similarities between the armies of Lebanon and BiH are illuminated as exemplars of armies in post-conflict environment for divided societies. They are used in comparison to the characteristics of armies in semi-consociational systems and the problems that these militaries face in such cases.

In the final chapter, I reiterate the arguments in this book, and the academic contribution to the literature of power sharing, CMR, and deeply divided societies. I emphasize the need to take this work into account for future cases of societies with deep divisions and the attempt to reconstruct armies in post-conflict environments.

CHAPTER 2

Civil-Military Relations, SSR, DDR, and Power Sharing

The theory of civil military relations (CMR) faces critical challenges due to the fact that it is mostly applicable to the political systems of Western Europe and North America, that means cases which do not lack an overarching national identity. In addition, the literature on DDR and SSR does take into account the power sharing arrangements and the requirements needed in such deeply divided societies to create national armies with laws that govern the use, composition, and division of power in armed forces. As shown in this chapter, the literature of CMR is western-centric, it deals with societies that are politically homogenous, culturally syncretic where identities are not politicized. Therefore, applying CMR on cases in divided societies, with power sharing arrangements does not provide a proper explanation of the relationship between civilian authorities and armies. This book opens a new dimension in the literature by attempting to establish a theoretical framework which explains the threats of armies in deeply divided societies when they function according to western-centric norms, and how this feeds into instability. The alternative then is to propose a theory by which armies in deeply divided societies with power sharing arrangements can be created in post-conflict environment to promote stability. It is impossible to talk about the military without referring to CMR, and because the book looks at post-conflict environment, I relate CMR to Demobilization, Demilitarization, Reintegration (DDR) and Security Sector Reform (SSR). In addition to that, I distinguish between armed forces in full consociations (postwar Lebanon and Bosnia-Herzegovina) and semi-consociations (prewar Lebanon, post-invasion Iraq and Burundi), providing power sharing as framework for the implementation of the proposed theory. The chapter starts by giving a detailed account of the literature of CMR, DDR, SSR and power sharing.

1   Civil-Military Relations

CMR provides analytical tools that helps us to understand, explain and predict four interrelated dimensions of civil-military relations: the intervention of the military in politics, the role and function of the armed process in shaping defense policies, the effect of the armed forces on decisions requiring international and domestic force usage, and finally the effects of the armed forces on the mindset and social consciousness of the officer corps through education and culture.[1] The literature on CMR dates back to Samuel Huntington's work on militaries and their relationship to civilian authorities in the western world. What began as an academic study on CMR in the USA and other Western-European countries became a paradigm in itself. Most of what have been written since then have been an explicit or implicit response to Huntington's arguments.[2] Huntington argued that armies should be put under objective civilian control because it maximizes military professionalism.[3] This form of military control emphasizes the "militarization of the military," that is to make it a tool for the state to be directed by the civilian authority, but recognizes the autonomy of military professionalism.[4] By professionalizing the military, the institution becomes politically sterile and neutral, and the highly professional officer corps stands ready to carry out the wishes of civilian authorities.[5] Hence, the army becomes an important instrument that allows the civilian authority to achieve political goals. Huntington's theory resembled for some scholars a "normal" theory of civil-military relations, which holds that during wartime, civilians determine the goals of war and leave the army to run the actual war,[6] that is to say soldiers are military bureaucrats.

On the contrary to Huntington's "objective" civilian control of the army, the subjective civilian control maximizes civilian power over the armed forces through civilian control by governmental institutions, social class and constitutional provisions (identified with democratic government).[7] It achieves its goal by civilizing the military, rather than militarizing it, that is to make the institution a mirror of the state and society, and preventing the rise of an independent military sphere.[8] Consequently, the army becomes an institution that holds social values, without the need to separate it from society.

---

1   Mustafa Uluçakar and Ali Çağlar, "An analysis of two Different Models of Civil-Military Relations: The Case of Turkey," *Uluslararası İlişkiler* 14, no. 55 (2017): 43.
2   Peter D. Feaver, "Civil-Military Relations," *Annual Review of Political Science* 2, (1999): 212–13.
3   Samuel P. Huntington, *The Soldier and the State: The Theory and Politics of Civil-Military Relations* (Harvard: The Belknap Press of Harvard University Press, 1957), 83.
4   Ibid.
5   Ibid., 84.
6   Mackubin Thomas Owens, "Scholar and Gentleman, Sam Huntington, R.I.P.," *National Review Online*, 29 December 2008, https://www.nationalreview.com/2008/12/scholar-gentleman-mackubin-thomas-owens/, accessed 29 August 2021.
7   Samuel P. Huntington, *The Soldier and the State*, 80–3.
8   Ibid., 83.

Huntington rejected this line of thought because he believed that it is better to separate the armed forces from society and restrict its role to the defense of the nation, depending only on political direction in that matter.[9] The subjective military control was a theme sponsored by Janowitz, as opposed to Huntington's preference of an objective form of military control. Janowitz argued that guaranteeing civilian control of the military requires "meaningful integration with civilian values,"[10] making the military part of society.[11] This integrative approach requires an increasing legislative oversight, extending civilian control into the lower levels of military organizations, and increasing civilian involvement in the professional education of the officer corps.[12] Janowitz's theory promotes the concept of "citizen-solider" which in his view should minimize the potential of civil-military conflict.[13]

The work of Huntington is subject to many criticisms. To start with, his thesis reveals a main preoccupation that the United States, in case of a prolonged competition with the Soviet Union during the Cold War, would be handicapped and in a disadvantaged position due to its liberal ideology.[14] Huntington then tried to respond to this challenge by advocating the objective control of the army and the need to separate the military from society. Moreover, Huntington emphasizes the importance of Clausewitz's concept of "independent military standards,"[15] which means that armed forces should be allowed to develop their own grammar without extraneous influence.[16] But two problems arise from this analysis: first, it is dangerous to consider that professionalism alone will prevent armed forces from developing into a force that seeks political domination. Military standards are not necessarily valid across time and place,[17] and armies may nurture an anti-democratic character by a military doctrine that becomes the essence and source of inspiration that defines the institution. This is the case of some countries that used to be liberal democracies, like Venezuela, under Hugo Chavez and his successor, Nicolas Maduro, whereby the army has developed "independent military standards" that are

---

9   Keith Hopkins, "Civil-Military Relations in Developing Countries," *The British Journal of Sociology* 17, no. 2 (1966): 7.
10 Morris Janowitz, *The Professional Soldier* (New York: The Free Press, 1964), 420.
11 Keith Hopkins, "Civil-Military Relations in Developing Countries," 7.
12 Morris Janowitz, *The Professional Soldier*, 439.
13 Keith Hopkins, "Civil-Military Relations in Developing Countries," 11.
14 Suzanne C. Nielsen, "Civil-Military Relations Theory and Military Effectiveness," *Public Administration and Management* 10, no. 2 (2005): 64–5.
15 Ibid., 65.
16 Samuel P. Huntington, *The Soldier and the State*, 57.
17 Suzanne C. Nielsen, "Civil-Military Relations," 65.

aggressive to democracy. In Egypt for example, the army is almost independent from civilian authorities in its budget and ability to run economic institutions. In Myanmar, the specific military standard of the army allowed it to overthrow a democratically elected government because it has increasingly sidelined the military institution in politics. Similarly, the 15 July 2016 failed military coup in Turkey was due to Recep Tayyib Erdogan's challenge to the independent military standards that used to allow the army to intervene by a military coup to protect the secular nature of the state.[18] Second, the problem in Huntington's theory is that it revolves around the American experience, assuming that this kind of separation can be used to prevent military intervention in all other countries.[19] In turn, Janowitz has focused on sustaining democratic values but neglected the importance of defending the democratic nature of the state.[20] He did acknowledge that boundaries between the military and civilian spheres were blurred and this would give rise to tension between both groups, however he does not address what is needed to resolve such a conflict.[21]

It is important to note that the main problem of both theories is that they fail to acknowledge that the crisis of civil military relations is not in developed countries, but rather in the newly independent states in the developing world after World War II and their socio-political contexts. Unlike the developed countries who, to a large extent enjoy diversity (politically, culturally, religiously and ethnically), hence their syncretic nature. On the other hand, most developing countries have to deal with the politicization of ethnic identities which is what Theodor Hanf referred to as "ethnurgy."[22] Huntington and Janowitz dismiss altogether the impact of internal ethnic cleavages on armed forces and civil military relations, despite the fact that in developing countries, the army is sometimes used to assist police agencies in internal security, and in either case, the army might become a sphere of contestation between ethnic groups. Hence, with the army becoming involved in internal security and in the context of deeply divided societies, the military can play a decisive role in

---

18   The failure was mainly due to the absence of consensus among military leaders to carry the coup.
19   Rebecca L. Schiff, "Civil Military Relations Reconsidered: A Theory of Concordance," *Armed Forces and Society* 22, no. 1 (1995): 7–9.
20   James Burk, "Theories of Democratic Civil-Military Relations," *Armed Forces and Society* 29, no. 1 (2002): 14.
21   Ibid.
22   Theodor Hanf, "Ethnurgy: On the Analytical Use and Normative Abuse of the Concept of 'Ethnic Identity'," in *Nationalism, Ethnicity and Cultural Identity in Europe*, ed. Keebet von Benda-Beckmann and Maykel Verkuyten, (Utrecht: European Research Centre on Migration and Ethnic Studies, 1995), 43.

political and military conflicts that occur in such states. Once the army favors one group over the other, its intervention may exacerbate violence, and the army will either disintegrate into different factions according to sectarian affiliation, as in the cases of Nigeria, Lebanon,[23] and Yugoslavia have shown, or take over the political system directly through a military coup as in Burundi, Iraq and Myanmar. To make matters worse, colonial powers have often heavily relied on minorities to control the military. Examples of which are Syria (Alawites), Burundi (Tutsi), and Iraq (Sunnis), thus providing a solid foundation for these communities to use the army to achieve political hegemony.

Another problem in Huntington's and Janowitz's theories of civil military relations is that they completely disregard the impact of the composition of the army and the command structure on stability on the country. It is irrelevant here if the army is isolated from society or successfully integrated into it, what is at stake is the legitimacy of the army in the eyes of the population when used for internal policing, which we can look at by determining the ethnic composition of the army, the prerogatives of the army commander who ends up belonging to the stronger community in the military, and to what extent politicians respect the chain of command. In some cases, the overall composition of the army may represent sharply the representation of ethnic groups in a state. However, it is critically important to look at the composition of the officer corps, army command, and their prerogatives because ultimately that is where military power resides. Such a situation can lead to ethnic tensions in the army and also in relationship with civilians, as the outlook of the army may be that of a military instrument in the hands of the group that dominated the officer corps. There are other cases where some societies were more privileged than others in military representation and control, like the Serbs in Former Yugoslavia and Maronites in prewar Lebanon. According to Horowitz, such scenarios can generate ethnic resentment,[24] because the domination of any powerful institution by a specific group may be a weapon to achieve ethnic purposes,[25] like enhancing their socio-economic status or enforcing their political domination over others by using the military to exclude non-dominant communities from political power. For instance, the Tutsis in Burundi excluded the Tutsi majority from the army, Sunnis in Iraq dominated over the military upper hierarchy and decision-making.

---

23   Donald L. Horowitz, *Ethnic Groups in Conflict* (Los Angeles: University of California Press, 1985), 443.
24   Ibid.
25   Ibid., 467.

In addition to what has been discussed, Huntington and Janowitz did not reflect on the circumvention of the chain of command by civilian authorities. Both theorists disregarded these circumstances despite their importance, because it is likely that politicians can use their prerogatives to give military orders without respecting the chain of command. An important example is that of Iraq under Prime Minister al-Maliki, who continuously gave orders (through phone calls) to mobilize the army thus disrespecting the chain of command.[26] Similarly, in today's Burundi, there is an alternative chain of command controlled by the president and his CNDD-FDD partisans. What can make matters worse is the fact that some of the battalions or units used for domestic order may be homogenous, or loyal to politicians in power. Thus, circumventing the chain of command could happen by ordering a battalion/unit that belongs to the same ethnic group as the civilian leader definitely undermines the legitimacy of the armed forces. This is one important reason to consider the loss of legitimacy of the armed forces in Burundi and Iraq, which means the military is the target of armed attacks by rebels.

A recent explanation of civil-military relations is the concordance theory, which concentrates on the cultural and institutional conditions, including separation, integration or some alternative that prevents or promotes domestic military intervention. Concordance theory does not presume civilian control over the military, promoting instead partnership and dialogue between a nation's major institutions according to the prevailing culture.[27] It claims that when an agreement prevails among elites, domestic military intervention is less likely to happen.[28] Therefore, concordance theory argues in favor of cooperation between three pillars in society: the military, political elites, and citizens.[29] The theory includes four main components: social composition of officer corps, political decision making process, recruitment method, and the military style.[30] Regarding the social composition of officer corps, the theory does not call for a broad representation from society; the political decision making process refers to the channels that determine the needs and allocations of the military (like military budget, materials, size and structure); recruitment methods deals with the enlistment of citizens into the armed forces and the methods that can be persuasive (based on patriotism and ethos) or coercive

---

26 Zaid al-Ali, *The Struggle for Iraq's Future: How Corruption, Incompetence and Sectarianism Have Undermined Democracy* (New Haven: Yale University Press, 2014), 131.
27 Rebecca L. Schiff, "Concordance Theory: A Response to Recent Criticism," *Armed Forces and Society* 23, no. 2 (1996): 277.
28 Keith Hopkins, "Civil-Military Relations in Developing Countries," 11–2.
29 Rebecca L. Schiff, "Civil-Military Relations Reconsidered," 7.
30 Ibid., 13.

(based on enlisting citizens against their will); finally the military style is about the outlook of the army, the ethos that drives it, and what people think of it.[31] These indicators reflect the specific conditions that influence the three partners to agree or disagree on civil-military issues.[32]

The main concern of concordance theory is to try figure out why the military intervenes in politics and sets the conditions that promote or inhibit such an intervention.[33] According to the founder of the theory Rebecca L. Schiff, "concordance moves beyond institutional analysis by addressing issues relevant to a nation's culture." She molds her theory according to the experience of India and Israel. Schiff's work, however, is short of application in post-conflict cases with power sharing arrangements, where societies are deeply divided. For instance, her case studies, India, Israel and later Argentina, are not societies divided by ethnic, racial, religious or linguistic cleavages. Her claim that "concordance does not presume that civilian institutions must control the military,"[34] opens the door for militaries to take over because partnership between civilians, political elites and military commanders is not always guaranteed in post conflict developing countries, particularly in societies deeply divided trying to establish a democratic system after civil wars. In addition, researchers have to take into account how hard it is to open a dialogue between civilians and military commanders on equal footing, without a set of constitutional laws and regulations that governs the interaction between both groups. It is important to keep in mind that military commanders have the upper hand in most developing countries when they discuss terms with civilian authority, simply because they control the guns. One can look at Egyptian president Sisi and the now ruler of Myanmar general Min Aung Hlaing. Both were appointed by democratically elected leaders and due to failure in the dialogue, they simply launched a coup against them. Moreover, the argument that citizens can participate in shaping civil-military relations is dangerous, especially in today's world with demagogues and populist leaders actively influencing citizens. It is not safe to assume that people or the masses may be able to take the right decisions especially in such technical and delicate topic. There is no guarantee that this formula which fuses citizens into the equation will not be exploited by political elites, or to some extent, radicals and demagogues. This is the case of many deeply divided societies whereby elites, as Lijphart says, have almost full control over their constituents, which can allow the former to influence

---

31 Ibid., 14–15.
32 Ibid., 13.
33 Ibid., 7.
34 Rebecca L. Schiff, "Concordance Theory: A Response," 277.

civil-military relations through mobilizing their constituents. If constituents are mobilized against one another by different elites to shape CMR, one can witness the fragmentation of the armed forces, thus moving to another and more dangerous problem.

An important point in concordance theory is its concentration of the concept of culture without defining what the author means. It is important to note that culture can be interpreted in different terms according to the discipline. For instance, a sociologist's view on culture is not the same as a political scientist. Also, nations may share similar cultures (as in Western culture), but differ in their political systems and civil-military relations. To further complicate matters we ask the following questions: What if we had different cultures in one society? How can this component of concordance theory be taken into consideration accordingly? In addition, the composition of the army according to the founder of concordance theory does not have to be broad representation, and leaves it to system to figure out how to represent groups. Again this concept reflects a Western perception that disregards the role of politicizing ethnic identities in the developing world, particularly in deeply divided societies. Hanf considers that diversity in the Western world is syncretic, that is there is celebration of diversity, while in other parts of the world, diversity becomes a source of contestation because communities politicize them, thus creating the phenomenon of ethnurgy.[35] As a result, politicized communities will compete over resources including positions in the army, and so if social composition of the army does not reflect demographic balances in the country, either the army will be used later for domestic political purposes (as in Lebanon in 1952, 1958, 1975 and Iraq in 2011, 2015, 2019) to crush the opposition. Moreover, if the army is not inclusive, it will carry along the burden of being a tool to serve the interest of the dominant community in the armed forces, thus threatening of the institution.

The final point on concordance theory revolves around the concept of political decision making and the army. Schiff explains that political decision-making deals with the budget, material, military size, and structure.[36] What is at stake here is the structure of the army and its institutions as they resemble whether communities will actively share power and agree on military matters or whether one group will dominate security affairs. As mentioned earlier, ethnurgy requires a broad representation of communities in the army to provide legitimacy by ensuring that groups are present in the

---

35 Theodor Hanf, "Ethnurgy," 46.
36 Rebecca L. Schiff, *The Military and Domestic Politics: A Concordance Theory of Civil-Military Relations* (New York: Routledge, 2009): 45.

rank and files as well as officer corps in a balanced way. However, this requires that the military structure is based on internal-military checks and balances. This is achieved by creating military committees and institutions that look at defense strategy, recruitment and promotion of military personnel, whereby these committees are representative of the different segments of the population. Concordance theory does not look at that kind of internal-military structure, mainly because it does not take into account the predicament of deeply divided societies.

After reviewing the main theories of civil-military relations, it is obvious that they do not fit to study this topic in deeply divided societies. However, because this book is also looking at post-conflict societies and their national armies, it is important to review the literature on Demobilization, Demilitarization, Reintegration (DDR) and Security Sector Reform (SSR) to see if there is any relation or impact between this topic and the making – and functioning – of armies in post-conflict societies.

2   DDR and Security Sector Reform (SSR)

DDR programs are designed to transform societies ridden with conflict into peaceful and stable nations by implementing policies related to demobilization, disarmament and reintegration. Demobilization relates to the disbanding of militias in order to reduce as much as possible the number of combatants.[37] Disarmament is an integral part of demobilization as it aims to acquire the weapons used by militias and hand them over to the authorities, who in turn would be responsible to store, redistribute or destroy them.[38] Finally, reintegration is a socio-economic process by which combatants are transformed into civilians,[39] mainly by severing the dependency combatants had on their military support network during the conflict.[40] Another form of reintegration is to try to integrate former militiamen into a unified national army. The United Nations is considered to be the godfather of DDR policies, and as the Secretary

---

37   Colin Gleichmann, Michael Odenwald, Kees Steenken, and Adrian Wilkinson, *Disarmament, Demobilization and Reintegration: A Practical Field and Classroom Guide* (Frankfurt: Druckerei Hassmüller Graphische Betriebe GmbH & Co. KG, 2004), 15, https://www.cimic-coe.org/resources/handbooks/ddr-handbook-eng.pdf, accessed 15 February 2021.
38   Ibid.
39   Ibid.
40   Chris Alden, Monika Thakur and Matthew Arnold, *Militias and the Challenges of Post-Conflict Peace: Silencing the Guns* (London: Zed Books,2011), 14. For details on DDR see pages 14–17.

General Kofi Anan put it, "these programs are vital to stability in post-conflict situation."[41] From 2001, the DDR has become a formal part of at least 25 peacekeeping missions, which made it a compulsory element of all new peacekeeping and peace enforcement operations.[42]

The literature of DDR talks about three generations of programs affiliated to post-conflict societies. The first generation of DDR programs are generally designed after conflicts between states or within a state. It can be designed following a definitive victory of one party or after a peace agreement between the combatting groups.[43] In this first generation, also referred to as traditional DDR, the focus is placed on disarmament and demobilization of warring parties,[44] by providing modest benefits to combatants, and giving them the choice to join a new security force or return to society as a civilian. The different programs for reintegration include educational and vocational training or micro-business grants to support ex-combatants to integrate into the market.[45] Second generation DDR program implementation is more advanced than the first generation and takes a more holistic and inclusive approach. In this context, DDR programs include entire communities in the reintegration process.[46] The program itself is designed according to the needs of local communities; it includes a shift in emphasis from operational security to community development.[47] Finally, the third generation of DDR program concentrates on how to address factors that influence the vulnerability of individuals to recruitment by armed groups. This generation if characterized by focusing on social and political engagement.[48] Thus, it aims at preventing groups from re-arming by sponsoring social programs and at the same time empowering the political context by encouraging people to engage and create a more peaceful environment.

---

41   Robert Muggah, "The Anatomy of Disarmament, Demobilisation and Reintegration in the Republic of Congo," *Conflict, Security and Development* 4, no. 1 (2004): 29–31.
42   Kees Kingma, *Demobilisation and Reintegration of Ex-combatants in Post-war and Transition Countries* (Eschborn: Deutsche Gesellschaft für Technische Zusammenarbeit, 2001), 1.
43   Robert Muggah and Chris O'Donnell, "Next Generation Disarmament, Demobilization and Reintegration," *International Journal of Security and Development* 4, no. 1 (2015): 4.
44   "Disarmament, Demobilization and Reintegration: Compendium of Project 2010–2017," *International Organization for Migration*, 3, (2019), https://publications.iom.int/system/files/pdf/ddr_compendium.pdf, accessed 15 February 2021.
45   Ibid., 4.
46   "Second Generation Disarmament, Demobilization and Reintegration Practices in Peace Operations" United Nations, 18 January 2010, https://peacekeeping.un.org/sites/default/files/2gddr_eng_with_cover_0.pdf, accessed 15 February 2021.
47   "Disarm Disarmament, Demobilization and Reintegration," 4.
48   Ibid.

The problem with DDR programs is that they are often reactive and executed in a way that isolates demilitarization process from a broader national process linked to state consolidation, economic recovery, governance and identity politics.[49] DDR alone is not enough to achieve stability and create a peaceful society. Therefore, DDR has been linked to Security Sector Reform (SSR), which emerged as a new field in security studies after the fall of the Soviet Union. SSR aims at conceptualizing policies to reform the security forces, based on the experience of Central and Eastern Europe.[50] SSR is defined by a range of activities and processes by which integrated and reformed security forces and institutions (armed forces, police, intelligence services, oversight bodies) are brought under state and civilian political control,[51] within a larger framework of rule of law and respect for human rights. This is important to guarantee the professionalism of the security sector. SSR is a holistic manner that takes into account state and human security, the role of security agencies in the wider processes of governance democratization and conflict prevention.[52] At present, SSR constitutes the following:

1. "Political- involves capacity building for civil and executive oversight institutions; the strengthening of civil society structures, including parliament and government monitoring mechanisms; the reform of control bodies, such as those responsible for planning and budgetary issues; providing support to NGOs and the press; and seeking to ensure the principle of effective civilian oversight and civil supremacy over the military and security apparatuses.
2. "Social- entails the cultural transformation in security sector institutions including leadership, management and administrative ethos and traditions; the strengthening of public security; training in the preparation of security reviews and assessment of citizen security needs; the proper control of arms transfer, especially measures to curtail the illicit proliferation of small arms and light weapons.
3. "Economic/Development- constitutes measures to consolidate disarmament, demobilisation and reintegration of former fighters; the civil

---

49 Chris Alden, Monika Thakur and Matthew Arnold, *Militias and the Challenges of Post-Conflict Peace*, x-xi.
50 Christopher von Dyck, *DDR and SSR in War-to-Peace Transition* (London: Ubiquity Press, 2018), 5.
51 Martin Edmonds, Greg Mills and Terence McNamee, "Disarmament, Demobilization, and Reintegration and Local Ownership in the Great Lakes: The Experience of Rwanda, Burundi, and the Democratic Republic of Congo," *African Security* 2, no. 1 (2009): 33.
52 Andy Knight, "Linking DDR and SSR in post-conflict Peacebuilding in Africa: An Overview", *African Journal of Political Science and International Relations* 4, no. 1 (2010): 33.

utilisation of resources formerly used for military purposes; the demilitarisation of post-conflict states.
4. "Institutional- includes organisational restructuring that focuses on the professionalization of security forces; pairing back of the size of security forces; training of armed forces in the application of international norms and laws; improving organisational and management processes to ensure effectiveness and efficiency in the security area."[53]

A number of DDR and SSR programs have been challenged due to the lack of a well-defined context and flexibility. This has led to questions concerning their effectiveness when weighed against major investments that such activities entail.[54] There is also the question of national ownership to programs that are funded and sometimes run by foreign donors. Thus, strong emphasis on national ownership of these programs is critical to address challenges of legitimacy and sustainability, which means they should be designed to fit the circumstances of each particular country.[55]

SSR policy-makers tend to focus on three short to long term tasks: restoring order by neutralizing non-state armed groups (similar to DDR's demilitarization), re-establishing formal state security forces, and restoring state institutions that oversee and monitor these security forces.[56] Proper implementation of SSR policies and success of DDR requires some sort of nexus – combination between the two. The relationship is then synergistic and symbiotic, one cannot advance without the other.[57] However, researchers disagree whether DDR is a pre-requisite to effective SSR,[58] or the two processes are distinct but overlapping in war-peace transition spectrum to restore central state authority and reduce the power of irregular armed forces.[59] Regardless whether SSR and DDR should go side-by-side or one should be prior to the other, the nexus studies do not provide an explanation on the details of how to re-establish security apparatuses after civil strife, particularly with respect to armed forces. Moreover, it seems that nexus studies do not take into account the nature of the political

---

53 Ibid., 34.
54 Cornelis Steenken, "DDR and SSR Based on UN Integrated DDR Standards Monopoly of Force: The Nexus of DDR and SSR," in *Monopoly of Force: The Nexus of DDR and SSR*, ed. Melanne A. Civic and Michael Miklaucic, (Washington D.C.: National Defense University Press, 2011), 288.
55 Ibid., 293.
56 Christopher von Dyck, *DDR and SSR in War-to-Peace Transition*, 11.
57 Martin Edmonds, Greg Mills and Terence McNamee, "Disarmament, Demobilization, and Reintegration," 33.
58 Ibid., 33–4.
59 Christopher von Dyck, *DDR and SSR in War-to-Peace Transition*, 5.

system and how it impacts security provisions and institutions. Hence, SSR and DDR lack a conceptual basis to explain the relationship between the nature of the political system and security apparatuses. SSR's political, social, economic, and institutional constituents are vague: How do you achieve and implement these concepts? What formula should be considered? How do we evaluate the legitimacy of armed forces? What are the oversight bodies and how are they formed? What are their prerogatives? Hence, there is a critical need to emphasize these questions in a new theory of armed forces in divided societies that relate DDR and SSR to the wider political context of power sharing.

3   Post-Conflict Power Sharing and Security Apparatuses

The power sharing context that this book looks at is consociationalism which defines the cases of post-war Lebanon and Bosnia-Herzegovina, and semi-consociationalism in prewar Lebanon, post-invasion Iraq, and today's Burundi. Consociationalism is a form of power sharing derived from Arend Lijphart's study on stability in divided societies. He defined consociational democracy as "a government by elite cartel designed to turn democracy with fragmented culture into a stable democracy."[60] This kind of political system is built upon four pillars: grand coalition, mutual veto, proportionality and segmental autonomy.[61] A grand coalition can be the representation of all groups in the executive (in parliamentary systems), or advisory grand councils with significant functions, or a grand coalition with the President and some top office politicians like Prime Minister, Speaker of House, Speaker of the Senate, (or others) in presidential systems.[62] Beside that, mutual veto is introduced as a guarantee that no minority will be outvoted by the majority when its vital interests are at stake,[63] and these two characteristics represent the primary ones of a consociational democracy. As for the secondary characteristics, proportionality deals with the representation of each community in the civil service and public sector according to its size vis-à-vis the whole population, and segmental autonomy is a reference to self-rule of minorities in areas of their exclusive

---

60 Arend Lijphart, The Politics of Accommodation: Pluralism and Democracy in the Netherlands (California: University of California, 1974), 79.
61 Arend Lijphart, Democracy in Plural Societies: A Comparative Exploration (New Haven: Yale University Press, 1977), 3–4.
62 Arend Lijphart, "Majority Rule Versus Democracy in Deeply Divided Societies," Politikon: South African Journal of Political Studies 4, no. 2 (1977): 118.
63 Ibid.

concern,[64] like religious, cultural and linguistic affairs. Semi-consociational democracy, is a form of power sharing political system one relies on proportionality and segmental autonomy, in the presence – or absence – of a ceremonial grand coalition without veto powers.[65] Semi-consociational democracies are defined by three characteristics. First, they tend to have grand coalitions that are largely ceremonial, and executive powers are concentrated in either the presidential or prime ministerial office, allowing the community that controls these positions to be overwhelmingly stronger than others combined. Second, one community has the upper hand in the army, and finally there is some sort of communal hegemony in cultural and economic terms.

Post-invasion Iraq, Burundi and prewar Lebanon are examples of semi-consociational systems. In Iraq, the most powerful executive position in the Iraqi government is that of the prime minister – reserved for the largest ethnic community, the Shiites. Sunnis received the position of the Speaker of the House and the minister of defense, while Kurds received the ceremonial position of the federal presidency, considering that they enjoy political, cultural, security and some sort of economic autonomy in the Kurdish Regional Government (KRG). According to the constitution, the prime ministers names his cabinet members and dismisses them with a majority vote from the parliament.[66] He is also the commander in chief of the army, giving him the right to deploy the armed forces,[67] and prime minister Nouri al-Maliki used the army to crush the opposition several times, like sending the army to discipline Sunni tribes in Anbar and crushing the wave of protests in Iraq after during the Arab uprisings that began in 2011. Moreover, because the prime minister is the commander in chief, he exercised exclusive control over intelligence sector.[68] These powers are similar to that of the president of Burundi. According to the constitution, he heads the government, names and dismisses cabinet members, he negotiates treaties, has the right to name judges, controls the public administration and the ministers report to the president. In civil-military relations, the president is the commander in chief of the army, orders the deployment of the army to preserve law and order in the country, and is only obliged

---

64   Ibid., 119.
65   Eduardo Wassim Aboultaif, "Revisiting the Semi-Consociational Model: Democratic Failure in Prewar Lebanon and Post-Invasion Iraq," *International Political Science Review* 41, no. 1 (2020): 109.
66   Constitution of Iraq, art. 78.
67   Ibid.
68   "Iraq: Intelligence Agency Admits Holding Hundreds Despite Previous Denials," *Human Rights Watch*, 22 July 2018, https://www.hrw.org/news/2018/07/22/iraq-intelligence-agency-admits-holding-hundreds-despite-previous-denials, accessed 26 February 2021.

to send a notification to the parliament to explain the reason for deploying the army and the timeframe of deployment.[69] Finally, in prewar Lebanon, the president happened to share many prerogatives of the prime minister in Iraq and the president of Burundi. He names and dismisses ministers, negotiates and ratifies treaties, bringing them to the knowledge of parliament whenever he sees the time is right, and resides over the government.[70] The president is the commander in chief, he can order the deployment of the army without noticing the government or the parliament, and above all has exclusive control over the intelligence.[71]

Semi-consociational systems lays ground for the emergence of a communal hegemon, one which has the ability to subordinate other groups politically, culturally and economically. The ability of the Shiites in Iraq, Hutus of Burundi and Maronites in prewar Lebanon to dominate political life and establish themselves at the center of economic activity proves that. This is reinforced by the communal control that these societies exerted over the armed forces, which is a critical factor that allows a group to emerge as a hegemon and exercise control over other communities.[72] While semi-consociationalism appears to operate according to consociational logic, it is clear that it fails in warding off the tendency of communal hegemony. The center of this semi-consociational mode lies in the control of the army, hence the importance of establishing a framework of armies in divided societies while distinguishing full and semi-consociations.

The communal hegemony of Maronites in prewar Lebanon in political, economic, cultural and military sectors of society, in the absence of any sort of executive veto rendered the system semi-consociational. In post-invasion Iraq, the Shiite community has established itself as a hegemon by controlling the most important offices in the state, like the position of Prime Minister and key positions in the army, in the absence of veto powers for the Kurds and Sunni-Arabs in the government. Hence, the country functions in a semi-consociational model. Similarly, Burundi falls in this category due to the concentration of executive powers in the Presidential office. Moreover, the army has come under the heavy influence of the Hutu President and there is a complete absence of any veto rights for the Tutsi minority, or even for smaller or less powerful Hutu parties. Hence, there is absolutely no military power sharing in these cases.

---

69   Constitution of Burundi, art. 256.
70   Constitution of Lebanon before the Taif Amendments.
71   Ibid.
72   Eduardo Wassim Aboultaif, "Revisiting the Semi-Consociational Model," 120.

On the contrary, postwar Lebanon and Bosnia-Herzegovina are perfect examples of consociational democracies due to the presence of grand coalitions, veto powers represented by executive quorum, proportionality and segmental autonomy. In Lebanon, the government and parliament are equally divided between Muslims and Christians.[73] Governmental sessions require a two-thirds quorum, and major decisions are taken by a two-thirds majority from the total number of ministers. Hence, consensus is a key element in the executive. Moreover, the president no longer has the right to deploy the army, and instead it requires a government decision, which means that the system demands consensus in security. In Bosnia, the tripartite presidency consists of a president from each community: Serb, Croat and Bosniak, with each community holding a veto in the federal chamber, in addition to territorial autonomy for each ethnic community. The importance of the Bosnian experience in civil-military relations is the success in unification of the three armed forces and depoliticization of the unified army.

An important development in the consociational literature is the distinction between liberal and corporate consociational democracies. The former model rewards salient political identities that emerge in elections without the need to divide seats of government of parliament to specific group, instead it leaves it open to electoral alliances,[74] while corporate systems accommodates groups according to their ascriptive criteria (religion or ethnicity) on the assumption that group identities are fixed and these groups are internally homogenous and externally bounded.[75] McCulloch lists the countries with a corporate consociational democracy: Burundi with a 6 : 4 representation of Hutu to Tutsi in the parliament, Belgium with a 6 : 4 representation between Flemish and Walloons in the parliament and parity at the executive level, the 7 : 3 ratio of Greek Cypriots to Turkish Cypriots for the legislature and public service in Cyprus between 1960 and 1963, the Bosnian collective Presidency of three members representing each of the constituent people (Bosniak, Bosnian-Croat and Bosnian-Serb), with the upper house containing five representatives of each group, the Lebanese parity between Christians and Muslims, and finally the corporate measures in South Tyrol.[76] On the other hand, there are three cases of liberal consociation democracies represented in Iraq,

---

73 Constitution of Lebanon, art. 24(a).
74 John McGarry and Brendan O'Leary, "Iraq's Constitution of 2005: Liberal Consociation as Political Prescription," *International Journal of Constitutional Law* 5, no. 4 (2007): 675.
75 Ibid.
76 Allison McCulloch, "Consociational Settlements in Deeply Divided Societies: The Liberal-Corporate Distinction," *Democratization* 21, no. 3 (2014): 503.

Afghanistan and Malaysia, with other four cases of mixed liberal-corporate consociations in Northern Ireland, Macedonia, Kenya and Switzerland.[77]

Another topic in the consociational literature is the role of exogenous factors that John McGarry and Brendan O'Leary refer to when they explain power sharing in Northern Ireland. They explain the importance of "benign external intervention" in explaining the establishment and success of power sharing.[78] Third parties have played important roles in implementing power sharing agreements elsewhere also: Bosnia and Herzegovina, Lebanon, Macedonia and Iraq. Nevertheless, the degree to what we can refer to as a success in providing peace by third parties in these cases remains vague because competing regional or international powers often use these fractured political landscapes for proxy wars to empower their position in the region. McEvoy believes that elites follow the rationalist mechanism of strategic calculation, whereby elites carefully calculate and seek to maximize given interests, adapting their behavior to the norms and rules favoured by the external agents.[79] Hence, she concludes that the cases of Northern Ireland and Bosnia-Herzegovina provide empirical evidence that power sharing agreements are formed and maintained when external actors' rewards for compliance meet domestic actors' institutional preferences.[80]

After evaluating the development of the literature of consociationalism and the relationship of each case study with power sharing and CMR, we can see that consociationalism, *par excellence*, completely neglects the importance of managing armed forces in such political systems. Lijphart's work concentrate on power sharing institutions and the distribution of political power,[81] without studying the impact of a politicized army on stability. A well-established consociational system is subject to harassment and even destruction if the army is completely controlled by one ethnic group. Hence, it is critically important to theorize about armed forces in consociational systems. Among the first scholars to study security sector reforms within consociational systems are John McGarry and Brendan O'Leary in *Policing Northern Ireland Proposals for a New Start*. The issue with this book is that it deals with the police rather than the

---

77 Ibid., 506.
78 John McGarry and Brendan O'Leary, "Consociational Theory, Northern Ireland's Conflict and its Agreement. Part 1: What Consociationalists can Learn from Northern Ireland," *Government and Opposition* 41, no. 1 (2006): 48.
79 Joanne McEvoy, "The Role of External Actors in Incentivizing Post-Conflict Power-Sharing," *Government and Opposition* 49, no. 1 (2014): 49.
80 Ibid.
81 Caroline A. Hartzell and Matthew Hoddie, "The Art of the Possible: Power Sharing and Post-Civil War," *World Politics* 67, no. 1 (2015): 40.

army. Nevertheless, some of the authors' recommendations which could be used for the case of armed forces are, like:
1. Creating an independent police training agency with an independent public official, which should operate in consultation with human rights agencies.
2. Members of the police are not allowed to be members of a secret society or sectarian organization.
3. Security forces should be for all the people and must be as inclusive as possible.[82]

Other scholars have looked at armed forces in power sharing settlements (not necessarily consociational). Leonard Wantchekon considers that any post-conflict power sharing agreement that generates democratic political order is likely to require internal security arrangement or an effective state building mechanism.[83] Similarly, Caroline Hartzell believes that a credible settlement of any war should address the question of who will control the armed forces after its reconstruction.[84] Hence, the term "military power sharing" has been coined by Hartzell and Matthew Hoddie,[85] who rightly claim that successful efforts to implement provisions to share or divide military power are strongly associated with peace in the long term.[86] According to the authors, an agreement includes military power sharing or power dividing mechanisms if it includes any of the following:[87]

1. "The creation of the state's security forces through the integration of former antagonists' armed forces on the basis of a formula representative of the size of the armed groups.

---

82 John McGarry and Brendan O'Leary, *Policing Northern Ireland: Proposals for a New Start* (Belfast: The Blackstaff Press, 1999), 72, 75, 98, 110.
83 Leonard Wantchekon, "Credible Power-Sharing Agreements: Theory with Evidence from South Africa and Lebanon," *Constitutional Political Economy* 11, (2000): 346.
84 Caroline A Hartzell, "Explaining the Stability of Intrastate Wars," *Journal of Conflict Resolution* 43, no. 1(1999): 7.
85 The authors also talk about territorial, political and economic power sharing. See also Anna K. Jarstad and Desiree Nilsson, "From Words to Deeds: The Implementation of Power-Sharing Pacts in Peace Accords," *Conflict Management and Peace Science* 25, no. 3 (2008): 207.
86 Matthew Hoddie and Caroline Hartzell, "Civil War Settlements and the Implementation of Military Power-Sharing Arrangements," *Journal of Peace Research* 40, no. 3 (2003): 304–9.
87 Caroline A. Hartzell and Matthew Hoddie, *Crafting Peace: Power-Sharing Institutions and the Negotiated Settlement of Civil Wars* (Pennsylvania: The Pennsylvania State University Press, 2007), 99.

2. The creation of the state's security forces on the basis of equal numbers of troops drawn from the antagonists' armed forces.
3. The appointment of members of armed faction(s) that do not dominate the state, or of weaker armed factions, to key leadership positions in the state's security forces.
4. The retention by antagonists of their own armed forces or the creation of their own security forces."

Military power is central to any post-conflict society. The question of who controls the military and other security apparatuses after civil wars is of particular concern to the ex-combatants.[88] Military power sharing, then, is one critical dimension in security agreements between warring parties to distribute authority within the coercive apparatus of the state. It empowers peace by bringing everyone aboard and making sure that the interest of the warring parties is best secured by being part of the state, particularly the security forces. Moreover, it can provide a guarantee that no ethnic group will dominate the army and use it against others in the future.[89] This is done by a set of measures used together or separately depending on the situation. One way is to establish a proportional formula that reflects the size of the armed factions in order to integrate them to the security apparatus accordingly. Another is to distribute military power by appointing members of subordinate group(s) to key positions in the security apparatus. Finally, opposing sides may remain armed or retain their own security forces.[90]

The role of armies in divided societies with consociational systems has been underestimated. The military is the strongest institution in preserving law and order, and these hierarchical units that are well trained in the use of violence play an important role in preserving peace. In cases where ethnic groups use violence against one another, the army can force a settlement by being neutral and protect governmental institutions, as happened in Lebanon in 1958 and 2008. If the army favors one group or another, its intervention may exacerbate the violence,[91] and eventually lead to the disintegration of its units along sectarian/ethnic lines. Donald Horowitz provides the cases of Burma, Nigeria and Lebanon as examples of this phenomena. Florence Gaub considers that the under – and overrepresentation of certain groups in the army will eventually

---

88 Caroline A. Hartzell, "Mixed Motives? Explaining the Decision to Integrate Militaries at Civil War's End," in *New Armies from Old: Merging Competing Military Forces After Civil Wars*, ed. Roy Licklider, (Washington D.C.: Georgetown University Press, 2014), 22.
89 Caroline A. Hartzell and Matthew Hoddie, "The Art of the Possible," 42.
90 Ibid.
91 Donald L. Horowitz, *Ethnic Groups in Conflict*, 443.

impact army cohesion especially during the conflict.[92] Any sort of underrepresentation of a group in the army can be perceived as a bitter experience that add to the collective grievance of this particular community within the larger political picture. As Horowitz note, one should keep in mind that armies in deeply divided societies cannot reverse the cumulative effect of ethnic divisions making the institution unable to play its integrative role.[93] Therefore, the ability of ethnic loyalties to supersede soldierly professionalism becomes evident in times of ethnic crisis,[94] particularly when there is bloodshed. Hence, the insulation of armed forces is of critical importance to prevent ethnic tensions that emerge from outside the army from leaking into it.[95]

4   Conclusion

The theories of CMR, DDR, SSR and power sharing are not enough to explain the role of armed forces in divided societies. There is a complete absence of a theory that can explain this, hence the importance of theorizing about the subject. The theory proposed in this book has to take into account the military doctrine of the army, broad representation through proportionality, the structure of the army which includes the oversight bodies, and the political decision of deploying the army in times of upheaval. The cases of Lebanon, Iraq, Bosnia-Herzegovina and Burundi allow for proper theorizing on the matter considering that they are all examples of post-conflict environments with power sharing political systems. In the next chapter, I begin the analysis of the empirical section of the book by talking about the army in Lebanon.

---

92   Florence Gaub, *Military Integration after Civil Wars: Multiethnic Armies, Identity and Post-Conflict Reconstruction* (London: Routledge 2010), 6.
93   Donald L. Horowitz, *Ethnic Groups in Conflict*, 443.
94   Ibid., 464.
95   Ibid., 465.

CHAPTER 3

The Lebanese Armed Forces

The Lebanese Armed Forces (LAF) represents an institution that resembles the backbone of the Lebanese state. This does not imply that the army controls the political system; instead it is a safety net that prevents the Lebanese polity from falling into a state of anarchy. The institution has been in a constant state of reconstruction, deconstruction and resurgence following difficult conflicts,[1] which shows its ability to adapt and reproduce itself according to the local and regional difficulties. This is a healthy sign that the military doctrine and army institutions allow for swift response to different challenges.

The army was established by the French Mandate, and later became a national army when the country gained independence, with General Fouad Shihab being the first Army Commander (AC). Shihab built a professional, neutral and apolitical army characterized as an institution above politics. Hence, Shihab rejected embroiling the army in any role against the opposition in 1952 and 1958. However, the election of Shihab as president in 1958 and his distrust of Lebanese politicians forced him to rely on the military to achieve political aims, particularly the military intelligence (Deuxième Bureau). In the 1970s, as a reaction to Shihab's reliance on the military, the political class disbanded the political attachment to the army. Less than six years later, the army was involved in the civil war that led to several splits in addition to a widespread perception that it was a tool of hegemony for the Christian community against the Muslims. Nevertheless, Lebanese politicians understood the need to preserve and build a national army, and so the process of reconstruction went from the late 1970s throughout the 1980s, crystallizing in the "Total Integration" project in 1991 after the end of the civil war.

The army played in different times a political role, sometimes defying orders from civilian authorities (including the president), because their aim is to be a peacemaker, representing a nation above sectarian divisions.[2] This chapter looks at the development and crises in the LAF. I begin by exploring the origins

---

1   Juan Rial, "The Question of the Military in Lebanon," *Latin American Security and Defence Network*, July (2004): 1, https://www.resdal.org/ing/assets/Paz_y_Seguridad_01_ing.pdf, accessed 16 March 2020.
2   Anne Marie Baylouni, "Building an Integrated Military in Post-Conflict Societies: Lebanon," in *The Routledge Handbook of Civil-Military Relations*, ed. Thomas C. Bruneau and Florina Cristiana Matei (London: Routledge, 2012), 244.

of the army during the Mandate period, then move on to explain the development of the army after independence and how it responded to domestic and regional challenges. After that, I talk about the civil war and the destruction of the legitimacy of the LAF, and finally the post-Taif context which shows the resurrection of the legitimacy and status of the army as a national institution. Throughout the chapter, I will pinpoint to the elements of transformation in the army regarding its composition, decision-making in the military institutions, civil military relations, and proportionality composition of the LAF.

1   Origins: The LAF during the Mandate Period

The genesis of the modern Lebanese polity began with the *Mutassarifiya* of Mount Lebanon (1860 till 1914). The *Mutassarifiya* was a semi-autonomous political entity in Mount Lebanon, established in 1860 by the great powers (Russia, Prussia, Great Britain, France and Austria) as a response to the massacres committed between Druze and Christians. The first security agency established in the *Mutassarifiya* to provide law and order was known as the Judiciary Police, with 150 officers and 740.[3] The Judiciary Police became later the Internal Security Forces (ISF) after the establishment of Greater Lebanon in 1920.

During World War I (WWI), the French established plans with the British to divide the Arab regions in the Middle East between themselves. This plan was referred to as the Sykes-Picot Agreement, which eventually allocated Lebanon and Syria to the French, while Iraq, Transjordan (later known as Jordan) and Palestine to the British. To achieve this, the French authorities established the *La Légion d'Orient* (The Eastern Forces) on 17 November 1916, allowing Lebanese, Syrians and even Armenians to enlist in this force.[4] Around 236 Syrian and Lebanese citizens enlisted in the Eastern Force, and the French organized them in one military company.[5] The main reason for the low enrollment in the French-dominated Eastern Force was due to the Ottoman ban on the movement of people in Lebanon and Syria, which coincided with the British-French embargo on the Syrian-Lebanese-Palestinian coast. Hence, the Lebanese and Syrians who enlisted in the Eastern Force were mainly immigrants.

---

3   Asad Rustom, *Lubnan fi 'Ahd al-Mutasarifiyah* [Lebanon during the Mutassarifiya], (Beirut: Dar an-Nahar, 1973), 90.

4   *Tārīkh aj-Jaish al-lubnāni: al-Jeze' al-Awal 1920–1945* [The History of the Lebanese Army: First Part 1920-1945] (Yarzeh, Lebanon: Lebanese Army Command – Directorate of Orientation, 2009], 1st Edition, 43–46. The French included the Armenians in an attempt to benefit for their presence in Syria and Lebanon following the Armenian genocide.

5   Ibid., 47.

The French and British joint attack on Syria, Lebanon and Palestine in September 1918 forced the Ottomans out of the region. Consequently, France deployed its troops in Syria and Lebanon in an attempt to implement the Sykes-Picot Agreement, and in the process, they transformed the Eastern Forces into the *Armée du Levant* (The Army of the Levant, known as AL) on 27 October 1919.[6] This new army was composed of the Syrian Division and the Cilician Division: the former for Syrian and Lebanese and the latter for Armenians. Later, the French disbanded the Armenian division on 1 September 1920. The French authorities rebranded the AL into the *Troupes Auxiliaires du Levant* (Auxiliary Troops of the Levant) on 5 July 1920 before the Maisalun battle.[7] The AL included 12 officers and 695 soldiers, and the reason for the low number of soldiers was due to the absence of a legal framework for the presence of the French forces in addition to the political duality on the landscape whereby beside the French, the Arab government of Prince Faisal was still functioning in Syria until the battle of Maisalun 24 July 1920, when France expelled King Faisal and his Arab forces from Syria. The number of enrolled soldiers sharply increased into 5435 by June 1921: 185 officers (47 of them from Lebanon and Syria) with 6500 rank and files (5854 from Lebanon and Syria).[8]

The French authorities constantly refurbished and rebranded the armed forces of Syria and Lebanon, and in 1925, the army was named *Troupes Supplétives du Levant* (Supplementary Troops of the Levant).[9] Interestingly, the cost of maintaining these forces were provided by the national governments of Syria and Lebanon,[10] while the leadership and command of these forces were in the hands of the French High Commissionaire. Promotion was an exclusive power in the hands of the French authorities, and only promotion in the Sharpshooter Company was subject to the approval of the Lebanese president after the adoption of a Lebanese constitution in 1926. Anyone from a Syrian, Lebanese, Circassian and Armenian origins living in the region under the French mandate was allowed to be enlisted in the army.

The final stage of rebranding and transformation of the armed forces in Lebanon during the mandate period began on 20 Mars 1930, when the High Commissionaire issued resolution number 3045, which stated that the name of the armed forces herein after would be *Troupes Spéciales du Levant* (Special Troops of the Levant). The number of soldiers grew from 9,500 in 1930 to 14,000 in

---

6   Ibid., 48.
7   Ibid., 59.
8   Ibid., 56.
9   Ibid., 62.
10 Ibid.

1935, all of whom were under the supervision of French authorities.[11] The aim of this restructuring was to create an army obedient to the French but paid by the national governments of Lebanon and Syria to replace French troops in the region. The Special Troops had an important stance when the Allied Forces (British and Free French officers) were fighting the Vichy army in Lebanon. A group of Lebanese officers gathered in the coastal town of Zouk-Mikhael and signed "The Historical Document" on 26 July 1941, stating that they refuse to serve except under a national flag and receive orders from a national government.[12] They resumed their military service only after receiving a promise from France that it would deliver Lebanon its long-awaited independence.

Despite that, the Lebanese army failed to intervene during the events that led to independence in November 1943. The French authorities imprisoned the President, the Prime Minister, three ministers and a depute because the Parliament amended the constitution and abolished all clauses referring to the French mandate. The remaining ministers moved the seat of the government temporarily into Bshamoun and established the National Guards as an auxiliary force to protect the government. It clashed with the French forces who brought reinforcements from Senegal, and one Lebanese military volunteer by the name of Said Fakhredin was killed. Due to international pressure, France released the politicians and agreed to give Lebanon and Syria its independence. All of this happened with the Special Troops standing aside, mainly because they were still controlled by the French and did not have the capabilities to fight the French reinforcement sent to the country as a reaction to the constitutional amendments by the Lebanese.

2   The Army after Independence

Lebanon gained its independence on 22 November 1943, but its army was transferred from the French supervision to the national government on 1 August 1945. This became the Army Day, a public holiday which is as important in the official calendar as Independence Day on November 22.[13] At the eve of independence, the national government had a task to create a professional army. In this section, I look at the creation of the national army, I then evaluate the

---

11   Ibid., 64–65.
12   *Al-Wathīka ad-Dusturiyah* [The Historical Document], 26 July 1941.
13   Vincent Geisser, "The People Want the Army": Is the Lebanese Military an Exception to the Crisis of the State?," in *Lebanon Facing the Arab Uprisings: Constraints and Adaptation*, ed. Rosita Di Peri and Daniel Meier, (London: Palgrave Macmillan, 2017), 100.

success and the problems that the institution faced in order to explain how the country ended up in a civil war and the disintegration of the LAF.

2.1 The Formation of the Lebanese Army

When Lebanon received its armed forces from the French authorities, the army was divided into three main branches: army, navy, air force, in addition to other subsidiary institutions.[14] All these branches were integrated under the leadership of the army commander, but without a horizontal link between any of the branches,[15] probably in an attempt to coup-proof the regime. The forces received its orders not from the brigadier generals, but from the AC regardless of circumstances.[16] In 1946, Lebanon established its military academy to train officers, because during the mandate, Lebanese officers were trained in the military academy in Damascus or Homs.[17]

By the time the national government received its army in August 1945 from the French mandate authorities, the army lacked discipline and a corporate identity, because the French authorities wanted a weak army that responds only to its orders without any threat to the interest of the mandate. Hence, President Bechara al-Khoury told Army Commander (AC) General Fouad Shihab to make a genuine, strong and national army out of this rabble that they inherited from the mandate.[18] At that time, officers were not trained to establish a balance between their corporate and professional duties, along with their political inclinations. Therefore, officers engaged in heated debates between supporters of Bechara al-Khoury's Constitutional Bloc and Emile Edde's National Bloc,[19] which was more sympathetic with the French authorities. Sometimes things would come close to violence and AC Shihab had to intervene several times in order to stop the officers from attacking one another.[20]

Shihab needed a founding myth to create and legitimize the military as a national institution, which would also help him in producing a soldier loyal

---

14　Amine Saliba, "The Security Sector in Lebanon: Jurisdiction and Organization," *Carnegie Endownment*, 8 December 2015, https://carnegieendowment.org/files/Security_Sector_in _Lebanon2.pdf, accessed 16 March 2020.
15　Ibid.
16　Ibid.
17　Ahmad Allou, "Tatawor Binā' aj-Jaish al-Lubnāni Bain 1945 wa 1975," [The Development of the Construction of the Lebanese Army between 1945 and 1975], *The Army's Magazine*, no. 398–399, August 2018, https://t.ly/nV73, accessed 16 March 2020.
18　Iskandar Riyāshi, Ru'asā' Lubnān Kama 'Araftahum [The Lebanese Presidents as I Knew them], (Beirut: al-Maktab al-Tijāri lil-Tibāʻh wat-Tauzīʻ wal-Nasher, 1961), 208.
19　Oren Barak, "Commemorating Malikiyya: Political Myth, Multiethnic Identity and the Making of the Lebanese Army," *History and Memory* 13, no. 1 (2001): 64.
20　Ibid.

to the institution in a country that was deeply divided according to sectarian affiliation. Therefore, Shihab's opportunity came in the first Arab-Israeli war in 1948. According to Oren Barak, the war provided the army with an opportunity to prove its capabilities and win much needed legitimacy and prestige.[21] The army participated in the battle of Malikiyya, whereby the LAF controlled the strategic town of Malikiyya inside Palestine for few months before losing it to the Haganah in October 1948.[22] The army's stance, however, with its outdated weaponry against a more sophisticated and better equipped military organization provided Shihab with a founding myth to build upon a professional army.[23]

Shihab advocated an institution that was aloof from sectarianism and politics.[24] In this manner, he followed Huntington's method of separating the army from the political and private sphere. He benefitted from the vast prerogatives that the AC enjoyed to exercise control over the army.[25] Among these provisions were to lead the army, all its institutions, military schools and regional commands.[26] The AC also had the right to ask the head of the police and general security agencies to provide him with information about national security.[27] Everything that had to do with administrative work of the army had to be under the direction of the AC, and he could assign the administrative and logistical inspectors who answer only to him. Shihab used these prerogatives to establish a professional army that was apolitical, mainly because he witnessed the violent and heated debates between officers in the early days of independence. The Syrian coup in 1949 empowered Shihab's position and argument that the army should be completely aloof from internal political divisions. Thus, Shihab created an army distanced from politics by barring soldiers from running in parliament and municipal elections, stipulating that they could be elected to public office only six months after their retirement, and they were forbidden to vote while performing their military duties.[28] In this way, Shihab tried to fortify the army against political influence, at least by

---

21 Ibid., 66.
22 Ibid., 67.
23 Ibid., 67–68.
24 Florence Gaub, "Rebuilding Armed Forces: Learning from Iraq and Lebanon," *Strategic Studies Institute* 2011, 24, https://www.globalsecurity.org/military/library/report/2011/ssi_gaub.pdf, accessed 16 March 2020.
25 Oren Barak, *The Lebanese Army: A National Institution in a Divided Society* (New York: State University of New York Press, 2009), 37.
26 "The Law of the Army [Kānūn aj-Jaish]," no. 66, 10 April 1953 and no. 33, 19 January 1955.
27 Ibid.
28 Oren Barak, The Lebanese Army, 38.

preventing soldiers from upholding political activity, as per decree no. 136 of June 1959 (when Shihab became President).[29] According to Shihab, military education should be accompanied with humanitarian and social education in order to make the soldier a good citizen and a role model for others.[30] Here we can see that he moved closer to the Janowitzian mode of integrating the military with the social sphere. Apparently, he had extremely high expectations from the military personnel and the institution. However, the danger of this Janowitzian approach was that politicians did not leave the army outside the political scene and tried to push the LAF to support the regime against the opposition in several instances. Hence, the army faced many problems and challenges during the period from independence until the civil war in 1975.

2.2 Problems and Challenges

The main problem that the army faced after independence until the start of the civil war in 1975 was the dominant position of the Christian community, particularly the Maronites. By the time the army was transferred to the Lebanese government, 57.8% of soldiers were Christians compared to 38.9 percent who were Muslims.[31] The percentage was more skewed in favor of the Christians at the level of officer corps: 71.8 percent were Christians with 47.6 percent of them being Maronites, while the total share of Shia and Sunnis was 11.6%. The Druze element in the officer corps was significant, at around 14.6 percent,[32] even though they constituted less than 5 percent of the total population. By 1975, Christians constituted 55 percent of the officer corps - where 34.8 percent were Maronites – the Druze preserved their share of 14 percent, the Sunnis had a moderate increase and the Shiite share rose to 15.3 percent.[33] The main reason for such a disparity is socio-economic: Sunnis preferred to engage in business domain as it was more profitable in Lebanon, and they were already well established in that domain; Shiite candidates had issues in passing the entrance exam at the military academy because they either lacked educational institutions in their regions or the ones they had were under-developed. Meanwhile, the Druze benefitted by being over-represented in the officer corps and

---

29 Juan Rial, "The Question of the Military in Lebanon," 2.
30 Ahmad Allou, "Tatawor Binā' aj-Jaish al-Lubnāni Bain 1945 wa 1975".
31 Sami Rihana, *Histoire de L'Armée Libanaise Contemporaine : Les Troupes Spéciales du Levant et L'Armée de l'indépendance 1926–1946*, Vol. I (Beirut: Imprimerie Rahbani, 1984), 175; Oren Barak, *The Lebanese Army*,26.
32 Oren Barak, *The Lebanese Army*, 26.
33 Ibid., 27.

the Maronite community enjoyed a plural majority in this body,[34] as they benefitted from the missionary schools in their regions.

The shortage of Muslim officers meant that their Christian counterparts had a majority in the army's twenty-four battalion commanders and they dominated the combat units because Muslims were not inclined to take on combat posts.[35] Nevertheless, among the 73 principal posts in the army by early 1970s, 39 were held by Christians and 34 by Muslims.[36] As a result, in order to create a balance between Muslim and Christian in the posts held among officers, Muslims felt frustrated from being barred from sensitive posts like the position of director of intelligence, while Christians felt embittered because their Muslim counterparts benefited from faster promotion in an attempt to create a balance between both communities in the higher ranks.[37]

At the level of military prerogatives, there was a sense of marginalization among the Lebanese Muslims because the main powers rested in the hands of the AC and the President, both of whom happened to be Maronite Christians as per the National Pact of 1943. For instance, prior to the Taif Agreement of 1989 that ended the civil war, the Maronite President had the exclusive right of deploying the army in the country.[38] This problem leads us to the challenges that the LAF faced with the government, when it was asked in 1952 by president Khoury and 1958 by president Kamil Shamoun to crush the opposition. In 1952, the opposition to Khoury grew and the Patriotic Socialist Front (PSF), which included a wide range of political figures like Kamal Joumblatt, Kamil Shamoun, Raymond and Pierre Edde, the Kataib party, the Syrian Social National Party (SSNP) and the Communist Party.[39] The PSF called for a general strike all over Lebanon in mid-September 1952. Khoury tried to use the army to end the general strike and asked AC Shihab to forcibly end the strike.[40] Shihab, however, ignored the pleas of the president claiming that his role is not to take sides in internal political feud. Shihab told the officers that that was none of the army's business, and to let the politicians wrack their brains, as the army's

---

34 See Oren Barak, "Towards a Representative Military? The Transformation of the Lebanese Officer Corps since 1945," *The Middle East Journal* 60, no. 1 (2006).
35 Oren Barak, *The Lebanese Army*, 32.
36 Fouad Aoun, *Ma'sāt aj-Jaish al-Lubnāni* [The Tragedy of the Lebanese Army], (Beirut: 1976); Oren Barak, *The Lebanese Army*, 32.
37 Oren Barak, *The Lebanese Army*, 33.
38 Eduardo Wassim Aboultaif, "The Lebanese Army: Saviour of the Republic?," *The Royal United Service Institute Journal* 161, no. 1 (2016): 75.
39 Eduardo Wassim Aboultaif, *Power Sharing in Lebanon: Consociationalism since 1820* (London: Routledge 2019), 81.
40 Eduardo Wassim Aboultaif, "The Lebanese Army," 72.

task is to defend the public institutions and safeguard independence, national unity, and discipline within the army.[41] Since the army would not intervene to crush the strike, and due to the absence of any influential Sunni political figure to head the government, Khoury resigned on September 18, 1952.[42]

A similar thing happened during the era of President Kamil Shamoun. The opposition to Shamoun gathered in 1957 under the banner of the cross-sectarian United National Front (UNF). The UNF turned to a full rebellion in 1958 after Shamoun was accused of being behind the assassination of a critical journalist by the name of Nassib al-Matni.[43] This time, however, Shamoun ordered the army to fight the rebels by the use of lethal weapons. Again, Shihab declined the order and committed the army to neutrality.[44] He ordered the army to control the cities, protect governmental buildings, the airport, patrolled main roads such as the Beirut-Damascus highway, and deployed his units as buffer between warring parties.[45] This decision preserved the integrity of the Lebanese army at a time when the country was falling apart.[46] In both cases, the decision by Shihab not to engage the army in violence against strikers (in 1952) or rebels (in 1958) saved the army from disintegration. Shihab's concern was that deploying the army in a Muslim or Christian region would threaten the unity of the LAF, because soldiers would sympathize with their co-religions, especially that the essence of the crisis was political, and not an existential threat to communities. The 1952 and 1958 crises reveal the destructive role of political intervention in the army by trying to force it to take sides in domestic political upheaval. Lebanon was lucky to have an enlightened AC as Shihab.

The civil-military relations were uneasy even before 1952. When the first Arab-Israeli war took place in 1948, there was a debate between Prime Minister Riad as-Solh and AC Shihab. The former was pushing towards an offensive role for the Lebanese army in Palestine, while the latter, who had more experience regarding the capabilities of the army and its prospective duties, argued that the army should have a defensive role. At first, as-Solh agreed with Shihab, but after the 3rd battle of Malikiyya, the Prime Minister began to push Shihab to take a more aggressive and offensive role in the war in order to please the masses and expand his political base, but Shihab refused.[47] Both men did not heed to one another, until president Khoury intervened and sided with Shihab,

---

41 Ibid.
42 Ibid.
43 Eduardo Wassim Aboultaif, *Power Sharing in Lebanon*, 82.
44 Ibid.
45 Eduardo Wassim Aboultaif, "The Lebanese Army," 73.
46 Kamal Salibi, *Crossroads to Civil War: Lebanon 1958–1976* (New York: Caravan, 1976), 2.
47 Oren Barak, *The Lebanese Army*, 47.

which then forced as-Solh to quit his pressure on the AC.[48] Had Shihab not stood against the pressure of the as-Solh, probably the status and legitimacy of the Lebanese army would have been jeopardized in the newly independent republic, leading to heavy casualties and a humiliating defeat. Politicians gave the impression to Shihab that they were using the army for domestic political purposes, which was an important reason why Shihab came to mistrust the politicians of Beirut.

Despite Shihab's benevolent status as an enlightened military commander who was elected as President in the aftermath of the 1958 rebellion, he committed a mistake that led to crisis in the relationship between the civilian and military authorities. Shihab's mistrust of politicians forced him to rely on the army as a tool to achieve political goals. With his presidential power, he used the military intelligence known as the Deuxième Bureau to influence politicians. The Bureau answered directly to the President, it exceeded its prerogatives granted to it, got involved in domestic affairs, intervened in parliamentary elections, assisted candidates supportive of Shihab and worked against his opponents.[49] Officers also exerted pressure to appoint district governors, directors of ministries and sometimes influenced the appointment of cabinet ministers.[50] This heavy involvement in domestic affairs during Shihab's Presidency (1958–1964) and his successor Charles Helou (1964–1970) forced many politicians to reconsider their political stance during the presidential elections in 1970. Hence, an anti-Shihabist candidate by the name of Suleiman Franjiyah won the elections and began the process of purging the political sphere from any influence from the Deuxième Bureau.[51] In March 1973, eleven army officers were tried and convicted along with five officers who were tried in absentia (but later pardoned). They were accused of corruption and so many vacant positions were open in the armed forces, which were filled by partisans of Franjiyah and other Christian leaders,[52] like AC Iskandar Ghanem who was closely affiliated with the president. This partisanship within the armed forces made the army obey the orders from President Franjiyah in 1975 to take sides in the civil war, which eventually led to the disintegration of the army according to sectarian

---

48   Ibid.
49   Ibid., 67.
50   Ibid.
51   Eduardo Wassim Aboultaif, "The Lebanese Army," 74.
52   Nayla Moussa, "Loyalties and Group Formation in the Lebanese Officer Corps," *Carnegie Middle East Center*, 27 January 2016, https://carnegieendowment.org/files/ACMR_Moussa.pdf, accessed 16 March 2020.

affiliation, thus losing its legitimacy and labelling it as a partisan tool that serves the interest of the Christian community.[53]

The other set of the challenges that the army faced was from the Palestinian Liberation Organization (PLO). After the six-day war in 1967, the Palestinians began attacking Israel from neighboring countries, including Jordan and Lebanon. The main base for the PLO was in Jordan, where they engaged in guerilla activities against the Israeli forces and succeeded in kidnapping airplanes and negotiating their release from Jordan. Meanwhile, the PLO also exploited the weakness of the Lebanese state and the sympathy of leftist parties and the Muslim community to attack Israel from Lebanese soil. The military activity of the PLO led to clashes between them and the Lebanese army, who monitored the former's activities in and around the Palestinian refugee camps. Moreover, it happened that PLO affiliated groups were caught by the army on their way to do a military operation against Israel. The army reacted to the PLO in a classical manner: they perceived themselves as the only legitimate institution with the right to acquire and use weapons, so attacking the PLO was normal for them. Nevertheless, the country was deeply divided between supporters and opponents of the Palestinian activities, and things escalated after the heavy retaliations of the Israeli forces against Lebanese military and civilian sites.

The series of clashes between the PLO and the Lebanese army led to the Cairo Agreement of 1969. The agreement was negotiated between AC Emile Bustani and Yasser Arafat, head of the PLO, in Cairo in the presence of the Minister of Defense Mohammad Fauzi and Minister of Foreign Affairs Mahmoud Riad. According to the agreement, Lebanon allowed the PLO to carry out military operations against Israel in a south-east region on the borders with Syria and Israel in Sultan Yaaqub, later referred to as Fatehland (after the main military organization in the PLO, Fateh). The agreement also gave the Palestinians the right to police the refugee camps, and coordinate with the army when needed but prohibiting the latter from entering the camps. Also, the army was to allow the freedom of movement of guerilla groups between camps and into the region designated for their military activities.[54] What made matters worse was when King Hussein of Jordan took a decisive action in 1970 and forcedly expelled the PLO from the country into Syria for what was known as Black September. Syrian then facilitated the PLO's infiltration into Lebanon, thus the number of PLO members sharply increased.

The Cairo Agreement represented the first instance in Lebanese history when the state relinquished part of its sovereignty for a non-state actor. The

---

53   Eduardo Wassim Aboultaif, "The Lebanese Army," 74.
54   "Cairo Agreement," 3 November 1969.

army was now caught in a maelstrom: it could not do its duty of monopolizing the use of weapons and at the same time it could not punish trespassers with weapons due to Lebanon's commitment to the Arab-Israeli conflict. In the process, parties opposing Palestinian guerilla activities began to militarize, which led to a domino effect, when supporters of the PLO also militarized in response.[55] In addition, the Cairo Agreement opened the door for the duality of weapons in the Lebanese scenery, beginning with the PLO and passing later to Hezbollah.

Despite these challenges and problems, the army played an important role in preserving national institutions and responding to security challenges in Lebanon. The first successful role was during the 1948 Arab-Israeli war and the ability of the army to stand against the Haganah despite being underequipped and not trained enough to answer these kind of challenge. The incident of Malikiyya, as mentioned earlier in this chapter, was properly used by Shihab to fuse in a sense of corporate identity and belonging to the nation, adding an important sense of legitimacy to the newly created army.

The second successful episode came in 1949 when the army foiled an attempt by the Syrian Social National Party (SSNP) to take over the country by a coup d'état. In early July 1949, Antoine Saadeh, leader and founder of the SSNP proclaimed a revolution against the sectarian regime of Lebanon.[56] However, the army reacted quickly, and in less than 48 hours, the "revolution" was put down, Saadeh had to flee to Syria but was then delivered to Lebanese authorities, and within few hours, he was summarily tried by a military tribunal and executed early morning of 8 July 1949.

The third successful episode was in 1952 and 1958. In both instances, Shihab shielded the army from the dangers of involving it in the quagmire of Lebanese domestic politics. It would have been destructive for the army to take sides with or against the opposition. His decision in 1952 to be neutral provided much needed legitimacy to the Lebanese people, while playing the role of the arbiter between loyalists to Shamoun and the opposition in 1958. Shihab was smart enough to impose his arbitrator status by defending governmental institutions, the presidential palace and particularly the Presidential Summer Resort in Deir el-Qamar (Shouf district) were Druze opposition forces launched an attack against it, and at the same time preventing the opposition from taking the strategic town of Shimlan which oversees the airport. Meanwhile, he met with one of the main opposition leaders Kamal Joumblatt in

---

55   Juan Rial, "The Question of the Military in Lebanon," 3.
56   Adel Beshara, *Lebanon: The Politics of Frustration – The Failed Coup of 1961* (London: Routledge, 2013), 37.

order to arrange the delivery of medicine and food to Lebanese citizens in the region controlled by Joumblatt's men.[57]

Another success was the response of the army against the second coup d'état by the SSNP on New Year's Eve (1961–1962). The harsh measures taken by the Lebanese authorities and the army against the SSNP in 1949 created a sense of bitterness of members of the party and delegitimized their perception of the Lebanese polity. Adel Beshara refers to that as the politics of frustration, and it eventually led the party to attempt a second coup d'état on New Year's Eve, 1 January 1962. The dangerous aspect of this event was the participation of army units in the coup attempt. The main conspirators of the coup were Abdullah Saadeh (Chairman of the SSNP), Captain Shauki Khairallah, a Junior Officer in the Lebanese army, and Captain Tawfik Awwad, head of the Second Independent Armored Company stationed in the south of the country. According to the plan, it was agreed that Captain Awwad would occupy the Ministry of Defense and establish there the headquarters of the new military regime under his command, then he would move on to arrest the Chief of Army Police and the Head of Gendarmerie; the SSNP would provide an infantry of 300 armed men to abduct the President and the Chief of Staff of the army, the commander of the Beirut Garrison, head of the Deuxième Bureau, chief of internal security, head of the Battalion Company, and the head of the Third Independent Armored Company.[58] In addition, the SSNP decided to abduct several important politicians including Kamal Joumblatt, Pierre Gemayel and Maaruf Saad, before cutting-off the telecommunications in Beirut.[59] This grandiose plan, however, failed because it was not properly executed, and the Deuxième Bureau already new and informed President Shihab about the SSNP's plans, but decided not take action against them in order "not to shake foreign confidence in the Lebanon," according to a cable in the British Foreign Office.[60] The collaborators lacked a concise ideological revolutionary spirit and poor logistical preparations,[61] both of which played an important role in the failure of the coup.

Shihab was not merciful in the aftermath of the coup attempt, mainly because of the partial involvement of military elements in the plan. Some 17,000 individuals believed to be sympathizers of the SSNP were arrested,[62] and

---

57 Eduardo Wassim Aboultaif, "The Lebanese Army," 73.
58 Adel Beshara, *Lebanon: The Politics of Frustration*, 122.
59 Ibid., 123–125.
60 Crosthwaire to F.O., No. 5, 5 January 1962.
61 Joseph A. Kechichian, "The Lebanese Army: Capabilities and Challenges in the 1980s," *Conflict Quarterly* 5, no. 1 (1985): 18.
62 Ibid.

the party itself was banned. Moreover, he empowered the Deuxième Bureau and relied more on it to deliver political goals, and his successor Charles Helou followed suit. Regardless of that, the ability of the army to defend the legitimate government and swiftly break the plan of the SSNP with Awwad and Khairallah meant that the army was capable of delivering its job.

The army, nevertheless, failed in upholding its legitimacy and neutral status by the beginning of the civil war. The pressure put on the army from all sides – the Lebanese right, the Christian community, the Lebanese left, and the Muslim community – after the Cairo Agreement of 1969, the militarization of Lebanese society, and the dominant status of partisan military men after the anti-Shihabist purge in 1970 led to the *fait accompli* of its participation in the Lebanese civil war against the Palestinians and their allies, the Lebanese National Movement (a coalition of left wing and Arab nationalist parties). This led to the ultimate destruction of the status, prestige and cohesion of the Lebanese army throughout the civil war period until its reconstruction in 1991.

3   Paying the Price: Disintegration during the Civil War

The Lebanese civil war began in April 1975, though skirmishes were taking places from 1973 onward. At the beginning of the war, the Lebanese army counted some 20,000 men,[63] but then many of its personnel deserted or chose not to serve because of the danger of crossing from one region to another. Above all, the decision that led to the disintegration of the army was taking sides at the early stages of the civil war. At the beginning, Prime Minister Rashid Karami did not favor any military intervention by the army, fearing that such move would cause the army to side with Christian militias since the officer corps of the army was dominated by the Christian community.[64] However, the Minister of Interior Kamil Shamoun wanted to uphold the government's legal prerogatives and intervene in the fighting,[65] something that he failed to do in 1958 when he was President. The army in 1976 did not have an enlightened AC like Fouad Shihab, and so on 16 January 1976, the Lebanese Air Force intervened by the orders of President Franjiyah, attacking Palestinian-Leftist

---

63   Are Knudsen and Tine Gade, "The Lebanese Armed Forces (LAF): A United Army for a Divided Country?," in *Civil-Military Relations in Lebanon: Conflict, Cohesion and Confessionalism in a Divided Society*, ed. Are Knudsen and Tine Gade, (London: Palgrave Macmillan, 2017), 5.
64   Joseph A. Kechichian, "The Lebanese Army," 19.
65   Ibid.

forces in Damour where Shamoun was besieged.[66] This marked a point-of-no-return since the army lost its legitimacy accordingly, and Karami's warning came into effect: the Muslim population and secular/nationalist groups saw the army as a tool of Christian domination. Consequently, the Lebanese army lost its legitimacy.

The impact of the army's intervention was huge. First, Lieutenant Ahmad al-Khatib (Sunni Muslim) defected with his squad and formed the Arab Army of Lebanon on 21 January 1976.[67] Second, when President Franjiyah refused to pardon the rebels,[68] General Abdel Aziz Ahdab (Sunni Muslim) defected on 11 March 1976 and issued announcement "Number One" after taking over the National TV claiming that he staged a coup d'état.[69] The Muslim reaction in the army led also to a Christian reaction in the same month, by which a Christian Colonel established the Free Lebanon Army (FLA) in the north of Beirut (a Christian dominated region), and few days later another Christian officer, Major Saad Haddad announced the creation of the South Lebanon Army (SLA), sponsored by the Israelis in order to end the Palestinian military presence in the country.[70]

The army's composition in the spring of 1977 was still in favor of Christians. AC Victor Khuri stated that the command of the army was composed entirely of Christian elements,[71] which only empowered the argument that the Lebanese army was a tool used by the Christian community to fight others. What made matters worse was that 75 percent of soldiers did not report for duty, either because they went home to defend their towns and villages, or waited for the crisis to end, or even could not join their units because it was too risky to cross from one region to another,[72] so only 10 percent of the soldiers were in their positions.[73] Hence, to overcome that problem, homogenous units in the army emerged,[74] and they were stationed in regions identical to their religious affiliations. For instance, brigade no. 11 was a Druze one stationed in the Shouf area (Druze dominated), brigade no. 12 was Sunni and stationed in Saida, brigade no. 5 was Christian and stationed in East Beirut, brigade no. 6 was Shiite and stationed in the Bekaa Valley, and only few were mixed like brigade no. 3

---

66 Ibid., 20.
67 Oren Barak, *The Lebanese Army*, 100.
68 Oren Barak, "Towards a Representative Military?," 78.
69 Oren Barak, *The Lebanese Army*, 103.
70 Juan Rial, "The Question of the Military in Lebanon," 3.
71 *Al-Hawadith*, 27 November 1978.
72 Oren Barak, *The Lebanese Army*, 104.
73 *Al-Hawadith*, 27 November 1978.
74 Oren Barak, *The Lebanese Army*, 104.

stationed in downtown Beirut,[75] beside the famous Green Line separating East Beirut from the Muslim dominated West Beirut.

The army's legitimacy was hampered by a series of events that contributed further to the partisanship narrative. The army did not take any active role in fighting the Israeli attack in 1978 during Operation Litani. It also stood still during the Israeli invasion in 1982. Moreover, the army continued to fight alongside Christian militias during the Mountain War in September 1983, between the Druze dominated militia of the Progressive Socialist Party (PSP) against the Lebanese Forces and the army. Then on 6 February 1984, the PSP alongside the Shiite Amal Movement expelled the Lebanese army from West Beirut, which was followed by the success of the PSP again in expelling the Lebanese Forces and the army from the Shahar region in Aley district. The repercussion of these battles was that the army lost its legitimate status vis-à-vis the Muslim population, and militias began to regulate the affairs of people living under their domain of influence. The Internal Security Forces, however, were allowed to function in these regions but only in coordination with militias.

In the Christian regions, the army's status was also diminished after the Lebanese Forces fought with the Lebanese army under the command of Michel Aoun between 1988 and 1990. The final battle in January 1990 was destructive for the Christian community, as the Christian hub of east Beirut witnessed extensive shelling by both sides in what was known as the "war of elimination." This incident demoted the army into the status of other Lebanese militias in the country. Aoun, the AC who was named Prime Minister of a military government by President Amin Gemayel in 1988 after the latter's term ended without the ability of the Lebanese Parliament to elect a successor, moved to the Presidential Palace in Baabda and rejected cooperation with other militia leaders. When the Taif Accord was signed and a new President was elected (Rene Mouawad), he refused the Accord and rejected Mouwad's authority. Mouawad, however, wanted Aoun to be re-incorporated into the system and achieve a peaceful settlement of the conflict with him. Nevertheless, the President was assassinated in November 1989, and a new President, Elias Hrawi, a friend of Syria, was elected and did not object to the use of force to expel Aoun out of the presidential palace in Baabda. Consequently, the final blow delivered to the army was on 13 October 1990, when the Syrian army launched a grand assault against Aoun and his troops, leading him to take refuge in the French embassy and later into exile in France (until 2005). The defeat on Aoun opened the doors for the Taif Agreement to be implemented, thus militias

---

75   Juan Rial, "The Question of the Military in Lebanon," 4.

decommissioned, and all groups agreed on the need to reconstruct the Lebanese army and re-legitimize its role in the country.

4 Structural and Institutional Reforms of the Lebanese Armed Forces (LAF)

The reconstruction of the LAF began during the civil war and it had two processes: a structural one that dealt with the composition and component of the personnel in the LAF, and an institutional one that looked at the diffusion of military decision-making and new bodies created to look at military issues. During the civil war, both processes did not produce any coherent solution that legitimized the status of the army, mainly because militias were still active, their claims were legitimized by their constituents and supporters, in addition to the contested legitimacy of the LAF. Hence, the attempts aimed at reconstructing the LAF failed and the effective measures to transform the LAF into a national institution was launched after the Taif Agreement and the end of the civil war, when militias were disbanded and the LAF emerged as the sole military vehicle in the country. However, the structural and institutional reforms facilitated the reconstruction of the army after the civil war.

Hezbollah was an exception to the decommissioning of militias because it was perceived as a resistance of Israeli occupation. Nevertheless, the cohabitation of the LAF and Hezbollah is a complex relationship particularly after the Syrian withdrawal from Lebanon in 2005.

4.1 Structural Reforms in the LAF

There were three schools of thought among high-ranked officials in the LAF as to whether they had to create a new army composed of homogenous units (Muslim and Christian), as per the argument of Fouad Malik, or four sub-national armies (Druze, Shiite, Sunni and Christian) promoted by Ibrahim Tannous operating under one command, or a unified national army with heterogeneous battalions and units, a view sponsored by Michel Aoun and Johny Abdo, along with Nabil Farhat.[76] The school of thought that prevailed was that of the Aoun, Abdo and Farhat, and so the army began the process of reconstruction accordingly.

The first attempt to reconstruct the LAF was in 1977, when the government issued a decree on the 10th of February, giving career officers an opportunity

---

76 Oren Barak, *The Lebanese Army*, 117.

to resign in exchange for generous financial compensations. The aim was to persuade a number of Maronite Colonels to resign their posts and substitute them with junior,[77] less politicized officers. In addition, army deserters were given the chance to rejoin their ranks, however some 9,000 soldiers were discharged, and in return 12,000 new volunteers were recruited.[78] The LAF promoted 817 army officers in a communally-balanced way and also without discriminating between those who obeyed the government and those who did not.[79] The aim of this move was to show soldiers that the army was neutral and took a distance from all groups, and for the first time, the LAF had equal number of Christian and Muslim officers.[80] The Lebanese Front (coalition of right wing and Lebanese nationalist parties) rejected this move because it hampered Christian privileges in the army and questioned the loyalty of the previous members of the AAL (from the Muslim community) who were promoted.[81] This shows that the some elements in the Christian community wanted to preserve not only the status quo within the political system, but also inside the army to secure their dominant position in the country. Meanwhile, the LAF went forward with its reforms, and initiated a series of mixed training camps, referred to as Friendship Camps,[82] to serve as a melting pot for soldiers who were joining the army. The LAF implemented its plan, with the support of Syria's Arab Deterrence Force, which was a military force sponsored by the League of Arab States to assist the LAF in providing security and order. The Deterrence Force arrested some members of the AAL, including its founder Ahmad al-Khatib, and then the LAF expelled him from the army.[83] Then came the turn of Saad Haddad, the founder of the South Lebanese Army who was expelled from the army and his salary suspended a day after he proclaimed the State of Free Lebanon in the area under Israeli control in the southern part of the country.[84] The LAF properly exploited the Khatib-Haddad saga to punish mutineers from both communities.

Despite these critical decisions, it was hard to achieve unity and professional cohesion in the army. Officers were still loyal to their respective communities, and coexistence between officers from different religious backgrounds was extremely hard. At one point, AC Victor Khuri had to escort the

---

77   Joseph A. Kechichian, "The Lebanese Army," 21.
78   *Annahar*, 15 February 1977.
79   *Al-Wasat*, 4 April 1994.
80   Oren Barak, Oren Barak, "Towards a Representative Military?, 86.
81   al-Jundi al-Lubnani Bulletin, December 1979 and August 1981.
82   *Ash-Shirā'*, 14 May 184.
83   Joseph Kechichian, "The Lebanese Army," 21.
84   Ibid.

Chief-of-Staff (COS) Munir Tarabay to his work and make sure that he gained the respect of his subordinates.[85] The position of COS was reserved for the Druze community since 1958, but because of the troublesome relationship between the Druze and the Maronite communities during the civil war, coexistence in the officer corps proved an extremely hard task to uphold. The result, then, was a complete failure of these structural reforms, especially after the Israeli invasion of Lebanon whereby the LAF stood still and did not take any role in defending the country. To make matters worse, the LAF collaborated again with Christian militias like the Lebanese Forces, and this led to the furious reaction of the Druze, Sunni and Shiite communities in 1983 and 1984.

The second attempt to tackle the structural reform came after the Israeli invasion of 1982. In this phase, the government again opened the door for the resignation of army officers, and the army received training from the Americans. The new AC, Ibrahim Tannous received support from the government of Amin Gemayel to seal an arms deal of 150 million dollars, it bought tanks from Jordan, upgraded its air force and expanded the number of personnel of the army. Moreover, the army was entrusted with the security of West Beirut (Muslim dominated) and in regions around the capital.[86] The number of personnel in the military increased from 25,000 to 35,000, with the aim to form an army of citizens, introducing conscription as a strategy to overcome communal, confessional and religious belonging.[87] The Service to the Flag Law was passed in 1982, mandating a one year service for young male,[88] but the problem with the conscription law was that it could be evaded by financial compensation,[89] and it had to wait until the war's end to be properly implemented.[90] Nevertheless, despite this ambitious plan, the 12 brigades organized as the new armed forces were fairly homogenous in terms of religious integration and were distributed according to regional compatibility.[91] In addition, the army began to confiscate weapons and exercise governmental authority at a time when communities and militias did not reach a compromise for the end of the civil war. Hence, the army's moves were seen by the Muslim section of the population as an attempt by the Christian authorities in the state to deprive them of the ability to fight and protect themselves. As a result, the War of the Mountain in 1983, the uprising in West Beirut on 6 February 1984, and

---

85 *Al-Wasat*, 4 April 1994.
86 Oren Barak, "The Lebanese Army," 123–125.
87 Juan Rial, "The Question of the Military in Lebanon," 4.
88 Anne Marie Baylouni, "Building an Integrated Military," 246.
89 Juan Rial, "The Question of the Military in Lebanon," 4.
90 Anne Marie Baylouni, "Building an Integrated Military," 246.
91 Juan Rial, "The Question of the Military in Lebanon," 4.

the Shahar battles in Aley district on 14 February 1984 led to the failure of the restructuring of the army. Worse still, the 4th brigade of the LAF stationed in the Shouf area was completely destroyed, and in today's Lebanon the brigade is annulled, while the Shiite Amal movement controlled the Shiite dominated 6th brigade of the LAF.

The final part of the structural reforms was political, related to the Taif Agreement that ended the Lebanese civil war. The accord provided the government with authority over the armed forces, by which the president is the Supreme Commander of the armed forces who practices his authority through the government.[92] Unlike the constitution of 1926 that gave the president with supreme powers over the army, particularly to deploy it for domestic purposes, the Taif agreement stated that the decision for deployment requires a two-thirds majority vote in the government. Hence, this special majority mechanism means that the deployment of the LAF is subject to national consensus and weakens the threat of possible de-legitimization due to political circumstances.

4.2 The Institutional Reforms

The second type of reform is referred to as institutional because it dealt with the way decision making ought to be taken in the military, along with the set of committees and military bodies created for this purpose. This set of reforms began on the 3rd of March 1979 with the new National Defense Law (NDL).[93] The law arranged the relationship between the civilian and military authority, and diffused power within the LAF itself by creating the following bodies: the Higher Defense Council, the Military Office, the Army Command, the General Command of Administration, the General Inspection, the Military Council and the Disciplinary Council.

4.2.1 The Higher Defense Council

As per article 7 of the NDL, the military council is a joint civilian-military body that consists of the President, Prime Minister, Minister of Defense, Minister of Foreign Affairs, Minister of Finance, Minister of Interior and Minister of Economy. The council is headed by the President of the Republic with the Prime Minister acting as Vice President. The council may decide to include a minister or more in its meetings as per section 3 of article 7. The role of the council (stated in art. 8) is to take the necessary measures to implement the defense

---

92 National Defense Law, 16 September 1983.
93 "Lebanese Armed Forces," *Global Security*, https://www.globalsecurity.org/military/world/lebanon/command-structure.htm, accessed 16 March 2020.

strategy of the government. The minutes of the council is left secret and concentrates on the following: conscription and military service, educational and economic mobilization (agricultural, industrial, financial and commercial), health and medical mobilization, general mobilization of the state, citizens and civil defense, guidance and awareness mobilization, and finally to distribute defensive roles to the different ministries. The President asks the council to meet, if not, then it can gather as per the demand of a minimum of two-third of its members. Regarding the Prime Minister, his role is to follow up and implement the decisions taken by the council and to command the general secretary of the higher defense council.

4.2.2   The Military Office

According to the NDL, art. 17 specifies that a military office is to be established in the Ministry of Defense, to be headed by an officer of the rank of Captain or above, named by an executive decree according to the proposition of the Minister of Defense. This office includes the Administrative Control that inspects the legality of the military activities in the ministry of defense. The Military Office audits the use of tools and instruments for public work, and follows up with the media and public affairs, military attaché, military courts, and the retired military personnel.

4.2.2.1   *The Army Command*

The Army command consists of the commander in chief of the army and the General staff that consists of the chief of staff (COS), the deputies of the chief of staff, and the directorates, branches, bureaus and specialized units. The AC, COS and the deputies are named by an executive decree from the government, with the AC having a say in the naming of the COS and his respective deputies. The role of the AC is to overlook conscription and optional volunteering, organizing and managing military units and bureaus and specifying their mission, performing general mobilization and on the alert operations when they are decided, preparing plans and combat orders, putting forth their logistic programs, determining the need of the Army and maintaining the state of equipment and supplies upon their delivery from the general administration, and finally commanding military operations. The military intelligence is directly related to the AC except in issues relating to military security, then it is related to the COS. Military intelligence provides all sort of information to the Prime Minister. The role of the COS is to assist the AC in assuming his responsibilities and performing his missions, and that through the control of the work of the General Staff and the coordination among them. Moreover, The COS supervises the combat level of the army through the following supervision and the implementation of the military decisions, overseeing the readiness of the army as to men and equipment, suggesting means and ways to develop the work of the General Staff and improve the level of services for the combat units, and finally supervising the training and managing of the affairs of the reserve force.

In case of disagreement between the AC and the COS, the former has the right to ask the higher military council (through the good office of the minister of defense) to decide on the divisive issue. However, this has never happened as all COS have respected the military hierarchy on the army.

4.2.2.2   Military Council

The council consists of the AC as president, COS as vice president, the general director of administration, general inspector, the secretary of the higher defense council and a general officer assigned by the council of ministers based on the recommendation of the minister of defense. The role of the military council is to organize all the institutions under the command of the ministry of defense, naming the regional commanders of the brigade, divisions, units, platoons, and academic schools. These decisions are issued by a decree from the ministry of defense when they are in accordance with the recommendations from the AC, and in case of disagreement between the military council and the AC, the higher defense council decides on the matter.

The military council also enjoys the right to suspend officers in the rank of major and above for more than one month, promoting officers to the rank of captain and above in all military institutions. These decisions are issued by a degree from the council based on the recommendation from the minister of defense. The council also decides on the seniority, decorations, the criteria for civilian volunteer in the military, establishing military academies according to the recommendation of the AC, referring officers to the disciplinary council, choosing soldiers to continue their military training and education or for special assignments abroad, approving the list of candidates to the military academy. In addition, the council inspects arms deals in tis different stages, and has the right to approve the conditions or amend them. Finally, it has the right to submit the budget of the ministry of defense, empowering national defense and amending the defensive policy of the state, and naming the military attaché.

As for the organization of the military council, it meets according to a plan scheduled by the head of the council at the beginning of each year. A council may meet at other instances based on the invitation of the minister of defense, the invitation of the head of the council, or if half of the members ask for a meeting to take place. Because the decisions taken in the council are of critical importance to the armed forces, the quorum of the meeting is 5 members.

Decisions are taken by a majority of votes, and when there is a tie, the vote goes to the side to which the AC supported. The deliberations are kept secret, and when the AC is absent, the COS takes his role instead.

4.2.2.3 Republican Guard

The Republican Guard brigade works independently from the army command. Its aim is to cover the movements of the president and his guests. The Republican Guard coordinates with other security agencies in order to ensure the president's protection.[94]

4.2.2.4 Military Intelligence Directory

The director of the intelligence unit is made in accordance with the preference of the president and the approval of the AC. The chief directly follows the AC when it comes to operations and has no link to the COS except in administrative duties. The chief has the right to order the Counter Sabotage Regiment (*Mukafaha*) to deploy without informing anyone except the AC, and it is considered one of the army's best strike force. The Military Intelligence Directory may intercede in all security matters even in crimes that are not related directly to national security.[95]

4.2.2.5 Ministry of Defense

The Ministry is located in Yarzeh, and it shares the location with the Army Command and the military museum. The role of the ministry has been downgraded according to the NDL, and has become more administrative and political, rather than military and security oriented. Its main role is to monitor the work of the LAF according to the reports it receives from the military inspection. As for other important military arrangements, like transferring military personnel from one region to another, deployment, promotion, demotion, recruitment, training and international cooperation, they are in the hands of the institutional bodies created in the LAF where all communities are represented instead of it being in the hands of the minister.[96]

It took Lebanon more than 33 years to arrange its civil-military relations and properly organize its armed forces with the NDL. The law categorically specified the functions, duties and the way for the LAF to conduct its internal affairs and manage its relationship with the civilian authorities. The most

---

94 Amine Saliba, "The Security Sector in Lebanon"; National Defense Law, 16 September 1983.
95 Amine Saliba, "The Security Sector in Lebanon".
96 National Defense Law, 16 September 1983.

important reform was in the Taif Accord which required the government to deploy the armed forces rather than that right being held exclusive by the president.[97] Hence, prior to deployment of the LAF, there should be national consensus for this security provision. As a result, this empowered the legitimacy and endorsement of the LAF by all communities, whenever it was deployed (as seen in the forthcoming part of the chapter), to prevent the many – and dangerous – divisive politics in this deeply divided society from infiltrating the rank and files of the army. Moreover, important security and military decisions in the army were to be shared in the Military Council and Army Command where all major communities are represented (Druze, Shia, Sunni, Catholic, Maronite and Orthodox).

In 1988 the Lebanese parliament could not choose a successor to Amin Gemayel, leaving the president with no choice but to build on the precedence of 1952 when Bechara al-Khouri assigned AC Fouad Shihab for a transitional military government until the parliament elected a new president. Similarly, Gemayel named AC Michel Aoun as prime minister and head of a military government, which was boycotted by the Muslim generals. Aoun had political ambitions and rejected the Taif Agreement, used the army to forcefully end the domination of militias, particularly the PSP in the mountain and the Lebanese Forces in the Christian areas. He then moved on to fight the Syrian army, relying on support from Saddam Hussein. Eventually, Aoun was defeated by the Syrian army on 13 October 1991, when the Americans gave Assad the green light, as per the demand of then Lebanese President Elias Hrawi, to oust Aoun from the Presidential Palace. Aoun then sought refuge in the French embassy, after which he left for exile until 2005. The civil war ended and the new regime was left to reconstruct the army.

5   Reconstructing the *LAF*

The LAF underwent large reconstruction immediately after the civil war, starting in 1991. The salient point by which this process began was the military doctrine, endorsed by the Taif Accord. For the first time in its history, the army doctrine outlined "friend and foes:" for Lebanon, Israel is the enemy of all the Lebanese people and the state, and not for a group without the other. This is an important breakaway from the past, when communities in Lebanon perceived the role of Israel from different perceptions especially that the LAF did not

---

97   The Taif Accord.

engage in any skirmish against Israel during the 1982 invasion. Moreover, the friends of Lebanon according to the doctrine are those countries, particularly Syria, that support the Lebanese cause against Israel. Of course, mentioning Syria as a state that has special relations with Lebanon was due to Syria's hegemonic role in the country after the civil war. In addition, the LAF stated (along with the Taif Accord) that the identity of Lebanon – and hence its army – is Arab. Thus, any sort of prospective peace between Lebanon and Israel should take into account the resolution of the Arab-Israeli conflict.[98] The doctrine also took into account the domestic complexity of deep political divisions in Lebanon, emphasizing that the decision making in the Army Command is based on the Taif Accord, and considers above everything else national unity between the components of the Lebanese state.[99] This clear-cut and well defined military doctrine means that the LAF functions according to what preserves national unity, is in accordance with the Arab world, and responds to the threats of its enemy, Israel. A new educational program was developed for this purpose and soldiers (along with militiamen incorporated into the army) were indoctrinated accordingly, with primary allegiance to the nation rather than religion. The aim was to create a new Lebanese solder capable of transcending above sectarian differences.[100]

Beside the doctrine, the LAF has developed a series of directives that serve as a framework for defensive, security, developmental and disaster-oriented issues. With respect to defensive matters, the LAF draws its role as one that should be always ready to respond to Israeli threat, provide security for the south of Lebanon, and cooperate with the United Nations Interim Force in Lebanon (UNIFIL) to implement resolution 1701 which banned any role for non-state actors to function in the south. With respect to security duties, its role is to fight terrorism and Israeli espionage, destroy Israeli spying cells, illegal weaponry stores, respond to security threats, fight organized crime, monitor the land and sea borders to prevent smuggling, protect civil strikes and demonstrators, provide a peaceful environment for local and general elections and remove cluster bombs that were left behind the Israeli army. Regarding developmental and humanitarian duties, the LAF has a humble role in building infrastructure in specific regions. Finally, in the times of natural disasters,

---

98   Wafik Kanso, "Taʿdīl ʿAkidat aj-Jaish Khark li-Wathikat al-Wifāk al-Watani," [Amending the Military Doctrine is a Breach to the Pact of National Reconciliation], *al-Akhbar*, 20 October 2007, https://al-akhbar.com/Archive_Local_News/182600, accessed 16 March 2020.
99   The Army Journal, March 2007, no. 261, https://t.ly/LYZd, accessed 16 March 2020.
100 Anne Marie Baylouni, "Building an Integrated Military," 248.

its role is to build mobile and immobile bridges, rebuilding electrical lines and providing water supply, fixing roads, opening new roads in underdeveloped regions, contribute to fire extinction, cleaning rivers and sea regions from petroleum related contamination, disaster management in coordination with the government, save citizens stuck due to floods or storms, provide vaccine to underdeveloped regions along with clothes and food.[101]

The LAF began to restructure its military units in 1991 by transplanting companies in different brigades, other than the ones they were in during the war, taking into account the need to put these companies in brigades that have different religious affiliations. The plan did not work because only five companies out of 66 were reshuffled in the process.[102] Hence, the LAF took a more audacious step by reforming its units not at company level, but at the individual one in order to destroy any existing company cohesion produced by the war based on religious and regional affiliation.[103] The policy was also accompanied – unlike the previous step – with an extended information campaign, labelling the reform as "total integration" or "Operation Global Integration." The reform began in 1992 and transformed all brigades into heterogeneous ones, and soldiers were posted elsewhere than they were posted during the war.[104] Moreover, a six month rotation of units between regions was instituted in an attempt to severe primordial tries and confessional loyalties.[105] The aim of this move, according to Florence Gaub, was to bring back the self-confidence of the army, break any political attachments of its units, free the LAF from any religious imprint, create trust between people and the army, balance the size of the brigades, and introduce the idea of nation and fatherland.[106]

During the total integration plan, the government also prepared to integrate some militiamen into its public agencies and military, as per the executive decree on 5 May 1992. It was agreed that 4,000 militiamen were to be integrated into the army, and 2000 for other state institutions as stipulated by Law no. 88 on 13 June 1992.[107] The problem was that militias began to compete to take the largest share of these numbers. The Lebanese Forces alone, for instance, asked for 8,600 soldiers and 100 officers to be recruited from its side; the Druze PSP

---

101   "The Duties of the Army," https://t.ly/-9f, accessed 20 March 2020.
102   Florence Gaub, "Multi-Ethnic Armies in the Aftermath of Civil War: Lessons Learned from Lebanon," *Defence Studies* 7, no. 1 (2007): 8.
103   Anne Marie Baylouni, "Building an Integrated Military," 248.
104   Ibid.
105   Are Knudsen, "The Lebanese Armed Forces," 7.
106   Florence Gaub, "Multi-Ethnic Armies," 8.
107   Ibid., 11.

and the Shiite Amal movement asked for 2,800 soldiers and 50 officers each.[108] In the end, the state incorporated 6,000 soldiers: 5,000 of them were Muslims and the remaining Christians, in order to balance the number of Christian and Muslim soldiers in the LAF, and also because the leaders of the Lebanese Forces had a different philosophy of the military reform, which wanted separate battalions between Muslims and Christians.[109] It is important to note that none of the militiamen incorporated into the LAF were prominent members of their respective organizations,[110] thus the army was free from any military figure that was intimidating to different communities. However, in order to preserve a balance between Muslims and Christians, the latter were compensated with the large majority of newcomers recruited to the LAF, which stood around 89.8 percent from the 3,664 new recruits to the LAF who were not part of any militia.[111]

Among the other things that the LAF underwent after the civil war was the introduction of law number 97 in 1993, which established a one-year military service for young men over the age of 18. It was later reduced to 6 months in 2005 and then annulled in 2006. In addition, the LAF acknowledged the importance of female personnel in its ranks. In 1992, female officers cadets were recruited, and today they participate in combat units and provide administrative assistance.

Regarding communal representation in the LAF, it is important to note that the army became more representative and no single community had a dominant position in the LAF. The official policy of the army was to establish a clear balance between Muslims and Christians. The conditions may change regarding rank and file due to demographic considerations, so the percentage of soldiers may be 60–70 percent Muslims and 30–40 percent Christians, but at the level of officer corps parity is the norm,[112] and it is applied to the cadets enrolling at the Military Academy.[113] By 1992, Muslims had a slight majority in the officer corps of around 52.2 percent,[114] and this is mainly due to the demographic shift in favor of the Muslim community after the civil war. According to Nerguizian, "Maronites counted 29 percent, Shiite and Sunni were each

---

108 Ibid., 10–11.
109 Anne Marie Baylouni, "Building an Integrated Military," 248.
110 Florence Gaub, "Multi-Ethnic Armies," 11.
111 Sean Boyne, "Lebanon Rebuilds its Army," *Jane's Intelligence Review* 7, no. 3 (1995): 122–125.
112 Aram Nerguizian, "Between Sectarianism and Military Development: The Paradox of the Lebanese Armed Forces," in *The Politics of Sectarianism in Postwar Lebanon*, ed. Bassel F. Salloukh (London: Pluto Press, 2015), 118.
113 Nayla Moussa, "Loyalties and Group Formation".
114 Oren Barak, *The Lebanese Army*, 177.

22 percent, Greek Orthodox were 11 percent, Greek Catholics were 8 percent, 7 percent for the Druze, with the remaining balance composed of a mix of smaller sectarian groups."[115] The LAF made sure to create a balance in the line of command, so if the commander of a unit, brigade, battalion or platoon is a Muslim, the second in command should be Christian, and vice-versa. Also, units that had the reputation of being dominated by Muslim or Christian soldiers, new commanders were appointed who belonged to another community.[116] Despite these sectarian arrangements, the officer corps remained competent, professional and well trained in the postwar context.[117] The success of the LAF in representing itself as a cohesive national institution above sectarian lines was expressed in the study on the LAF in 2002, whereby 75.3 percent agreed with the statement "Lebanese trust their army."[118]

The reconstruction process of the LAF after the civil war was done without any international assistance.[119] Nevertheless, Syria was overseeing the process by exploiting the Treaty of Brotherhood, Cooperation and Coordination signed in 1991 which allowed Syria to scrutinize security affairs in Lebanon, and by its military presence in Lebanon, its intelligence infiltrated the public, private and military spheres.[120] Hence, it was impossible to take security decisions without Syrian blessing, represented by the Syria's Security and Surveillance Apparatus in Lebanon, led by Ghazi Kanaan and later Rustom Ghazali. The treaty was also used to strengthen ties between the armies of the two countries. For instance, from 1991 to 1994, around 261 officers were sent to Syria for training, as opposed to 171 who were sent to the USA and 75 sent to France, Europe and other Arab countries, and those who went to Syria benefited in their career advancement.[121]

The Lebanese phenomena of armed forces is peculiar because the legitimate army, which in theory should monopolize the use of force and weapons,

---

115 Aram Nerguizian, "Between Sectarianism and Military Development," 119.
116 Oren Barak, *The Lebanese Army*, 176.
117 Aram Nerguizian, "Between Sectarianism and Military Development," 113.
118 Florence Gaub, "Rebuilding Armed Forces Learning from Iraq and Lebanon," *Strategic Studies Institute*, May 2011, https://www.globalsecurity.org/military/library/report/2011/ssi_gaub.pdf, accessed 16 March 2020.
119 Ibid.
120 Sohpie Kara, "Lebanon: The Limits of Controlling a National Army in a Sectarian State," in *Reforming Civil-Military Relations in New Democracies: Democratic Control and Military Effectiveness in Comparative Perspectives*, ed. Aurel Croissant and David Kuehn, (Gewerbestrasse: Springer, 2017), 198.
121 Nayla Moussa, "Loyalties and Group Formation".

coexists with a non-state actor, that is Hezbollah. The party was established in Lebanon after the Israeli invasion in 1982 with Iranian and Syrian support. Its ideology is that of Khomeini's *Velayat al-Faqih*, the rule of the Jurisprudent, which promotes that concept that the religious men (Shiite) are the leaders of the Islamic nation (*Ummah*). Khomeini's ideology found resonance in Lebanon's 1982 invasion when a group of young Shiite clerics from Lebanon, visited Tehran and received support from Khomeini to fight Israel, in return for their allegiance to Khomeini's doctrine. Hezbollah grew in number by utilizing religious propaganda and social services, through the financial and military support from Iran with Syria's blessings. The party that began as an "Islamic Resistance" against Israel, was then elevated to the status of "National Resistance" when the Taif Agreement ended the presence of all militias and non-state armed forces, with the exception of Hezbollah. It was believed that Hezbollah can carry the burden of liberating Lebanese territory from Israeli occupation while Lebanese parties rebuild the political, economic and security spheres in Lebanon. Meanwhile, Hezbollah argued that it would not interfere in domestic affairs and acknowledged the legitimacy of the Lebanese entity by participating in local and national elections. Hezbollah received national endorsement which culminated in the Israeli withdrawal from south of Lebanon in May 2000.

The LAF learned to coexist with Hezbollah, considering that the doctrine of the army acknowledged Israel as an enemy state, aggressor, and because of its reconstruction process, it could not fight Israel, so the task was delegated to Hezbollah. But when Israel withdrew, Syria, along with Emile Lahoud who was then the President of Lebanon, decided not to deploy the army in the liberated territories of southern Lebanon, under the pretext that the Lebanese army is weak and cannot defend the state from Israeli aggression. Then the issue of the Shebaa farms popped up as an excuse to legitimize the presence of Hezbollah's status as an armed non-state actor.

Syria's hegemony and marginalization of the LAF continued until the withdrawal of the former in 2005. The LAF was absent from the south of Lebanon for three decades, and its return was based on UN Security Council Resolution 1701, which ended hostilities between Lebanon and Israel, called for the deployment of the LAF in the southern borders of the country, Israeli withdrawal, and the decommission of Hezbollah's armed arsenal. The withdrawal of Syria and the July war accelerated the perception domestically and internationally on the need to empower the LAF and support its military capabilities. This leads researchers to investigate the strategy the LAF used to overcome challenges in the post-Syria context.

6 Challenges and Responses

According to Antointe Messara, a former member of the constitutional council who played a role in the writing of the Taif Agreement, the army is a supranational community body responsible for restoring order after crises that endangered the entire system.[122] Messara believes that the army's role in the political sphere is that of moderation, avoiding polarizations and playing a sort of arbitrating role between opposing groups.[123] I agree with Messara's evaluation of the LAF, but the question that a researcher has to ask is how can the army achieve that role of moderating force in an unstable, polarized polity without itself being polarized? The LAF does that in four ways: empowering its military capabilities to respond to security challenges exclusively (no coordination with Hezbollah in this matter); proclaiming national consensus to its military operations; preventing spill-over of sectarian politics into the institution; and finally, gender and human rights issues, to achieve international recognition as a professional and modern army.

6.1 *Military Capabilities*

After Syria's withdrawal, the LAF needed to upgrade and empower its military equipment to respond to challenges effectively. A successful response to security challenges means that the army is capable of upholding Lebanese security, and it also sends a firm answer to critics who believe that the army is weak to respond to Israeli threats. For this purpose, the LAF has found in the USA and other European states an important partner to improve its military equipment. Since 2005, the total assistance of USA to the LAF in military and defense cooperation amounted to 2.29 billion dollars, including 29.4 million dollars in International Military Education and Training (IMET), 11.1 million dollars in Counter Terrorism Fellowship Program (CRFP), and 52.5 million dollars in Defense Threat Reduction Agency funding for Land Border Security Program since 2014.[124] This is in addition to US equipment provided to the LAF, like towed and self-propelled Howitzers, M113 armored personnel carriers, coastal security craft, A-29 super Tucano and Cessna attack aircraft, Huey I and II helicopters, scan eagle unmanned aerial systems, Bradley fighting vehicles, M48

---

122 Juan Rial, "The Question of the Military in Lebanon," 2.
123 Antoine Nasri Messara, *La Gouvernance d'un Système Consensuel : Le Liban Après Les Amendements Constitutionnels de 1990* (Beirut: Librairie Orientale, 2003).
124 "Fact Sheet: US-Lebanon Military Assistance and Defense Cooperation," https://lb.usembassy.gov/fact-sheet-u-s-lebanon-military-assistance-and-defense-cooperation/, accessed 20 March 2020.

and M60A3 main battle tanks, personal protective equipment, bomb disposal robots, millions of rounds of ammunition of various types and calibers along with assault rifles, machine guns and grenade launchers.[125] From 2010 till 2016, US military aid amounted to just over 1 billion dollars.[126] According to LAF estimate, more than 80 percent of its equipment come from the US government,[127] making the LAF the sixth-largest US military aid recipient in the world.

In 2012, the United Kingdom had also provided substantial support for the LAF to develop its border security forces. The UK used its Rapid Land Border Security Assistance Project to mentor, equip and sustain the newly formed land border regiments of the LAF in an attempt to control its territorial borders with Syria,[128] mainly to stop infiltration of terrorists into the country. Between 2012 and 2014, the LAF established a network of Protector Border Observation Posts (PBOP), buttressed by a series of mobilized observation towers, which were provided by the British.[129] Each Sangar-style PBOP is equipped with a sophisticated system of day and night electro-optical surveillance systems, anti-RPG netting, protection from overlapping HESCO barriers, in addition to other offensive and defensive countermeasures.[130] The LAF used these newly equipped weapons and strategies to repel attacks from the Jabhat an-Nusra and Islamic State.

6.2 *Legitimacy and National Consensus*

Lebanon faced many domestic and regional challenges that required balanced, impartial and prudent decisions to move forward without risking open conflict between different communities. The most critical threat to Lebanon's stability came after 14 February 2005 with the assassination of former Prime Minister Rafik Hariri. The country was polarized between supporters and opponents of Syria's hegemony in Lebanon. The opponents of Syria gathered momentum on 14 March, unleashing human waves who gathered from all over Lebanon in downtown Beirut. Hours before the demonstration, the army was deployed, and President Lahoud called AC Michel Suleiman, asking him to end the demonstration, even if he had to use force. AC Suleiman, however, recalled the 1952 and 1958 incidents, and implemented the Shihabist doctrine

---

125 Ibid.
126 Simone Tholens, "Border Management in an Era of 'Statebuilding lite:' Security Assistance and Lebanon's Hybrid Sovereignty," *International Affairs* 93, no. 4 (2017): 870.
127 "Fact Sheet: US-Lebanon Military Assistance and Defense Cooperation".
128 Aram Nerguizian, "The Lebanese Armed Forces, Hezbollah and Military Legitimacy," *Center for Strategic and International Studies*, 4 October 2017, 11.
129 Ibid.
130 Ibid.

of non-intervention in domestic affairs, but rather to protect demonstrators and public order. The result was that because of the army's decision not to prevent the flow of people into the Martyrs' square in downtown Beirut, the anti-Syrian alliance succeeded in gathering more than a million people in a show of force and a message to the international community that they are the majority. The army, at that moment, reclaimed its lost status since the civil war: the much-needed legitimacy in the eyes of its citizens.

The event in 2005 was followed by the July war in 2006. Hezbollah conducted a ground operation (Operation Truthful Promise) inside Israeli territory officially recognized by the international community as being under Israeli sovereignty (borders of 1948). In the process, Hezbollah succeeded in kidnapping two Israeli soldiers in order to exchange them with Lebanese prisoners in Israel, and that led to the July war that lasted for 33 days. In this war, the LAF was largely a bystander, but suffered heavy casualties, some 46 soldiers were killed in action due to Israel's aggression, particularly after Hezbollah attacked an Israeli military ship in front of the coast of Beirut. It was believed that the Lebanese army gave the coordinates to Hezbollah which then attacked the ship from the coast of Khaldeh, south of Beirut. The army's prestige in Lebanon was somehow dwarfed by Hezbollah prominence. Some army officers, however, believed that Hezbollah did not have the right to act independently in such strategic matter, and should have consulted and cooperated with the LAF before going to war.[131]

The LAF uses this fact in order to buttress their argument that it could not credibly call to disarm Hezbollah if it lacks the means to defend the country.[132] This line of thought was strongly promoted during the Nahr al-Bared campaign in the summer of 2007. That year, members from a terrorist organization called Fateh al-Islam whose headquarter was in the Palestinian refugee camp of Nahr al-Bared in Tripoli, assaulted the Lebanese army, slayed around 12 soldiers, and stole large sums of cash from a bank. The LAF in response received full support from the government to put an end to the terrorist organization, whose leader, Shaker al-Absi, was a prisoner in Syria and upon his release was smuggled into Lebanon. The campaign exhausted the LAF not because its personnel were not ready, but due to the fact that they lacked the necessary equipment to launch

---

131   Marie Kortam, "aj-Jaish wal-Mujtama': Shar'iyat aj-Jaishal-Lubnāni fi Daulat wa-Mujtama' al-Tawa'ef [The army and Society: The Legitimacy of the Lebanese Army in the State and Society of Religious Communities], *Civil Society Knowledge Centre - Lebanon Support*, 1 August 2016, https://t.ly/kz37, accessed 16 March 2020.

132   Joseph A. Kechichian, "A Strong Army for a Stable Lebanon," *Middle East Institute*, 1 September 2008, https://www.mei.edu/publications/strong-army-stable-lebanon, accessed 16 March 2020.

such an operation. Around 40 percent of its total ammunition stocks was used in the first week of fighting, and Syrian fuel was donated to power many of the LAF's trucks and tanks.[133] The cost was that 170 Lebanese soldiers died in action,[134] because their strategy was to avoid civilian casualties as much as possible. The successful tactical military operations, along with the fierce fighting spirit of LAF soldiers convinced Western and Arab countries to provide support to the army. Otherwise in such circumstances, in the absence of military equipment, the fighting spirit and professionalism of the LAF would not be enough to defend the country from terrorist groups such as Fateh al-Islam, and hence the army would have to rely on Hezbollah for domestic protection as well. After the success of the campaign, the army's popularity soared with opinion polls showing strong support for its fight against militant groups.[135]

Another event that required prudent action by the LAF was in May 2008. The Lebanese government decided to confiscate the private communication equipment of Hezbollah and asked the army to take action accordingly. The unexpected response by the party was to perceive such a move as an existential threat which triggered a military response on the parties behind this move, mainly Saad Hariri's Future Movement and Walid Joumblatt's PSP. Militants from Hezbollah attacked Sunni areas that came under the influence of Hariri, and laid siege to his house in Koraitem and to Joumblatt's residence in Clemencau (both in Beirut) on 7 May. A couple of days later Hezbollah decided to control the Druze city of Shwaifet and Aley, strategic areas that oversee the southern suburbs of Beirut with Hezbollah dominance, and at the night of 10–11 May, they tried to overtake the strategic position in Barouk area in Shouf region, Joumblatt's stronghold, which oversees the Bekaa valley and the south of Lebanon. Hezbollah's attacks on Shwaifet, Aley and Shouf were repelled by the Druze community, and the crisis ended when the government delegated the decision to confiscate the communication network of Hezbollah to the LAF command, but the latter decided not to carry the order due to the prevailing circumstances.

The way out of the crisis was successful via the LAF which provided the necessary decision to end hostilities. This reflects the serious commitment of the LAF to preserve national under any circumstances. Another thing to take into consideration is the neutral approach that the LAF command took during the skirmishes in different parts of the country, where it stood as a buffer between opposing sides. Again, their action was based on the delicate calculation that it

---

133 Ibid.
134 Are Knudsen, "The Lebanese Armed Forces," 12.
135 Ibid., 13.

is better not to intervene militarily but preserve the army's unity and cohesion on the long run, than to intervene and transform the crisis into one within the LAF command and structure, which would have had heavy repercussions on the unity of the LAF. If the army had intervened, it was highly likely that it would have disintegrated according to sectarian lines, leading the country to a total abyss.

Regarding Israel, the LAF has shown that it does not have any sort of inferiority complex vis-à-vis the Israeli army. For instance, in 2010, the LAF exchanged fire with the Israeli army killing one soldier.[136] The source of tension was due to the Israeli forces cutting down a tree on the borders to enhance their surveillance over the region. At another instance in 2018, the two armies came face to face when few Israeli soldiers crossed the UN demarcated blue line, and were later pushed back by Lebanese soldiers while pointing their guns at their counterparts.[137]

The army's next challenge was in Tripoli, where due to the Syrian civil war, sectarian tensions rose between the Sunni dominated Bab al-Tibbeneh region and the Alawite Jabal Mohsen. Over 20 rounds of conflict took place between both groups from 2011 to 2014,[138] but the army did not receive the political backing needed to end the fight. Only after the formation of a new government – that of Tammam Salam, which took 11 months to be formed – could the army receive the consensus needed to enforce peace. The army allowed many of the militants to surrender in return of a fair trial, while few like the Alawite militant Rifaat Eid fled to Syria,[139] and other Sunni continued fighting until they were captured by the army. The peace plan imposed by the LAF was well received by the people of Tripoli,[140] which reflects the general consensus that the army is the guarantor of peace and stability.

The coming challenge of the LAF was to stop the infiltration of terrorists from Syria, who wanted to use Lebanon's territory to launch operations into Syria. The crisis began in the summer of 2014 when members from Jabhat an-Nusra and Islamic State simultaneously attacked police station in Arsal and the army barracks, taking several soldiers captive and killing others. Due to the different stances of Lebanese groups regarding the Syrian civil war, and the deep division between Lebanese supporters and opponents of Syria's Assad,

---

136 Anne Marie Baylouni, "Building an Integrated Military," 249.
137 "Army Soldier Orders Israelis to Step Back," *The Daily Star*, 18 December 2018, https://www.dailystar.com.lb/News/Lebanon-News/2018/Dec-18/472053-army-soldier-orders-israelis-to-step-back.ashx, accessed 16 March 2020.
138 Marie Kortam, "aj-Jaish wal-Mujtama'".
139 Ibid.
140 Ibid.

the LAF was not given the political endorsement to launch a counter attack on the terrorist groups until 19 August 2017. The operation code-named "Operation Dawn of the Outskirt" initiated by the army was meant to completely destroy the presence of terrorist organizations on the north-east borders of the country. Simultaneously, Hezbollah participated in the attack along the Syrian army from the Syrian borders,[141] but with no cooperation between them and the Lebanese army. Only 9 soldiers died mostly due to Improvised Explosive Devices (IED) and mines.[142] The operation was described as a "21st century maneuver warfare by a modern military,"[143] shattering the narrative in the minds of Lebanese that only Hezbollah can protect the borders of Lebanon,[144] and proving that it is better equipped and prepared to stand against militant terrorists.[145] Hence, reinforcing its counter-terrorism and border control capacities over the last 10 years reflected the LAF's status that it is better prepared to engage in asymmetric conflict than Hezbollah.[146]

The LAF has improved its military capabilities and shown that it is an institution that the Lebanese state and citizens can rely on to provide security and order. The army is relentlessly working to preserve its hard-won legitimacy. For this purpose, the institution sees itself in a continuous battle to preserve its status as an impartial and neutral force in the country, and at the same time to show that it is an institution that does not come under the influence of Hezbollah.

6.3 Confessional-Proofing in the LAF – Preserving Neutrality

There are no angels in Lebanese politics and definitely many politicians try their best to influence security matters in the LAF or decision making. There have been efforts by 8 March (pro-Syrian) and 14 March (anti-Syrian) alliances to penetrate the LAF, regulate and shape the orientation of the military.[147] From 2005 till 2009, 14 March alliance tried to marginalize officers who received training in Syria, and from 2009 onward, officers who had received

---

141 Aram Nerguizian, "The Lebanese Armed Forces," 23.
142 Ibid., 24.
143 Ibid.
144 Ibid., 28.
145 Sohpie Kara, "Lebanon: The Limits of Controlling," 206.
146 Maxime de Taisne, "Resilience of the Lebanese Armed Forces," *MENAS Analysis*, 8 November 2015, 4.
147 Aram Nerguizian, "Lebanese Civil Military Dynamics Weathering Regional Storm," *Carnegie Endowment for International Peace*, 21 November 2011, https://carnegieendowment.org/sada/46038, accessed 16 March 2020.

training in the US military education were sidelined.¹⁴⁸ The aim is to promote a specific political agenda by shaping the dynamics of civil-military relations in the country. However, across communal lines, there are officers who want to preserve the military's neutrality and insulate it from the impact of sectarian politics.¹⁴⁹ The army, up till now, is succeeding in denying politicians to have a swing in internal military affairs. This can be seen during the current events that unleashed the 17 October unrest all over the country, and how the army responded in ways that did not please the political establishment. While civilians peacefully occupied runways and streets, leading to a total paralysis of the country for three weeks to force the government to resign and adopt political and economic reforms, the LAF refrained from using violence and allowed citizens to demonstrate. It was after three weeks of peaceful demonstration that the LAF began to open roads, sometimes by force.

The incentive of the LAF to preserve its neutral status and avoid the politicization of its personnel is highly appreciated in Lebanon, especially that ordinary citizens generally respect the posters used by the army to propagate messages of cooperation between civilians and citizens. Rarely are these posters vandalized or covered in insults,¹⁵⁰ which shows the acceptance of the population to the messages the army intends to send to the populace. The LAF employs a professional marketing structure (poster campaigns and press releases), with colorful banners covering the urban landscape of cities and villages. Slogans are heavily used to play up romantic, heroic and patriotic registers, like: From the heart of the family to that of a nation; the dawn of martyrs is not absent; the military's hand brings people together; year after year, we continue to give; in the heart of the country and on the border;¹⁵¹ and so on. The aim is to civilize the public space and state institutions, making part of the population to view the army as a vector of civility, even civic-mindness,¹⁵² despite its precarious sectarian makeup. The message, hence, is that the army is not influenced by sectarian politics, and respecting the sectarian makeup of the state is aimed at providing a safety net for communities without influencing their professionalism, thus preserving their impartial stance in domestic affairs.

The army's aloofness to sectarian politics in Lebanon and its resilience to the projected influence by politicians on its rank, files and officer corps provide

---

148   Ibid.
149   Ibid.
150   Vincent Geisser, "The People Want the Army," 100.
151   Ibid., 96–99.
152   Ibid., 95.

a great deal of legitimacy. Moreover, by confessional-proofing the army, the LAF has become a decent and transparent military institution in the region.[153] Nevertheless, the LAF has to engage in limited confessional and political practices because of the politicization of identities in the country. For instance, the post of COS has been reserved for the Druze community since 1958, and after the Taif Accord, the strongest Druze chieftain Walid Joumblatt has to accept the nomination of the COS. Similarly, the position of AC has to be endorsed by Christian leaders. As for the LAF strategy to ease pressure of the military institution it is best scene in the adoption of a Military Council that includes a member from the six major communities: Maronite, Sunni, Shiite, Orthodox, Druze and Catholic. The problem that the LAF faces is when the government is unable to nominate names in the LAF due to political disagreements, as in September 2014, when AC Jean Kahwaji was supposed to retire, but due to the absence of consensus for the successor, his retirement was delayed for an additional year until 2015.[154] Despite sectarian issues, the appointed personnel to delicate positions in the LAF have acted in utmost professionalism away from sectarian considerations. This reflects the success of the indoctrination of the LAF personnel in the institution that emphasizes national belonging over sectarian loyalties.

The final set of challenges is related to gender and human rights. This is the set of challenges that the LAF is trying to catch up with, and recent developments show that there is still a lot to be done in order to improve the policies of the LAF in this matter.

6.4 *Gender and Human Rights*

Ministerial resolutions 376 and 839 issued in 1989 and 1991 respectively laid out the provisions for female enrollment in the armed forces. For instance, 10 percent quota is set for women volunteers across the departments in the Ministry of Defense. Women are to receive similar training to men,[155] but in the current circumstances the role of women is more inclined to be in administrative positions. By 2017, the LAF had around 1,000 volunteers out of 70,000 overall soldiers in the LAF.[156] After the attacks on Arsal by Jabhar an-Nusra and ISIS, female personnel were deployment in Wadi Hemayed checkpoint in Arsal which was considered to be one of the most dangerous checkpoints

---

153   Maxime de Taisne, "Resilience of the Lebanese Armed Forces," 1.
154   Nayla Moussa, "Loyalties and Group Formation".
155   Dina Arakji, "Females in the Ranks," *Carnegie Middle East Center*, 19 June 2019.
156   Ibid.

on the borders.¹⁵⁷ Previously, in the Nahr al-Bared campaign in 2007, female personnel were deployed but their role was restricted to searching and investigating female suspects.¹⁵⁸

With the new LAF AC General Joseph Aoun, the number of female personnel in the army has increased drastically. In 2008, there were three female generals and 17 colonels. By 2019 there were some 4,000 female soldiers and many of them were deployed for critical mission areas. Nevertheless, the current resolutions are not turned into laws, and so any future Minister of Defense can revoke the resolution.¹⁵⁹

Regarding human rights, the LAF launched its code of conduct on law enforcement on 29 January 2019, a very late move for an army that perceives itself as a modern one. The code of conduct was launched in assistance of the Regional Office of the High Commissionaire for Human Rights in the Middle East and North Africa.¹⁶⁰ AC Aoun declared that the military is committed to respecting human rights while performing security missions and enforcing accountability to guarantee the institution's commitment for this goal.¹⁶¹ However, the Lebanese government along with its security forces, are still accused of covering up many cases of torture in prisons and during investigation despite the law passed in 2017 that prohibits any kind of torture against prisoners or detainees, which is a violation of the LAF's part in preserving its commitment to human rights.¹⁶²

The code of conduct on human rights has been a double-edged sword for the LAF. During the first few weeks of the Lebanese uprising following the events of 17 October 2019, the LAF was put face-to-face with Lebanese protestors. Some politicians, including the President's notorious son-in-law, Gebran Bassil, pushed the army to take violent measures against the demonstrators. This is why the security amendment in the NDL that specifies that the army is to be deployed by national consensus and not an exclusive right to the Supreme Commander (the President), is of critical importance in deeply divided societies. Politicians sometimes tend to prioritize short term goals over national, long-term interests. In this case, the AC (who happens to be appointed by

---

157 Ibid.
158 Ibid.
159 Ibid.
160 "Lebanese Army Launches Code of Conduct on Human Rights," 29 January 2019, https://unscol.unmissions.org/lebanese-army-launches-code-conduct-human-rights, accessed 20 March 2020.
161 Ibid.
162 "Lebanon: Events in the Year 2018," *Human Rights Watch*, https://www.hrw.org/ar/world-report/2019/country-chapters/325424, accessed 20 March 2020.

President Michel Aoun, Bassil's father-in-law), along with the LAF command, refused the excessive use of violence to open the roads closed by peaceful demonstrators. This has allowed the demonstrators to look up at the army as a guarantor for their movement, despite the inaction of all security forces in Lebanon to protect demonstrators in many instances in downtown Beirut (Martyrs' Square) after several waves of attacks by loyalist to the dominant political parties. Nevertheless, after weeks of demonstrations, the LAF was forced to open highways and roads blocked by demonstrators because of the economic impact that had on the country due to weeks of closure, also due to fear that anti-demonstrators would take action, leading to violent clashes between the two groups. This process of opening up the roads led to hundreds of injured people and the death of two citizens,[163] one of them was shot in cold blood by a security agent in front of his family.[164] The large number of wounded people raises the question about the heavy use of violence by the LAF, but at the same time, one has to be weary of situation because in general, armed forces are trained to be "rough and tough" to protect the nation. Hence, this dilemma can only be resolved by training the army to be soft on demonstrators and tough on enemies. This requires a lot of training and indoctrination in human rights.

7 Conclusion

The LAF has passed through different phases: construction after the independence, disintegration during the civil war and reconstruction after the Taif Accord. The LAF's legacy, despite its disintegration and partisanship during the civil war, is a comforting one close to being splendid. It is important to keep in mind that when evaluating the legacy of the LAF, one has to consider the events that happened in 1952, 1958, 1975–1990, 2005, 2008 and 2017. Despite the tremendous challenges, deep internal divisions (be it political or sectarian), and the humble capabilities of the army, the military institution has successfully navigated through these challenges, and today the LAF is perceived as one of the few successful and transparent institutions in the country.

The structural and institutional reforms in the LAF were critically important to create an army that is representative of the Lebanese society with no single community being dominant in it. Moreover, the reforms provided the

---

163 Saateh Nouredin, "'An ath-Thaurah wa-Maujatuha ath-Thāniyah," [On the Revolution and its Second Wave], *al-Modon*, 20 January 2020.
164 Alaa Bou Fakher was shot in front of his son and wife in Khalde, when attempting to block the road, by a security agent. The LAF is holding an investigation into the matter.

LAF with a mechanism to diffuse power within its institution and arrange the relationship with the civilian authorities. Beside the reforms in the NDL, the Taif Agreement made it clear that the deployment of the army requires a two-third majority in the government, hence the decision was not exclusive in the hands of the president and required consensus.

Another point relates to the performance of the LAF. The success of the army in responding to different types of challenges post-civil war context and particularly after the Syrian withdrawal, means that mixed armies do function in professional. There is always the question to what extent can mixed armies create and sustain a corporate identity when sectarian or ethnic identification is stronger than the national one. In fact, armies in heterogeneous societies,

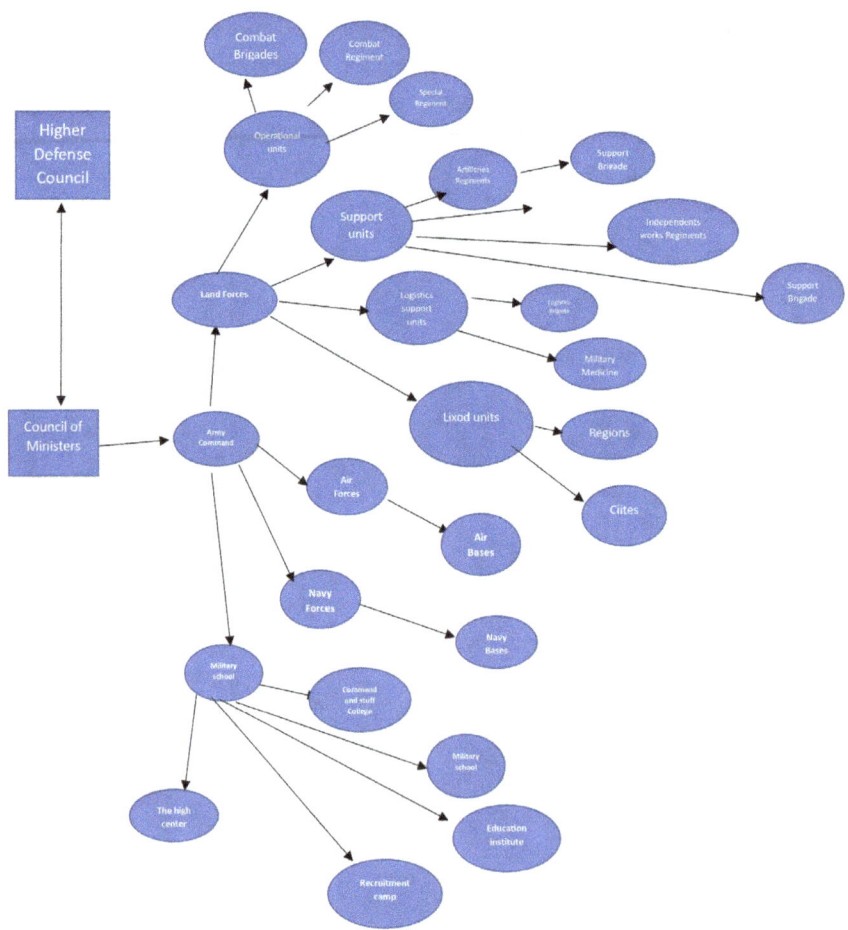

FIGURE 1   Chain of Command of the Lebanese Armed Forces

even in ones that are deeply divided, play a successful and important role in being a melting pot, at least post-civil war, confirms it.

Finally, Lebanon is yet to establish a national defense strategy to incorporate the militant party – Hezbollah – and benefit from its combat experience in fighting Israel. The aim is to monopolize the use of weapon and the decision of war and peace in the hands of the Lebanese state. Currently, the duality is unnatural and related to regional issues, particularly to the Iranian ambitions in the region. How the events in the future will unfold and what they will lead to is unknown, but the record of the LAF shows that it is a modern, successful and professional army that has the capability to be the only legitimate group with the monopoly of weapons.

CHAPTER 4

Armed Forces of Bosnia and Herzegovina

Perhaps one of the bloodiest, painful, violent and most aggressive civil conflicts in the 20th century took place in Bosnia-Herzegovina (BiH) during the third Balkan war. The conflict was unleashed by contesting forms of nationalism, embedded in the complicated history of the Balkan. The breakup of the state of Yugoslavia left three main ethnic groups of Bosnia in limbo regarding their ambitious political plans for statehood: Serbs, Croats and Bosniaks. For the sake of achieving the status of "a place among nations," elites employed and manipulated nationalism. Despite the peaceful coexistence of these ethnic groups in BiH during the Yugoslav era, the residues of historical enmity prior to Tito's Yugoslavia were not resolved. Hence, in the absence of a strong central authority, it became easy to awaken these nationalistic antagonisms. As the conflict progressed, the army became involved in civil strife, disintegrating along ethnic lines and unable to stop the paramilitary groups involved in the conflict that later on formed the nucleus of the Armed Forces of Bosnia-Herzegovina (AFBiH).

This chapter discusses the third case study of an army in a deeply divided society. I begin by explaining the establishment of the army of Yugoslavia and its ethnic composition and how it functioned during that period. After that I move on to talk about the disintegration of the army during the 1990s and the creation of the AFBiH after the end of the war. Each section consists of an in-depth analysis of the problems, reforms, ethnic composition and the civil-military relations during the period under study. It is important to note that in BiH, external factors related to joining NATO and membership in the EU have important implications on security sector reforms. Moreover, despite the internal political antagonism between the ethnic components of the state, there has not been any major military incident, and the military intelligence has shown a high level of professionalism in dealing with different challenges. This does not imply a perfect success-story of recreating a national army in a divided society, but it is worth mentioning that the trajectory of building a national army has been progressive even if at a slow pace.

1 The Yugoslav People's Army (Jugoslovenska Narodna Armija, JNA)

The armed forces of Yugoslavia originated from the Austro-Hungarian army after WWI when the Allied powers allowed Serb volunteers to join the newly created army of the Kingdom of Serbs, Croats and Slovenes in 1919, later known as the Kingdom of Yugoslavia in 1929.[1] This army had a Yugoslav identity and was dominated by the Serbs,[2] a trait that survived in Tito's socialist republic as well. During WWII, the army of the Kingdom, was no match to that of Nazi Germany, and so its defeat during WWII led to the rise of different paramilitary groups defined by ethnicity like the Serbian Chetniks, the Croatian Ustasha. The Communists Partisans led by Josip Broz Tito, achieved victory over the other ethnic paramilitaries, and later on, the defeat of Nazi Germany allowed him to establish the Socialist Federal Republic of Yugoslavia in 1945.

Tito's Partisan victory represented the founding myth and legitimacy for the JNA.[3] The Partisan were a paramilitary-guerrilla group, but they transformed rapidly into a regular army modeled after that of other socialist armies in Eastern Europe,[4] with the help of the Soviet Union.[5] Simultaneously, the authorities established the State Security Service (SDB) affiliated with the Federal Ministry of Internal Affairs in 1946,[6] and it was later on divided into six branches (a branch for each republic of the Federation) during the constitutional reform of 1974.[7] To counter balance the SDB, there was the Second Department of the JNA that dealt with intelligence and counterintelligence.[8] This reflected the totalitarian nature of the regime that relied heavily on the army to control its population and scratch away any possible opposition.

In terms of organization, the state established a republic and provincial-level military units (Teritorijalna Odbrana, TO),[9] which had commanders from their

---

1   M. Deroc, "The Former Yugoslav Army," *East European Quarterly* 19, no. 3 (1985): 363.
2   Ibid., 364.
3   Florian Bieber, "The Role of the Yugoslav People's Army in the Dissolution of Yugoslavia: The Army without a State," ed. Lenard J. Cohen and Jasna Dragovic-Soso, *State Collapse in South-Eastern Europe: New Perspectives on Yugoslavia's Disintegration*, (Purdue: Purdue University Press, 2007), 302.
4   Ibid.
5   Timoslav Dulic and Roland Kustic, "Yugoslavs in Arms: Guerrilla Tradition, Total Defense and Ethnic Security Dilemma," *Europe-Asia Studies* 62, no. 7 (2010): 1058.
6   Helge Luras, "Democratic Oversight in Fragile States: The Case of Intelligence Reform in Bosnia and Herzegovina," *Intelligence and National Security* 29, no. 4 (2014): 603.
7   Ibid.
8   Ibid.
9   Florian Bieber, "The Role of the Yugoslav People's Army in the Dissolution of Yugoslavia," 304.

respective republics and local provinces operating within their borders.[10] The TO was modestly equipped and weak in manpower terms, but its task was to activate and wage a military struggle if the country was occupied.[11] In peace time the TO was to be under the command of the JNA, but in wartime, the republics' national defense staff commanded all units in their respective areas that were occupied.[12] Later during the Balkan war, the TO and other affiliated units were used against the JNA and the militias of other communities. The chain-of-command system began with the presidency as supreme commander of all units, and below him were the republics, provinces and municipalities.[13]

The army preserved its operational independence from the political authority, but Tito's League of Communists infiltrated all ranks of the army. By controlling the army, the League of made the JNA a tool for preserving the Communist grip over the country.[14] For instance, the choice of the Minister of Defense and other high-ranking personnel would not be made without party consent, and traditionally the Minister of Defense would be a member of the Central Committee of the League of Communists.[15] Moreover, only party members were allowed to join the SDB,[16] thus making it extremely hard, if not impossible, for the army to take any independent move from the League of Communists. As a result, when Tito took adventurous and audacious decisions that could have destabilized Yugoslavia, the army had no choice to side with him because it was already infiltrated by his League of Communists, examples of which are the Soviet ideological and political dispute with the USSR (1948), the sacking of Aleksander Rankovic in 1966, and the purge of the Croatian party leadership in 1971. In return, Tito came to honor the army as "the chief guardian of the achievement of our revolution,"[17] and the army "must not merely watch vigilantly over our borders but must also be present inside the country."[18] Therefore, the JNA represented the military wing of the League of Communists.

---

10   Ibid.
11   Adam Roberts, *Nations in Arms: The Theory and Practice of Territorial Defence* (New York: St Martin's Press, 1986), 173.
12   Tomislav Dulic and Roland Kostic, "Yugoslavs in Arms," 1059.
13   Ibid.
14   Florian Bieber, "The Role of the Yugoslav People's Army in the Dissolution of Yugoslavia," 304.
15   Ibid.
16   Helge Luras, "Democratic Oversight in Fragile States," 603.
17   Adam Roberts, *Nations in Arms*, 203.
18   Slobodan Stankovic, "Yugoslav Army Adopts Wait-and-See-Attitude," RFE report 13 January 1986.

The ethnic composition of the JNA was imbalanced and in favour of the Serb community. By the time the army was used by Tito in 1971 to purge the Croatian nationalists, the officer corps and the state security service were each dominated by the Serbs, with a two-thirds (around 60 to 70 percent) constituting these two important military bodies.[19] This led the Croatians to perceive the army as a tool for Serbian hegemony in the Federation, and that was a main reason which explained (in their view) the JNA's hostility and uncompromising approach towards Croatian interests.[20] This incident and the use of the army accounted to a deep mistrust with which Croatian politicians viewed the JNA.[21] Tito responded to these feelings of alienation by introducing a constitutional amendment that enshrined proportionality in the high army ranks to ensure that the constituents of the Yugoslav republic would be fairly represented,[22] in addition to establishing the TO in each republic and province. Art. 24 of the constitution stated that "the composition of the strategic staff and the employment of the high command and leadership functions in the Yugoslav People's Army has to ensure the proportional representation of republics and autonomous provinces."[23] Moreover, there were other measures taken to ensure proportionality, like introducing a national (ethnic based) and republican quotas in military schools to counter the Serb domination.[24] Nevertheless, the Serbs continued to dominate the officer corps and by the time of Tito's death in 1980, the command of the JNA was under the control of Serbs, including the Ministry of Defense, Chief of the armed forces, and the Secretary of the League of Communist Committee in the army.[25]

In order to understand the implications of communal hegemony in the army in the Yugoslavian case, it is important to study the composition of the JNA. Table 1 shows the demography of Yugoslavia in the 1980s, and the ethnic distribution of the army ranks according to ethnic affiliation. The Serbs community represented less than 40 percent of the population, the Croats came

---

19 Slobodan Stankovic, "Tito and the Army," 25, 3 May 1980, https://storage.osaarchivum.org/low/2b/11/2b11a530-9551-48e8-a307-b4d2b8d05b3c_l.pdf, accessed 26 October 2020.
20 Robert W. Dean, "Civil-Military Relations in Yugoslavia," *Armed Forces and Society* 3, no. 1 (1976): 37.
21 Ibid.
22 Florian Bieber, "The Role of the Yugoslav People's Army in the Dissolution of Yugoslavia," 306–7.
23 Constitution of SFRY 1974, art. 242.
24 Miroslav Hadzic, *The Yugoslav People's Agony: The Role of the Yugoslav People's Army* (Farnham: Ashgate Publishing, 2002), 215.
25 Florian Bieber, "The Role of the Yugoslav People's Army in the Dissolution of Yugoslavia," 306.

TABLE 1 Ethnic composition of the AFBiH[26]

	Bosnian Serb	Muslim	Bosnian Croat	Other	Total
1992/93	67,000	50,000	50,000		167,000
1995/96	75,000	92,000	92,000		217,000
2000/01	30,000	30,000	30,000		70,000
2013	3,533(33.6%)	4,826(45.9%)	2,084(19.8%)	74(0.7%)	10,450
2016	3,528(33.6%)	4,820(45.9%)	2,079(19.8%)	73(0.7%)	10,500

SOURCE: VERA STOJAROVA, "UNIFYING THE ARMED FORCES OF BOSNIA AND HERZEGOVINA," 74.

next with 22.1 percent, Bosniaks (Muslims from Bosnia) 8.4 percent, Slovenes 8.2 percent, Albanians 6.4 percent, Macedonians 5.81 percent and Montenegrins 2.5 percent. Despite that, the Serbs had more than half the active army staff (57.17 percent), much more than their overall demographic composition in the whole country. Next in line were the Croats with 12.51 percent, almost half of their demographic percentage of the population, followed by the Macedonians with 6.74 percent, Montenegrins 5.82 percent and Muslims 3.65 percent, a high disproportionality from the demographic status of each community. Matters are even more complicated at the level of officer corps: the Serbs had 60 percent, Croats had 12.6 percent, Yugoslavs, Macedonians and Montenegrins each around 6 percent. Finally, the Serb domination of the officer corps was strengthened by their plural majority among recruits by having 31 percent of recruits, followed by 18.52 percent for Croatians, then 12 percent Muslims (Bosniaks), 9 percent for Albanians, 7 percent for Yugoslavs and the same for Slovens, then 6.11 percent for Macedonians.[27] As a result, the constitutional amendment was about ethnic representation in the army within a Serb hegemony. This eventually led to the loss of legitimacy of the JNA and its disintegration along ethnic lines when the war broke out in 1991.

A similar problem emerged within the officer corps whereby the Serbs constituted 60 percent of Majors, 63 percent of Lieutenant-Colonels, 64.5 percent of Colonels, and 50.3 percent of Generals, followed by the Croats with 10.4 percent of Majors, 10.8 percent of Lieutenant-Colonels, 9.4 percent of Colonels, and 14.4 percent of Generals. The Muslims' share varied between 2.3 percent highest at the level of Majors, 2 percent at the level of Generals and lowest at

---

26 Vera Stojarova, "Unifying the Armed Forces of Bosnia and Herzegovina," 74.
27 Ibid.

the level of Colonels with 1.2 percent. Interestingly, the Montenegrins who only represented 2.5 percent of the total population, had a high percentage of Generals with 12.4 (slightly lower than that of the Croatians), and a higher percentage than the Croatians at the level of Colonels (11 percent).[28] This was mainly due to the fact that the Montenegrins were associated with the Serbian ethnic identity, giving them privileges and at the same time guaranteeing that the dominant status in the army at all levels is for the ethnic Serbs. Moreover, the Serb hegemony in the army was also present in Croatia where all key positions in the fifth army in Zagreb on the eve of the war were held by Serbs, in contrast to the situation few years back where some 50 percent of the important military positions in the republic were held by Croats.[29] As a result, the dynamics of power relations within the officer corps was greatly in favor of the Serbs, making ethnic representation of other communities at this level no more than superficial and cosmetic.

Under such circumstances, the army was no longer in a position to represent itself as a guarantor of the Yugoslavian identity as it was dominated by the Serbs. With the democratic process underway in Yugoslavia, elites sought to heavily invest in their primordial-ethnic sphere and mobilized their constituents according to nationalism. This was an easy task in the Balkans as history, memory and ethnic demarcation were easily resurrected in the Balkan mosaic. Hence, Serbs with Milosevic came up with the notion of Greater Serbia, or a Yugoslavia controlled by the Serbs as the largest ethnic community, while the Croats and the Slovenes sought to depart from what they perceived an imagined Yugoslav nation to establish their own independent states. The JNA got caught in the nationalist maelstrom unleashed everywhere in Yugoslavia, it could not stop violence because it was deeply infiltrated by all national communities who eventually deserted into their own ethnic enclaves, and at the same time military leaders realized that the old Yugoslavia was dead, so they needed to find their own place in the framework of the new nation-states. Moreover, the JNA's historic control by the League of Communists meant that the army never managed to take independent actions from the political authority even to safeguard security and stability in Yugoslavia. Without a political order for this purpose, the army had no role in protecting the unity of the country. The result was one of the worst atrocities in human history, probably similar to that which occurred during the times of Hulago.

---

28 Ibid., 307.
29 Martin Spegelj, "The First Phase, 1990–1992: The JNA Prepares for Aggression and Croatia for Defense," in ed. Branka Magas and Ivo Zanic, *The War in Croatia and Bosnia-Herzegovina, 1991–1995* (London: Frank Cass, 2001), 21.

The third Balkan war officially began on 26th of June 1991, the day after Slovenia's declaration of independence.[30] In Croatia, Tudjman deprived Serbs of their status as a constituent minority of the republic thus leading to a Serb rebellion in Krajina.[31] In the first week of the war, around 1000 Croatian soldiers in the JNA deserted and joined the Croatian forces.[32] Later, when Bosnia-Herzegovina became the battlefield of the Balkan war, the Serbs and the Croatians were in open revolt, receiving support from their respective ethnic republics. In the end, what was left of the JNA became attached to the Serbian army.[33] This study will not endeavor to talk about all the armies that emerged from the JNA since Serbia, Croatia, Slovenia and other republics – with the exception of BiH – have created a homogenous state and do not have a power sharing system. Hence, the concentration in this chapter is on the army of BiH after the third Balkan war.

2   The Making of the AFBiH

After the four-year war in the Balkans, BiH emerged as a destroyed and a poor country, with a 200 billion USD worth of damage.[34] Around 80 percent of men in the country above the age of 37 at that time could be considered as former combatants,[35] and the World Bank placed this figure at between 400,000 and 500,000 men.[36] With this massive mobilization, some 30,966 Bosniak soldiers were killed or went missing during the war, other 20,830 Serbs and 5,625 Croats, which meant that 59 percent of the total victims were soldiers.[37] The war ended with a NATO military intervention sponsored by the United Nations, and the Americans brokered the Dayton agreement that promoted power sharing and territorial autonomy for each ethnic group. The Dayton agreement

---

30   Francine Friedman, *Bosnia and Herzegovina: A Polity on the Brink* (London: Routledge, 2004), 37.
31   Leslie Benson, *Yugoslavia: A Concise History* (Hampshire: Palgrave Macmillan, 2004), 157.
32   Florian Bieber, "The Role of the Yugoslav People's Army in the Dissolution of Yugoslavia," 324.
33   Leslie Benson, *Yugoslavia*, 162.
34   Dujko Hasic, Institute for War Crimes, in an interview to Radio Free Europe, 19 November 2002, www.danas.org/programi/haaska, accessed 9 October 2020.
35   Oliwia Berdak, "Reintegrating Veterans in Bosnia and Herzegovina and Croatia: Citizenship and Gender Effects," *Women's Studies International Forum* 49, (2015): 52.
36   Xavier Bougarel, "The Shadow of Heroes: Former Combatants in post-war Bosnia-Herzegovina," *International Social Science Journal* 58, no. 189 (2006): 479.
37   Lara J. Nettlefield, "From Battlefield to the Barracks: The ICTY and the Armed Forces of Bosnia and Herzegovina," *International Journal of Transitional Justice* 4, no. 1 (2010): 94.

introduced the Office of High Representative (OHR) with powers to override any law, legislation, decision, constitutional amendment and resolution. The OHR reports to a steering Committee of the Peace Implementation Council that consists of representatives from the key international community countries and organizations (UN, USA, EU, Organization for Security and Cooperation in Europe).[38] The accord created a three-member presidency at the national level, where each community elects its president, two federal entities, Republika Srpska (Serbs) representing 49 percent of the territory and the Federation of Bosnia-Herzegovina (FBiH) that represented a union between Bosniaks and Croats, with 51 percent of the land. Just prior to the war, Bosniaks represented 43.5 percent of the population, Serbs 31.2 percent and Croats 17.43 percent.[39] Each federal entity has its own president, constitution, parliament, government, and most importantly, for few years each federal entity had its own ministry of defense and a separate security force.[40] NATO's mandate allowed it to establish an international peacekeeping force, "the Implementation Force (IFOR)," with 60,000 soldiers in order to achieve a lasting cessation to the failed mission of the United Nations Protection Forces (UNPRPFOR).[41] IFOR conducted reform of the defense forces within the framework of the Joint Military Commission (JMC).[42] The JMC was staffed with representatives of the international community and entity-level personnel, and its role was to monitor allegations of ceasefire violations. The JMC allowed the international forces in the country to police violations of the Dayton agreement, and if any violation was documented, it would summon the entity armed forces to end hostilities.[43]

Since BiH became a federal state with extensive powers to each federal entity, the internal borders had to be properly demarcated. Once that was done, the Dayton agreement demanded that all armed forces withdraw into their respective entities.[44] The newly created army of Bosnia, hence, was divided into two

---

38 Graeme P. Herd and Tom Tracy, "Democratic Civil-Military Relations in Bosnia and Herzegovina: A New Paradigm of Protectorates?," *Armed Forces and Society* 32, no. 4 (2006): 550.
39 Tim Judah, "Bosnia Powerless to Halt Democratic Decline," *Balkan Insight*, 21 November 2019, https://balkaninsight.com/2019/11/21/bosnia-powerless-to-halt-demographic-decline/, accessed 27 October 2020.
40 Alex Jeffrey, "Building State Capacity in Post-Conflict Bosnia and Herzegovina: The Case of Brcko District," *Political Geography* 25, no. 2 (2006): 208.
41 Denis Hadzovic, "The Office of the High Representative and Security Sector Reform in Bosnia and Herzegovina," *Centre for Security Studies – BH*, (2009): 31, http://www.css.ba/wp-content/uploads/2011/06/images_docs_ar.pdf, accessed 27 October 2020.
42 Dayton Agreement, Annex 1-A.
43 Lara J. Nettlefield, "From Battlefield to the Barracks," 91.
44 Danijela Dudley, "Civil-Military Relations in Bosnia and Herzegovina," 124.

separate ethnic armies interacting only by high military ranking officers, with each ethnic community controlling the corps of their respective ethnic group. The army of Republika Srpska (VRS) was created by the allocation of forces of the Yugoslav Second Military District (created in 1992) under the command of General Tarko Mladic;[45] the army of Federation of Bosnia and Herzegovina consisted of three Bosniak corps and one Croatian corps,[46] and each community control had their respective battalions as there were no heterogeneous units, so they had separate chains of command. The Serb and Croat contingent were heavily influenced by Belgrade and Zagreb heavily, as the funding came mainly from there.[47] The three armies represented the remnants of wartime militaries,[48] and in the absence of a common command it was fair to say that the army had a sectarian, rather than national character.[49] A very important step towards military modernization was taken in FBiH which consulted the Military Professional Resources Incorporated (MPRI) to establish its ministry of defense, the joint command, introduced the Training and Doctrine Command, established modern training methods copied from the American military system, in addition to train and equip the FBiH army,[50] which received military equipment from France and the USA. The army of RS, however, did not benefit from this program since it was closely associated with Serbia's army and received funding, training and equipment from the latter. Hence, VRS was not well equipped as its counterpart in FBiH.

Despite implementing a detailed power sharing system for Bosnia with consociational principles, the Dayton agreement gave no special attention to military matters. For instance, the Parliamentary Assembly of BiH had no Committee for Defense and Security, and no power or oversight over any of the armies.[51] The national government had nothing to do with military affairs; instead it was the entity parliament of each federation – alongside the Croatian

---

45   Elliot Short, "The Orao Affair: The Key to Military Integration in Post-Dayton Bosnia and Herzegovina," *The Journal of Slavic Military Studies* 31, no. 1 (2018): 44.
46   Peter Fitzgerald, "The Armed Forces in Bosnia and Herzegovina," *SFOR Informer*, no. 127, (2001), https://www.nato.int/sfor/indexinf/127/p03a/chapter4.htm, accessed 31 August 2021.
47   "Bosnia and Herzegovina Public Expenditure Review," *World Bank*, no. 171 61-BiH, (1997).
48   Danijela Dudley, "Civil-Military Relations in Bosnia and Herzegovina," 124.
49   Bisera Turkovic, "Civil-Military Relations in Bosnia and Herzegovina," ed. Philipp H. Fluri, Gustav E. Gustenau and Plamen I. Pantev, *The Evolution of Civil-Military Relations in South-East Europe: Continuing Democratic Reform and Adapting to the Needs of Fighting Terrorism*, (Heidelberg: Physica-Verlag, 2005), 83.
50   Elliot Short, "The Orao Affair," 41.
51   Danijela Dudley, "Civil-Military Relations in Bosnia," 124.

Defense Council – that had authority over each of their respective armies.[52] Moreover, civil and military leaders had extremely limited interaction as they only met to discuss defense budget.[53] The Dayton agreement gave so much powers for entities over security and military issues to the extent that each one had their own defense laws and regulations on their armies which defined their defense establishments and institutions for their control. With such fragmentation of military affairs, it was obvious that many leaders were either calling for secession (in RS), or for further decentralization as the Croats in FBiH.

The only security related body created by the Dayton agreement was the Standing Committee on Military Matters (SCMM). The SCMM was established in 1995 as a coordinating body within the collective presidency and it consisted of the Presidents of BiH, their military advisers, the Ministers and Chiefs of Defense of both federal entities, along with some national and international observers.[54] The SCMM functions were activated in July 1999 but did not enjoy any important role, because of the lack of resources,[55] especially that BiH lacked a Ministry of Defense at the national level, and the irony was that entity governments had their own ministries of defense. In addition, the armies of each entity kept their own bank accounts separate, and a report by the International Crisis Group in 1998 stated that the Bosniaks received military funding from the Gulf (40 percent) and the remaining raised locally, while the Croatian elements of the army receied 83 percent of their fund from Croatia and the rest from émigrés and the Gulf.[56] The army of RS received 40 percent of its funding from Yugoslavia and until 2002 its officers' wages were paid by Belgrade.[57] Moreover, most funding to the military came from outside official budgets, through informal arrangements with local parties that gave soldiers access to food, fuel, equipment, and housing without any official record.[58] Eventually, smuggling and trafficking were commonplace in the whole territory.

---

52 Bisera Turkovic, "Civil-Military Relations in Bosnia and Herzegovina," 83–4.
53 Ibid., 83.
54 Francine Friedman, *Bosnia and Herzegovina*, 67.
55 David Lightburn, "NATO Security Cooperation Activities with Bosnia and Herzegovina," *NATO Review* 46 (1998): 31–4.
56 "Is Dayton Failing? Bosnia Four Years After the Peace Agreement," *International Crisis Group*, no. 80 (1999): 9.
57 James Gow and Ivan Zverzhanovski, *Security, Democracy and War Crimes: Security Sector Transformation in Serbia* (London: Palgrave Macmillan, 2013), 124.
58 "Bosnia and Herzegovina: From Aid Dependency to Fiscal Self-Reliance, A Public Expenditure and Institutional Review," *World Bank*, report no. 24297-BiH, (2002): 15, https://documents1.worldbank.org/curated/en/105351468198847162/pdf/multiopage.pdf, accessed 31 August 2021.

The military segmentation according to ethnic lines was also applied in the military intelligence. In the direct aftermath of the war, the Serbs created the State Security Service (SNS) attached to the Ministry of Internal Affairs in the RS, which was later renamed Intelligence-Security Service (OBS – Obavestajno Bezbednosne Sluzbe) in 1998. The Croats formed the National Security Service (Sluzba Nacionalne Sigurnosti) in Mostar, and in 1996 the Bosniaks established the Agency for Research and Documentation (Agencija za Istraivanje I Dokumentaciju).[59]

Elites in BiH had no choice but to move forward with structural and institutional reforms in the armed forces, overcoming the burden of the Balkan wars. There are different reasons that forced elites to follow this path: the Orao scandal, intelligence irregularities by Bosnian secret services, financial difficulties and the need for regional/international integration with the EU and NATO respectively. To start with the Orao scandal, an aircraft company that was found to be selling motors and reserve parts for airplanes to Saddam's Iraq.[60] That happened at a time when the Americans were arguing that Saddam had managed to circumvent international sanctions, and it angered the Americans as elements of Bosnia are supporting America's enemy in a way or another, making it look as if US either had no control over Bosnia, or its mission in the country was a complete failure. Moreover, it was common knowledge for the international community that the Croat and Bosniak intelligence service were highly politicized, protecting ethnic interest and they themselves were implicated in ethnic cleansing and organized crime.[61] So, if the RS had managed to smuggle spare parts to Iraq, then they definitely were doing dirty business under the American nose in the federation. The second reason was that the military intelligence of RS was spying on political, diplomatic and military activities of the US, NATO member countries and EU representatives in BiH.[62] It meant that someone was ready to sell sensitive information for American enemies or competitors at a time when the Bush Administration was going aggressively asserting their international prominence in international relations. Third, the reforms were needed by elites to enter the Euro-Atlantic security community, be on road towards EU membership, and receive invitation to join NATO's Partnership for Peace (PfP) at the June 2004 Istanbul Summit.[63]

---

59 Helge Luras, "Democratic Oversight in Fragile States," 604.
60 Bisera Turkovic, "Civil-Military Relations in Bosnia," 84.
61 Graeme P. Herd and Tom Tracy, "Democratic Civil-Military Relations in Bosnia and Herzegovina: A New Paradigm for Protectorates?," *Armed Forces and Society* 32, no. 4 (2006): 560.
62 Bisera Turkovic, "Civil-Military Relations in Bosnia," 94.
63 Graeme P. Herd and Tom Tracy, "Democratic Civil-Military Relations in Bosnia," 550.

It became important for BiH to join the EU and NATO to support its fragile economy. Also, all of this coincided with the inability of Zagreb and Belgrade to continue supporting the armies and intelligence service of the Croats and Serbs of Bosnia respectively.[64] Hence, by early 2000s, the country was ready for serious changes in its military affairs.

3   Institutional and Structural Reforms in the AFBiH

Once the irregularities of the AFBiH became widespread, whether at the level of intelligence, smuggling, border trafficking or in the Orao affair, reform in the military became inevitable. For this purpose, the OHR benefitted from the Bonn powers granted to the office in December 1997, which gave it the right to "impose laws in the absence of willingness of local governing parties to adopt them and to dismiss from office public officials."[65] With these powers, the OHR had the authority to dismiss officials, restructure constitutional commission, impose economic legislation, and establish an Independent Judicial Commission.[66] Elites also understood that they needed to cooperate with the OHR as the regional and international pressure to achieve military reforms were unprecedented. Between 2000 and 2003, the OHR seized the Bank of Herzegovina which was the main source of funding for the Croatian Army in BiH, abolished the Supreme Defense Council of RS, and abolished or amended constitutions and laws in each entity to remove references that infer entities are states in their own right rather than part of the state of BiH.[67] The SCMM benefitted from the OHR's support, and issued its famous five pledges:
- to implement defense reforms that will hasten European integration and contribute to regional stability.
- to strengthen State-level institutions that exercise civilian command and control over the Armed Forces of Bosnia and Herzegovina.

---

64   Danijela Dudley, "Civil-Military Relations in Bosnia," 130.
65   For further details on the Bonn powers of the OHR, see Tim Banning, "The 'Bonn Powers' of the High Representative in Bosnia Herzegovina: Tracing a Legal Figment," *Göttingen Journal of International Law* 6, no. 2 (2014): 259–302.
66   "PIC Bonn Conclusion," *Office of the High Representative in Bosnia-Herzegovina*, http://www.ohr.int/pic-bonn-conclusions/?print=pdf, accessed 27 October 2020.
67   "Decision Appointing a Provisional Administrator for the Hercegovacka Banka," *Office of High Representative in Bosnia-Herzegovina*, (2001); "High Representative Acts to Ensure That Military in Bih Are under Effective Civilian Control," *Office of High Representative in Bosnia-Herzegovina*, (2003).

- to provide comprehensive and transparent parliamentary oversight over State-level defense institutions.
- to ensure professional, modern and affordable Armed Forces.
- to restructure armed forces to be able to participate in the PfP, integrate into wider Euro-Atlantic structures, and engage in peace support operations.[68]

In addition to that, the OHR created the Defense Reform Commission (DRC) and tasked it with formulating a comprehensive plan on security reform and create a state-level defense structure in BiH.[69] The DRC consisted of 12 members which included the secretary general of the SCMM, entity presidents, ministers of Defense of RS and FBiH, representatives of the OHR, NATO, and other regional security organizations.[70] It was headed by James R. Locher III, a well-known American expert on military reform who had been brought in 1996 under the Train and Equip effort to counsel the FBiH Ministry of Defense on civil military relations.[71] Later in 2004, the DRC's role was extended by the OHR, and it became co-chaired by NATO representative Raffi Gregorian, and the Minister of Defense,[72] to further look at additional security sector reform as the changes done in the first round were not satisfactory for goals set for BiH. A new law was then adopted by the parliament on 1 January 2005, highlighting important institutional and structural reforms in BiH.

3.1 Institutional Reforms

The first and most important achievement by the DRC was proposing a Law on Defense, adopted by the Parliament on 1 December 2003 (amendment in 2005). The law institutionalized the democratic-civilian control of the army through a newly created state-level Ministry of Defense, that is by updating the SCMM into the level of ministry. The ministry consists of the office of the minister of defense, eleven departments, the verification center and the joint command of the AFBiH.[73] It also established that the Minister of Defense will

---

68   "The Path to Partnership for Peace," *Defence Reform Commission*, (2003): 44; http://richardbainter.com/PDF/Defense_Reform_Commission_2003.pdf, accessed 27 October 2020.
69   "Decision Establishing the Defense Reform Commission," *Office of the High Representative in Bosnia and Herzegovina*, (2003).
70   Ibid.
71   Christopher J. Lamb, Sarah Arkin and Sally Scudder, "The Bosnian Train and Equip Program: A Lesson in Interagency Integration of Hard and Soft Power," *Institute for National Strategic Studies*, no. 15 (2014): 52.
72   Ingrid Olstad Busterud, "Defense Sector Reform in the Western Balkans, - Different Approaches and Different Tools," *European Security* 24, no. 2 (2015): 338.
73   Bisera Turkovic, "Civil-Military Relations in Bosnia," 88.

have two deputies each, ensuring that all three ethnic groups in the country are represented at the highest level of the ministry. A similar arrangement was created with the chief of the joint staff and operation command, where each has two deputies.[74] In this way, the security system enjoyed a broad ethnic representation and power sharing mechanism in decision making, assuring that the army command and the ministry of defense will not be dominated by one ethnic group. The minister of defense was also subject to the supreme command and control authority of the collective presidency.[75] These institutional reforms were of critical importance as it allowed the subsequent law on defense of 2005, agreed upon in the second round, to abolish the entity ministries of defense. Moreover, the law abolished the entity armies and unified the AFBiH into one single army with one chain of command whose highest authority was the collective presidency.[76] Hence, military and defense issues became in the hands of the central authorities exclusively. In addition, just under the ministry of defense was the joint staff of the armed forces which takes directives and orders from the ministry. It consists of the chief of the joint staff, deputy chief of the joint staff for operations, deputy chief for resources, and military staff from the armed forces.[77] The deputies cannot be from the same ethnic group of the chief of joint staff. The law also established the Commander of the Operational Command and Commander of the Support Command.[78] The chief of the joint staff cannot be of the same ethnic community as the commander of the operational command or that of the support command,[79] neither can the commander of operational command or support command be of the same ethnicity.[80]

The democratic oversight of the army was in the hands of the national parliament which became responsible for declaring war and state of emergency, practice oversight over defense institutions and armed forces, passing legislation regarding budget, equipment, training and deployment, approving appointments of senior officers, and conducting investigations in all defense related matters.[81] The amended law of defense in 2005 prohibited the use of the military for party purposes, abolished conscription and it reiterated equal

---

74 "Law on Defence of Bosnia and Herzegovina," *Official Gazette of Bosnia and Herzegovina,*" 88/05.
75 Ibid.
76 Ibid.
77 Ibid.
78 Ibid.
79 Ibid.
80 Ibid.
81 Danijela Dudley, "Civil-Military Relations in Bosnia," 132.

representation in the ministry of defense.[82] In addition, the reforms led to a vetting and selection process for the entire army and Ministry of Defense, a rebalancing of the rank-structure along with forced retirement of older soldiers.[83] The law also established a parliamentary oversight of the army by the Joint Defense and Security Policy Committee.[84] The SCMM was preserved as an institution with an advisory role, since most of its important competencies were now attributed to the ministry of defense. Moreover, the law institutionalized the 1st of December (which is the date of unifying the armed forces in 2003) as the anniversary of the army.

At the level of symbols, the law required that the AFBiH shall have its flag, anthem and insignia.[85] The flag and anthem shall be that of BiH, and it allowed regiments, brigades, units and institutions to have their own insignia. General officers are prohibited from wearing their regiment's insignia, as it refers to that of their respective communities. Most importantly, the ministry of defense regulates the design of flags and insignias, which requires the approval of the presidency.[86] In this way, none of these symbols can become a source of intimidation by one community against the other.

Another major institutional reform deals with the integration of military intelligence. As each ethnic group enjoyed a separate military intelligence the first step was to unify that of FBiH (Bosniaks and Croats had their own intelligence), which happened in 2002.[87] This was followed by the unification of the intelligence of FBiH and that of the RS in 2004 by creating the Intelligence and Security Agency (OSA).[88] The Law on the Intelligence Security Agency of Bosnia and Herzegovina established the position of Director-General, Deputy Director-General and Inspector-General to be filled by a representative of an one ethnic group.[89] An unofficial agreement reached between the three communities divided the positions in a corporate manner, so the Director-General was to be a Bosniak, deputy Director a Serb and Inspector a Croat.[90] At the

---

82   Ibid.
83   Louis-Alexandre Berg, "From Weakness to Strength: The Political Roots of Security Sector Reform in Bosnia and Herzegovina," *International Peacekeeping* 21, no. 2 (2014): 158.
84   "Defence White Paper of Bosnia and Herzegovina," June 2005, 11 http://www.mod.gov.ba/files/file/dokumenti/defense/engwhitebook.pdf, accessed 27 October 2020.
85   Law on Defense of Bosnia and Herzegovina.
86   Ibid.
87   Helge Luras, "Democratic Oversight in Fragile States," 605.
88   Ibid.
89   Law on the Intelligence and Security Agency of Bosnia and Herzegovina, April 2004, http://www.vertic.org/media/National%20Legislation/Bosnia-Herzegovina/BA_Law_on_Intelligence_and_Security_Agency.pdf, accessed 27 October 2020.
90   Ibid.

time of unification of intelligence service, each registered employee underwent a vetting procedure and a new criteria for professional qualification were established.[91] In the vetting process, the court archives and intelligence in BiH and archives from the ICTY were used to vet the registered employees. This was motivated to provide legitimacy to the intelligence sector and break away with the notorious history of this institution during the war.

The law on the OSA states that it is responsible to gather intelligence both within and outside BiH regarding threats to national security, which are understood to mean threats against sovereignty, territorial integrity, constitutional order, fundamental economic stability, terrorism, espionage, organized crime, trafficking and weapons of mass destruction proliferation.[92] The OSA has four field offices: Sarajevo, Mostar, Banja Luka and Brcko, in addition to few minor detachments in smaller towns around the country.[93] The OSA is under the control of the Chair of the Council of Ministers, who, according to the law, "shall supervise, and be politically responsible for, the work of the agency,"[94] and he is responsible for establishing the Executive Intelligence Committee to advise him on his task, which in turn consists of ministers representing the three ethnic communities.[95] Beside the Prime Minister, the collective presidency is to direct the Inspector General on internal investigative matters, and they are entitled to receive intelligence, and approve international intelligence cooperation that involves the OSA.[96] The government as a whole is responsible for the Intelligence Security Policy Platform, the annual Activity Program, and for defining coordination and assistance between the OSA and other national bodies and institutions.[97] With respect to the parliamentary oversight, each chamber of the assembly appoints six members to a joint intelligence-security committee, and the chairman must not belong to the governing coalition.[98] The committee may call for hearings and conduct inquiries about the legality of the work of the agency, and it provided opinions on the top three position appointments and reviews the budget expenditure of the OSA.[99] The law also established the Joint Committee and Security Agency as a parliamentary

---

91   Helge Luras, "Democratic Oversight in Fragile States," 608.
92   Law on the Intelligence and Security Agency of Bosnia and Herzegovina.
93   Ibid.
94   Ibid.
95   Ibid.
96   Ibid.
97   Ibid.
98   Ibid.
99   Ibid.

oversight for the work of the OSA.[100] The law, then, has diffused military authority rather than making it concentrated in one office. Consequently, a community's occupation of important military positions is shared with deputies and also supervised by other legislative institutions, where opposition of each community is present.

Democratic control in the legislative and diffusion of military power in the executive are signs of good governance. The radical institutional reforms that were done in a short period helped transform the AFBiH into a national institution. However, it still required further a set of structural changes that would allow the army to function in a proper manner.

3.2 *Structural Reforms*

The main structural reform had to do with the chain of command. In the first round of reforms, the law of 2003 established two chains of command: an administrative one with entity level control of their respective armed forces, whose task was to train, equip and recruit personnel into the army. The second chain of command was operational which gave authority to state institutions over both armies.[101] Figure 2 shows the two types of chains of commands: The administrative command begins with the entity presidents, and passes through the entity ministries of defense, followed by the Joint Chiefs of Staff and Joint Command in FBiH as the army represented two ethnic communities, and ends in the army. In the case of RS, the chain of command began with the president, then the ministry of Defense, followed by the RS General Staff and ends in the army. This meant that the law had preserved the ethnic nature of the armies in BiH. The operational chain of command, however, was the national command of the army and began with the collective presidency, followed BiH's newly established ministry of defense, then the AFBiH joint staff, the AFBiH operational command, and finally the army units of both entities. This kind of division of authority into administrative and operational command created confusion at the lower levels of the army when it had to report back to its respective authorities. Also, parallel authority in such situations may create problems in issuing orders, as the entity levels may issue an order that is not compatible with that at the state level, hence, which order supersedes the other? Eventually, rather than creating a solid, strong and unified

---

100   Denis Hadzovic and Mirela Hodvic, "Draft Report on the Parliamentary Oversight of the Security Sector for BiH for 2012," *Centre for Security Studies*, (2013): 4, http://css.ba/wp-content/uploads/2011/06/images_docs2_nacrt%20izvjestaaja%20english.pdf, accessed 27 October 2020.
101   Danijela Dudley, "Civil-Military Relations in Bosnia and Herzegovina," 129.

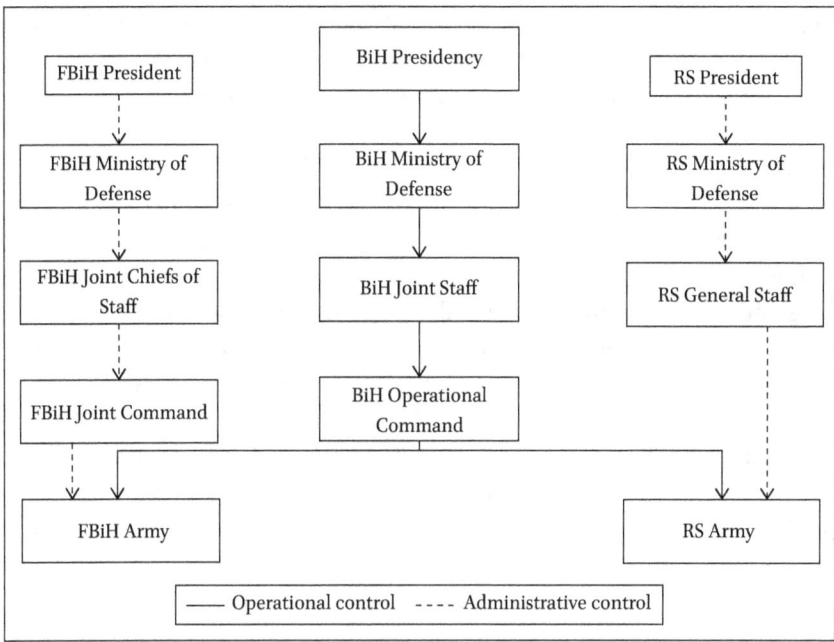

FIGURE 2   Chain of Command according to the 2003 law on defense

SOURCE: DANIJELA DUDLEY, "CIVIL-MILITARY RELATIONS IN BOSNIA AND HERZEGOVINA: STATE LEGITIMACY AND DEFENSE INSTITUTIONS," *ARMED FORCES AND SOCIETY* 42, NO. 1 (2016): 129.

army, the ambiguity created by the law could have led to civil-military conflict within each entity and between entities and state. As a result, a new reform was introduced in the second round to resolve this crisis.

The amended law of 2005 created a straightforward chain of command after abolishing the ministries of defense and unifying the two armies. The minister has two deputies: one for policy and planning whose role is to plan policies, provide internal cooperation, and oversee military intelligence as well as command, control and communications, while the other is for resource management who's responsible for personnel, finance, budget, procurement and logistics.[102] The law gave the state ministry of defense powers to oversee defense policy and strategy, operationally and administratively. The Ministry of Defense, enjoyed the following competencies: develop defense strategy, propose the defense budget, organize the armed forces administratively and logistically, provide equipment, development and training for its personnel,

---

102   "Law on Defence of Bosnia and Herzegovina".

implement defense policies, supervise all subjects in the army, and ensure transparency in the ministry.[103] The ministry also represents the state at the international level in all defense matters, makes recommendations to the presidency regarding the size and structure of the army, establish organization and formation commands and units in the army, establish planning for armed conflict, peace support operations, and response to natural disaster, plan and oversee implementation of all intelligence activities, employment, promotion and dismissal of military personnel, regulate the procurement of goods and services, manage and regulate the use of moveable and unmovable properties.[104] The supreme command of the army was now in the collective presidency, and decisions ought to be taken by unanimous vote. The presidency has the right to deploy the army by issuing directives to the minister of defense of this purpose, ask the military to assist civilian authorities in times of natural disaster, determine the size of the army and ethnic composition, appoint the chief and his deputies of the joint command, as well as that of the

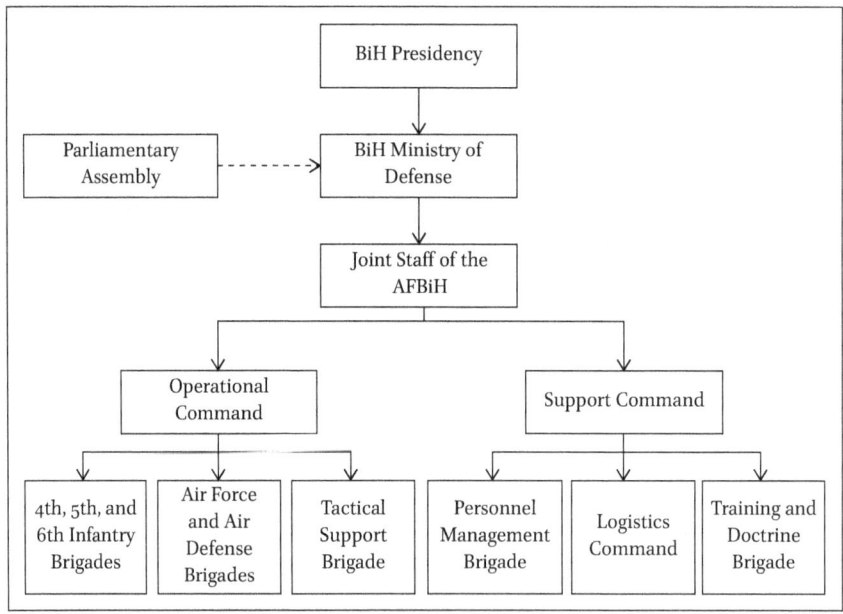

FIGURE 3   Chain of command according to the 2005 law on defense
SOURCE: DANIJELA DUDLEY, "CIVIL-MILITARY RELATIONS IN BOSNIA," 136

103   Ibid.
104   Ibid.

commander and deputy commanders of the operational command and support command. The presidency also enjoys the right to promote, appoint and remove general officers, remove the general chiefs and their deputies, appoint and remove military-diplomatic representatives abroad.[105]

Below the collective presidency comes the ministry of defense, followed by the Joint Staff of the AFBiH that controls the operational and support command: the former consists of the 4th, 5th and 6th infantry brigades, air force and air defense brigades, along with the tactical support brigades, while the latter is made up of the personnel management brigade, logistics command and the training and doctrine brigade.[106] This elevated the status of the armed force to become a national institution with one doctrine and command that functioned within the framework of consensus.

The joint staff is responsible for planning, organization, implementation of directives and orders from the minister of defense. It develops the military strategy, overlooks the engagement of military forces to ensure they are in accordance with the laws, develop military policies and provide support to the military staff of the ministry of defense.[107] The chief of the joint command acts as military advisor to the presidency and minister of defense, ensure the readiness of the armed forces, issue orders in accordance with the joint staff, oversee and ensure the execution of orders from the ministry of defense, recommends the promotion and appointment of colonels, brigadiers and generals. The deputy chief of the joint staff for operations is responsible for military intelligence, counter-intelligence, security operations, develop capabilities for the implementation of operational commands and plans, modernization of the army, and maintaining relations between civil authorities and the army. As for the deputy chief of the joint staff for resources, he enjoys responsibilities regarding human resources, supply, maintenance, transport and staff services, in addition to everything related to technology-based staff system.[108] The three positions are recommended of the ministry of defense and appointed by the presidency after consulting the SCMM.[109]

Regarding the role of the commander of the operational command, he oversees all tactical units, shall command operational units for any mission that requires deployment and employment of the army, and is the commander for training of the army and multinational exercises, he employs forces to carry

---

105 Ibid.
106 Danijela Dudley, "Civil-Military Relations in Bosnia," 136.
107 "Law on Defence of Bosnia and Herzegovina".
108 Ibid.
109 Ibid.

out specific orders from the command, appoints commanders of temporary units to accomplish specific missions.[110] The commander is under the authority of the chief of joint staff and has two deputies from the other two communities.[111] They are appointed in a similar manner as the members of the joint staff but their positions have to be confirmed by the parliament within 45 days of the presidential decision.[112] With respect to the commander of the support command, he is responsible for logistics, training and doctrine, personnel, prepares support plans for operations, organize departments within the command as he sees necessary, support deployment and redeployment of the army, coordinate and approve aspects of administration, including control over resources and equipment, recommend to the chief of joint command logistical requirements and standards for personnel training. He is also responsible for identifying training requirements, organize the implementation of individual training, maintain the immovable properties of the army, develop and implement plans to manage ammunition and weapons storage sites, advice on the procurement of goods and services, and is responsible to arrange personnel records management in accordance with regulations rendered by the ministry of defense.[113] He is also appointed in an identical manner like the commander of operational command.[114]

The duties of the AFBiH are laid out in the law of Defense. They are institutionalized in the army doctrine and military role which include participation in collective security operation, peace support (example of which is AFBiH's participation in peacekeeping in Iraq) and self-defense operations, combating terrorism, assisting civilian authorities in responding to natural disasters, and fulfilling BiH's international obligations (as in its relationship to the ICTY).[115] The army is answerable to the collective presidency, and it is now the largest multi-ethnic institution in the country.[116]

Another important structural reform is basically the parliamentary role in civil-military and security relations. For instance, the law of 2005 face the parliamentary tremendous powers represented in the right to declare war and state of emergency, full oversight of the armed forces and intelligence, issuing the military budget, deciding on military and technical issues like equipment, deployment, training of the army, approving appointments of senior officers,

---

110   Ibid.
111   Ibid.
112   Ibid.
113   Ibid.
114   Ibid
115   Ibid.
116   Elliot Short, "The Orao Affair," 38.

and above all, conducting investigations in military matters.[117] Moreover, the parliament is the legitimate body that approves the presidency to issue a declaration of war and a state of emergency.[118] Considering that veto powers are present in the political system especially in the parliament, declaring war and state of emergency, two vital cases of civil-military relations requires national consensus. Hence, the army cannot be used against one community, nor can it be mobilized to fight a war against Serbia, Croatia or Turkey, which are the cultural patrons of either communities in BiH.

Women are represented in the military, albeit in small percentages. Around 6.6 percent of AFBiH personnel are women. They are mostly school graduates who obtained military education by various individual and institutional educational programs.[119] At the level of ethnicity, the composition of the AFBiH promotes an ethnic quota to create a structural balance between different groups. A compromise was reached between the three ethnic communities in 2005 while negotiating the second round of security sector reform, battalions are formed on an ethnic basis,[120] and enlisted men can choose to serve in the infantry battalion nearest to home.[121] This means that there are nine mono-ethnic battalions within the three multi-ethnic infantry brigades, which are all under the AFBiH operational command.[122] Each regiment has a small headquarter staff, and their respective members wear should badges that signify their ethnic-military membership.[123] This is enshrined in art.6 of the law on service which states that each regiment should express the culture and heritage of its members' belonging.[124] In principle, from 2013 onwards, Bosniaks represent 45.9 percent of the AFBiH, followed by the Serbs with 33.6 percent and Croats with a 19.8 percent, with less than 1 percent for minorities. The numbers are shown in Table 1.

Another important structural reform deals with the military intelligence . The Director-General is the head of the Directorate of Operations, the Inspector-General carries internal oversight of the institution, both of them along with the Deputy Director-General are directly appointed and dismissed

---

117 "Law on Defence of Bosnia and Herzegovina".
118 Ibid.
119 Vera Stojarova, "Unifying the Armed Forces of Bosnia and Herzegovina – Mission Competed?," *Vojenské Rozhledy* 28, no. 4 (2019): 75.
120 Kurt Bassuener, "The Armed Forces of Bosnia and Herzegovina: Unfulfilled Promise," *Democratization Policy Council*, (2015): 8.
121 Ibid.
122 Ibid.
123 Ibid.
124 Ibid.

by the Council of Ministers.[125] In order to shield this vital institution from political interference, decisions in the OSA are made after careful deliberation.[126] Hence, the employs a professional-consensual mechanism to provide assurances for communities that it is impartial and not politicized.

After explaining the reforms of the AFBiH, it is important to analyze the work of the army. Moreover, BiH provides a good example of international and regional sponsorship in improving the status and professionalism of the armed forces. Mainly, the NATO and EU support has been critical in this matter.

4   Success and Setbacks

A very important achievement in Bosnia related to military affairs in post-conflict environment is demobilization. By the end of the war in 1995, there were around 400,000 soldiers in Bosnia, and within three months less than 100,000 soldiers stayed in the army.[127] By 2000, around 370,000 of them since 1995, so the army had around 30,000 soldiers,[128] and in 2002 the number was 12,000 out of which some 80 percent had served in the war.[129] In 2016, the army reported that it had around 10,500 soldiers.[130] A large part of this ability to demobilize came from international assistance, particularly from the World Bank's International Development Association (IDA), which designed the Emergency Demobilization and Reintegration Project (EDRP) for this purpose. The program aimed at reintegrating demobilized soldiers in FBiH and RS,[131] and support also refugees, war victims, disabled people, widows and the unemployed.[132] The program provided around 8.5 million USD for four projects: development of a labor market information data base (LMI), counseling and job-finding services, education and retraining services, and management assistance.[133] Other programs like the Pilot Emergency Redeployment Project

125   Helge Luras, "Democratic Oversight in Fragile States," 609.
126   Ibid., 614.
127   Lara J. Nettelfield, "From the Battlefield to the Barracks: The ICTY and the Armed Forces of Bosnia and Herzegovina," *International Journal of Transitional Justice* 4, no. 1 (2010): 95.
128   Jeremy King, *An Unprecedented Experiment: Security Sector Reform in Bosnia and Herzegovina* (London: Saferworld, 2002), 11.
129   Lara J. Nettelfield, "From the Battlefield to the Barracks," 95.
130   Vera Stojarova, "Unifying the Armed Forces of Bosnia and Herzegovina," 72–3.
131   Tobias Pietz, "Demobilization and Reintegration of Former Soldiers in Post-War Bosnia and Herzegovina: An Assessment of External Assistance," (2004): 33, http://edoc.vifapol.de /opus/volltexte/2008/547/pdf/hb135.pdf, accessed 28 October 2020.
132   "World Bank Technical Annex EDRP," *World Bank*, (1996): 3.
133   Tobias Pietz, "Demobilization and Reintegration," 37.

(PELRP) also provided by the World Bank assistance to demobilized soldiers in social reintegration after the Madrid Agreement in 1998 to reduce the size of the army in Bosnia.[134] This program provided help for demobilized soldiers in education, small enterprise, and agricultural support for business.[135]

Another important success in military affairs was the ability to integrate three previously combatting armies into one national institution, in addition to the military intelligence. It is important to note here that Bosnia has never existed as an independent state, and two ethnic communities in Bosnia, the Serbs and the Croats, have had plans to join their respective ethnic state around Bosnia. Moreover, there is a burden of history dating back to WWI, the antithetical historical narratives of Croats and Bosnians about their nationalism, and the massacres committed between Bosniaks, Croats and Serbs during the 1991–1995 Balkan war. Despite all of this, Bosnia, along with international support (and pressure), succeeded in developing a national army, with a unified command and ministry of defense, whose chain of command and supreme authority are clearly stated in the law on defense. This has allowed the international community to set up of the Peace Support Operations Training Centre which offers courses to Bosnian lieutenants, captains and majors, with courses that cover urban conflict, military doctrine and international humanitarian law.[136] This reflects the fact that the AFBiH is engaged in the process of modernization, at it is preparing its soldiers for "operations other than war," a reference to deployment in post-conflict peacekeeping missions, like their participation in Iraq.[137]

The Bosnian success in unifying its army allowed it to join the Partnership for Peace which was created to integrate the former communist countries into a pro-American alliance, as NATO enlargement was the top issue after the old war.[138] Also, NATO agreed on August 2007 – followed by another one in 2019 – to allow the exchange of highly-confidential data with BiH which is the highest possible level of access for countries that are not full NATO members, in addition to the protection of classified information.[139] According to NATO, BiH managed to attain a high level of access due to its efficient security

---

134   Ibid., 44.
135   "World Bank Project Appraisal Document for PELRP," *World Bank*, (2002): 3.
136   Lara J. Nettelfield, "From the Battlefield to the Barracks," 94.
137   Ibid.
138   Denis Hadzovic, "The Office of the High Representative," 32.
139   "NATO and Bosnia and Herzegovina Sign Agreement on Protection of Classified Information," *NATO*, 5 March 2019, https://www.nato.int/cps/en/natohq/news_164426.htm?selectedLocale=en#:~:text=NATO%20and%20Bosnia%20and%20Herzegovina%20sign%20agreement%20on%20protection%20of%20classified%20information,

establishment that protects confidential information as per NATO standards.[140] Hence, in 2010, BiH was conditionally invited to join NATO's MAP, a huge step forward considering that few years back the security apparatus of BiH was the center of scandals, and by 2007, the country gained access to sensitive confidential data from the most powerful military alliance in the world.

Regionally, the EU issued the road map for BiH's integration which contained 18 points including security-oriented reforms like creating a state-level border service, fighting illegal immigration, smuggling and corruption.[141] The EU's European Security and Defense Policy is used as a framework to negotiate Bosnia's integration into the union. Hence, BiH has been implementing the Stabilization and Association Agreement as it aspires an EU membership.[142] For this purpose, the European Union Military Force (EUFOR) has conducted a number of operations alongside AFBiH aimed at collecting illegal weapons, improving coordination with NATO, disrupting organized criminal activity, and supporting demining programs.[143]

Despite these successes, there are still a number of challenges and setbacks that BiH needs to overcome. To start with, the army does not serve as a melting pot for different communities mainly because of the monoethnic battalions and corps. In a deeply divided setting like BiH, with a history of hostility between different ethnic components, and in an environment where one ethnic group wishes to secede, it is critical to have mixed units. How can you convince a Bosniak or a Crota to defend the RS as if he is defending his collective identity, and vice versa, if there are no mixed units? Moreover, there is still a sense of politicization among members of the AFBiH. Before the unification of the army, there was an incident in the army of FBiH whereby the main Croatian political party in Bosnia, the Croatian Democratic Union (HDZ), requested that soldiers in the army to disobey order from non-Croat superiors.[144] The minister of defense of FBiH responded by disbanding the Croat component of the army and that Croat soldiers remove the Federation insignia from their

---

-05%20Mar.&text=On%205%20March%202019%2C%20NATO,on%20the%20Security%20of%20Information, accessed 28 October 2020.

140   Denis Hadzovic, "The Office of the High Representative," 51.
141   Ibid., 33.
142   "Bosnia and the European Union Military Force (EUFOR): Post-NATO Peacekeeping," *Congressional Research Service*, 15 January 2008, 1, https://www.everycrsreport.com/files/20080115_RS21774_698f21fa4b2b252e1e95db6fc83a8f4ccobaaacd.pdf, accessed 28 October 2020.
143   Ibid., 3.
144   Danijela Dudley, "Civil-Military Relations in Bosnia," 126.

uniforms.[145] To resolve this crisis, the minister was replaced by a moderate figure and the Croat deputy commander of the joint command of the army of FBiH resigned.[146] Still, some Croat soldiers in the army refused to obey the new deputy commander, and it took some time to de-politicize the incident and overcome its repercussions. Such a case demonstrated that ethnic loyalty within the army supersedes that of the national one, and breaking the chain of command by refusing to take orders from a superior because of ethnicity is a dangerous sign of decay in obedience that would eventually lead to disintegration. However, the OHR intervention afterwards and elite bargain led to the unification and reformation of the army which saved the institution.

Another incident happened prior to unification that showed deep fissures within the army. During a public-televised swearing-in ceremony for new Serb military recruits in RS, the recruits refused to swear allegiance to BiH, and some recruits opted to swear allegiance to RS, while others swore allegiance to RS first, followed by a second swearing allegiance to BiH.[147] However, just like the previous incident with the HDZ in FBiH, the RS army chief of staff was fired over the affair, and this incident happened to be the final fiasco that actually prompted the need for unification of the army in BiH.

After unification, there was still an element of cultural politicization that the army itself unintentionally sponsored. This was manifested in the ministry of defense funding for pilgrimage to Mecca and Orthodox trip to Greece for some soldiers.[148] Moreover, the army allows the use of nationalistic flags, symbols, heraldic signs and also anthems of other states.[149] In addition, RS organizes annually a parade of army, firefighters, cultural and sports groups to celebrate the Day of RS,[150] focusing mainly on a narrative on the role of the army of RS in founding the republic.[151] Add to that the practice of sending Serb soldiers for supplementary training in Serbia, Croats in Croatia and Bosniaks to Turkey.[152] Also, it is important to note that battalions in the AFBiH are ethnically homogenous, and it is only heterogeneous at the command level. Hence, symbols and cultural/ethnic affiliation represent an element of contestation within the army itself. There is a difference between respecting the faith and cultural/ethnic beliefs of each community within the army, which

---

145   Ibid.
146   Ibid.
147   Lara J. Nettlefield, "From Battlefield to the Barracks," 92.
148   Vera Stojarova, "Unifying the Armed Forces of Bosnia and Herzegovina," 78.
149   Ibid., 78–9.
150   Ibid., 80.
151   Elliot Short, "The Orao Affair," 46.
152   Vera Stojarova, "Unifying the Armed Forces of Bosnia and Herzegovina," 78.

is the case with the Mosques, Chapels, Priests and Sheikhs in the army, and revealing those symbols intentionally which could instigate feelings of superiority of one group over the other. It may seem, in such cases, that the soldier himself is loyal to the ethnic community that he belongs to, and consequently, attached to the regional-cultural patron (Serbia, Croatia or Turkey) as opposed to the BiH state. The question that arises then, is whether the army is a melting pot, by which soldiers from different faiths dedicate their lives for the survival of the BiH state or is it just a normal profession but with guns? If an army of a divided society fails to represent itself as a national institution, a melting pot for different groups, it cannot aspire for national legitimacy, simply because it has (or should have) a monopoly over violence.

Another type of challenge that bequest the AFBiH is its financial struggle. Soldiers in the country are paid as little as 300 euros per month, low rank officers around 400 euros and mid-officers around 550 euros.[153] As a result, there is a large outflow of personnel from the military institutions in an attempt to find better paid jobs.[154] Such financial difficulties have its impact in the BiH's membership process to NATO, as the coalition calls for a 2 percent expenditure on defense from the GDP, and Bosnia is struggling hard to achieve this requirement.[155] This means that BiH still needs financially related military support from international donors, without which the army cannot sustain its defense capabilities. In addition, NATO also demands that the state consolidates all military matters, but there is contestation between the central authorities and RS regarding defense properties situation in the latter, and so the dispute is over 69 defense properties, which RS claims should be owned by the entity because they lie within its borders.[156] The issue is still unresolved until the time of writing.

5   Conclusion

A historical feature of the army in Yugoslavia have been its Serbian character which hindered its legitimacy and played a role in triggering ethnic unrest. The

---

153 "Bosnia Faces Outflow of Military Personnel Over Low Wages," *Reuters*, 29 October 2019, https://www.reuters.com/article/us-bosnia-army-outflow/bosnia-faces-outflow-of-military-personnel-over-low-wages-parliamentary-commissioner-idUSKBN1X826J, accessed 28 October 2020.
154 Ibid.
155 Ingrid Olstad Busterud, "Defense Sector Reform in the Western Balkans," 339.
156 Mladen Lakic, "Bosnian Minister Floats Hopes of Progress Towards NATO," *Balkan Insights*, 14 November 2018, https://balkaninsight.com/2018/11/14/bosnia-s-fragile-hope-to-activate-map-for-nato-11-13-2018/, accessed 28 October 2020.

JNA failed mainly because it was not perceived as a national army, but rather a tool of ethnic hegemony of one group over the other. While proportionality is an important tool employed to guarantee fair ethnic representation in the army (as in the JNA in the 1970s), there is a difference between the need to represent ethnic groups and the exercise of authority over them. There is no point of having proportionality in representing communities in the army if the bulk of power and decision making will stay in the hands of a specific community. Hence, Tito's constitutional amendments regarding ethnic representation in the army failed, and the proof was the disintegration of the JNA along ethnic lines when the war began in 1991.

The AFBiH was formed in the aftermath of the 3rd Balkan war, and it inherited the main militias that fought during the period of 1991–1994. Despite the massacres and the burden of memory, the transformation of the army from three distinctive military formations, along with their intelligence, into one national and multiethnic constitution is astonishing. Also, the success in demobilizing the fighters from hundreds of thousands to a mere 10,000 soldiers or so is a step that has to be applauded. However, the challenges that the AFBiH still faces need to be tackled, especially ones that have to do with politicization of members, homogenous ethnic corps and the financial struggle of the country. The EU and NATO are playing the right role as a stabilizing external factor, but more is required to continue the successful process of modernizing the army and preserving what has been achieved.

CHAPTER 5

The Iraqi Armed Forces

The Iraqi Armed Forces (IAF) emerged as the backbone of the Iraqi state since the creation of Iraq in 1920. It became the defining element that shaped the nature and the future of the state. Consequently, the army became the target of Baathification of the Iraqi state. External actors in Iraqi, like the British (1920s) and the Americans (post 2003), played a central role in shaping and molding the IAF. Moreover, nationalism and ideologies transformed the army into a battleground between communists, Arab nationalists (*qawmiyin*), and Iraqi-firsters (*wataniyin*). Each ideological group tried to expand its base of supporters among the officer corps. The IAF then became a tool of political control and dictatorship by Saddam's Baath, only to be eradicated after the American invasion, which left the country without a proper national army. The reconstruction processes of 2003 and then 2011 (after the rise of the Islamic State in Iraq and Syria, ISIS), did not succeed in recreating a politically neutral and impartial national army capable of protecting Iraqis.

The IAF has had a history of intervention in Iraqi politics, which began under the Monarchy, culminated with the coup of Abdel-Karim Qassem, and then the army was subsumed by the Baath Party until the American invasion of 2003. The IAF relationship with the political players raises many questions about armies in societies that are divided according to sectarian and nationalistic lines. I intend to study the impact of the ideological competition and subsequent politicization of the armed forces on stability in Iraq, particularly before 1970. Whoever controlled the IAF could control the Iraqi state. The army, then, became the pillar of state consolidation. After that, I discuss the success of the Baath party in transforming the army into a party-institution that executed the interest of the Baath, particularly in protecting the "Baathified" Iraqi state and the interest of Saddam's loyal clique of civilian and military leaders. I then analyze the factors that led to the failure of the IAF reconstruction by the Americans post-2003 invasion, and the current status of the army after the second reconstruction attempt following the breakdown of the army due to the rise of ISIS.

1 Inception: The Establishment of the Iraqi Army

The Iraqi encounter with military education came during the last few decades of the Ottoman Empire. Sultan Abul-Hamid's zeal to modernize the Ottoman military and make it on equal foot with its European peers forced him to create military secondary schools throughout the Empire, to prepare students to enroll in the military academy of Istanbul. Among the regions that received military secondary schools in Iraq were Baghdad (two schools in 1876 and 1886), Mosul (1893), and Suleimaniya (1892).[1] There was a 10 percent quota reserved for cadets coming from the provinces that later formed Iraqi (Basra, Baghdad and Mosul) in the military academy in Istanbul.[2] Consequently, Iraqis had a chance to achieve social mobility for poor members of previously neglected regions in the Ottoman Empire, and the provinces that later formed Iraq in 1920 had an important share in this process. By 1921, around 1200 Iraqi officers were enrolled in the Ottoman army, and they happened to be taught cultural nationalism and patriotism from German officers teaching at the academy.[3] According to researchers, this German involvement in the military teaching process, along with the wars of nationalism in the Balkans, created a class of officers from the Arab world that were influenced by Arab nationalism, and Iraqi officers among them learned about the necessity of the army to intervene in politics when the situation warranted.[4] Hence, when the Arab revolt of Sherif Hussein began in Hijaz, Arab officers – particularly Iraqi ones – joined the ranks of the revolt in the name of Arab nationalism.[5]

After the defeat of the Turkish forces in 1917 and the triumph of the British forces in the Mesopotamia campaign, the British established their mandate in what was called the state of Iraq in April 1920. Iraq was composed of three Ottoman provinces: Basra (south), Baghdad (center), and Mosul (north). The country was ethnically diverse, with the Arab Shiite community being the majority, followed by Arab Sunnis, Kurds, and a small percentage of Christian minority. The British faced a major revolt in 1920 that put heavy pressure on their forces in Mesopotamia, then in an attempt to reduce the cost of controlling Iraq, they chose their ally Prince Faisal, who had lost Syria for the French, and so The

---

1 Mesut Uyar, "Ottoman Arab Officers between Nationalism and Loyalty during the First World War," *War in History* 20, no. 4 (2013): 531.
2 Ahmed Hashim, "Saddam Husayn and Civil-Military Relations in Iraq: The Quest for Legitimacy and Power," *The Middle East Journal* 57, no. 1 (2003): 13.
3 Ibid.
4 Ibid.
5 Reeva Simon, *Iraq Between the Wars: The Creation and Implementation of a Nationalist Ideology* (New York: Columbia University Press, 1986).

Hashemite Kingdom of Iraq was established in 1921.[6] Once King of Iraq, Faisal brought with him around 190 Iraqi officer who served under his command during WWI, they were referred to as "Sherifian Officers." Instantly, they moved into senior positions in the newly created kingdom, and formed the basis of a cosmopolitan and educated class by default.[7] Hence, from the early stages of Iraqi statehood, the military class played an important role in shaping the backbone of the state and nation.

The only institution that Feisal had inherited from the defunct "State of Iraq" was the army. The first units of the Iraqi army were raised on 6 January 1921, and they included 640 former Ottoman officers.[8] When Feisal took over as King of Iraq, he envisioned an Iraqi army that would protect his nascent Monarchy (hence the reliance on Sherifian Officers), protect the Kingdom from regional challenges, especially the one south-west from the Saudi Arabia's Ikhwan military force, and use this military institution as the backbone for nation-building.[9] The construction of a strong Iraqi army went in a very slow pace, Faisal's plan received a boost as of April 1922, when a conference was convened in Karbala by a Shia cleric Sheikh Mehdi al-Khalisi, along with 200 Shia religious leaders and tribesmen, asking King Feisal to provide protection from the Ikhwan raids.[10] It was then that the King began to unravel solid plans to create an indigenous Iraqi army, crucial for his state building plans as the backbone of an Iraqi nation.[11] Nevertheless, as an insurance policy – something he must have learned from his experience with the Sykes-Picot arrangements that led to his expulsion from Syria – Feisal did not pursue an anti-imperial policy, and so his regime was now protected by the British, and at the same time, by the Iraqi army.

Iraq built its first military college in 1924 with the help of the British,[12] and it played an important role in allowing sons of the lower middle class in the

---

6   Quincy Wright, "The Government of Iraq," *The American Political Science Review* 20, no. 4 (1926): 746.
7   Ahmed Hashim, "Saddam Husayn and Civil-Military Relations," 14.
8   Mohammad A. Tarbush, *The Role of the Military in Politics: A Case Study of Iraq to 1941* (New York: Routledge 2016). Up till today, army day is 6 January.
9   Hanna Batatu, *The Old Social Classes and the Revolutionary Movements of Iraq* (Princeton: Princeton University Press, 1979), 26.
10   Ibid., 333.
11   Ibrahim al-Marashi, "Iraq's Gulf Policy and Regime Security from the Monarchy to the Post-Baathist Era," *British Journal of Middle Eastern Studies* 36, no. 3 (2009): 450.
12   Steinar Sveinsson, *Iraq Podcast*, 23 April 2007 https://www.nato.int/docu/speech/2007/s070423c.html, accessed 11 July 2020.

1930s to join the armed forces.[13] These young officers were introduced to two main competing ideologies in Iraq: pan-Arab nationalism and "Iraq-first,"[14] which concentrated on the need to pursue Iraq's domestic interests and development. The only thing in common between both ideologies was the need to liberate Iraq from British domination. Consequently, the first generation of Iraqi officers who graduated from Iraq's military academy became politicized and radicalized. This eventually led to the first military coup in the Middle East in 1936 during the reign of King Ghazi bin Faisal. Ghazi was an enthusiast of a strong military, and he played a role in elevating the status of the military in Iraq; however, his plans backfired. Ghazi took over a year after his father signed the Anglo-Iraqi treaty in 1932, allowing Iraq to practice complete autonomy in domestic and regional issues. Among the "Iraqization" of the institutions were the armed forces - British retained considerable control over decision making until the signature of the treaty.[15] On 11 August 1933, Iraq intended to disarm an auxiliary unit previously used by the British as a levy officers from the Assyrian Hakkari tribe.[16] The Assyrians were unpopular among the armed forces because they were perceived as a force loyal to the British,[17] even though ties were cut between both groups after signing the treaty and the Assyrian units disbanded as a result. Nevertheless, most of the levies served as guards at British facilities (similar to private security),[18] which alarmed the Iraqi authorities. Instead of integrating the Assyrians into the army and political regime, Ghazi dispatched the army to the Assyrian region of Simele, and a skirmish with the local population resulted in razing, looting and the destruction of sixty to a hundred villages, with 6,000 Assyrians killed.[19] The main figure that was hailed as a national hero was Colonel Bakr Sidqi upon the success of the operation, and he was later promoted to General, so the army came to believe that it was carrying a sacred mission of achieving full independence of their country.

---

13 Ahmed S. Hashim, "Military Power and State Formation in Modern Iraq," *Middle East Policy Council* 5, no. 4 (2003), https://mepc.org/journal/military-power-and-state-formation-modern-iraq, accessed 11 July 2020.
14 Ahmed Hashim, "Saddam Husayn and Civil-Military Relations," 14.
15 Mark Heller, "Politics and the Military in Iraq and Jordan, 1921–1958: The British Influence," *Armed Forces and Society* 14, no. 1 (1977): 81.
16 Sargon Donabed, "Rethinking Nationalism and an Appellative Conundrum: Historiography and Politics in Iraq," *National Identities* 14, no. 4 (2012): 414.
17 Ibrahim al-Marashi and Sammy Salama, *Iraq's Armed Forces: An Analytical History* (New York: Routledge, 2008), 32.
18 Stephen Hemsley Longrigg, *Iraq, 1900 to 1950: A Political, Social, and Economic History* (Oxford: Oxford University Press, 1953), 197.
19 Ronald Sempill Stafford, *The Tragedy of the Assyrians*, (London: G. Allen & Unwin, 1935), 174–6.

The second target of the government was the Shiite dominated southern region, and in 1935–1936, Sidqi succeeded in his mission of dealing a fatal blow to the Shiite insurgents through the use of the Royal Iraqi Air Force (RIAF).[20] Meanwhile, the third target was the Kurdish regions north of the country, and a trend of insurgency began in the 1920s when the Iraqi army failed to deliver a decisive blow to the Kurdish insurgents.[21] Moreover, in June 1935, the parliament passed the conscription law, which was known as the National Service Law, and it meant that the number of soldiers in the army increased tremendously: by 1936, it had 800 officers and 19,500 soldiers organized in two divisions.[22] And so, establishing its legacy in such a mischievous manner that perceived a segment of the population as enemies and a threat to national integrity (Assyrians, Kurds and Shiite), the army, with Ghazi's support, became empowered by its conscription law and was ready to challenge the very authority that popped up its prestige and status: the Monarchy.

2   Bakr Sidqi and the Rise of as-Sabbagh

The army's success against the Assyrians, Shiites and Kurds led to a feeling of glorification of the army in the metropolitan. The politicization, radicalization and glorification of the Iraqi army crystallized its belief that it is the only institution which could establish stability in the country, and become the main arbitrator in Iraq. Hence, the army would be the dominant political player ruling from the shadows. On 29 October 1936, Sidqi and another conspirator, Abd al-Latif Nuri ordered the commander of the RIAF Mohamad Ali Jawwad to fly their airplanes over Baghdad and drop leaflets demanding that Ghazi replace the Prime Minister with Hikmat Sulayman.[23] The coup planners, however, revealed that they had no intention to overthrow the monarchy; instead they wanted to it to execute the political will of the army. When Ghazi refused to follow the army's lead, the latter threatened to bombard Baghdad, which they did eventually when they dropped bombs near the Prime Minister's office. Consequently, Prime Minister Yassin al-Hashimi resigned and in November 1936 Sulayman became the new Prime Minister.[24] This was known as the first military coup in the history of the Middle East, and it revealed the tragic mistake

---

20   Ibrahim al-Marashi and Sammy Salama, *Iraq's Armed Forces*, 34.
21   Ibid., 35.
22   FO 371/20013/E 6797/1419/93, 30 October 1936.
23   Ibrahim al-Marashi and Sammy Salama, *Iraq's Armed Forces*, 48.
24   Ibid., 49.

of Ghazi's overwhelming glorification of his armed forces. Sidqi's sudden and unexpected coup opened the door for the military to intervene in politics,[25] and many soldiers were impressed by the skills and secrecy in the way the coup was carried out.[26]

The ability to control the political system by the army did not unify its officer corps because of the competing ideologies that were entrenched in the institution. By the mid-1930s, ideological divisions between Iraqi officers began to take a sectarian and ethnic composition. Sunnis supported an active Iraqi involvement in Arab affairs, while Shiites and other ethnic officers (Kurds and Turkmen) supported an Iraqi-first approach.[27] Bakr Sidqi was an Iraqi Kurd from Kirkuk and Hikmat Sulayman was a Turkish sympathizer;[28] both admired Ataturk's principles of military intervention in the political sphere. They believed that Turkey's success in rebuilding its political system after the Caliphate, and the war of independence, should be attributed to the military. The Iraqi army was by that time an institution that sought to refashion itself on similar lines with Ataturk's principles of the need of the army to be politically active.[29] As a result, Sidqi and Sulayman believed in the importance of empowering the army. Hence, the army adopted the "Iraqi-first" ideology, without commitment to regional issues, which was a major blow to the pan-Arabist officers in the army, who perceived Sulayman's government as anti-Arabist, anti-nationalist and a separatist one, with a foreign policy that promoted Iraq's domestic interest at the expense of its pan-Arabist obligations.[30] Nevertheless, pan-Arab officers did not acquiescence because their ideology had already found a foothold in the army, and so a counter-coup took place in 1937 ending the brief period of Iraqi-firsters controlled the army and state. The conspirators of the second coup included Colonel Salahudin as-Sabbagh along other associates: Kamal Shabib, Mahmud Salman, Fahmi Said, Aziz Yamulki, Husayn Fawzi, and Amin al-Omari, who were known as the "Seven."[31] They

---

25 Karol R. Sorby, "The Coup d'état of Bakr Sidqī in Iraq," *Oriental Archive* 78, no. 1 (2010): 47.
26 Karol R. Sorby Jr., "Iraq's First Coup Government (1936–1937)," *Asian and African Studies* 20, no. 1 (2011): 24.
27 Ahmed Hashim, "Saddam Husayn and Civil-Military Relations," 14.
28 Majid Khaddouri, "The Coup d'État of 1936: A Study in Iraqi Politics," *The Middle East Journal* 2, no. 3 (1948): 292.
29 Fadel al-Barrak, *Daur aj-Jaish al-ʿIraqi fi Hukūmat ad-Difāʿ al-Watani wal-Harb maʿ Britaniya ʿām 1941* [The Role of the Iraqi Army in the Government of Defense and the War on Britain in Year 1941], (Beirut: ad-Dār al-Arabiya lil Mausūʿāt, 1987), 82.
30 Majid Khaddouri, *Independent Iraqi: A Study in Iraqi Politics Since 1932* (London: Royal Institute of International Affairs, 1960), 96.
31 Ibrahim al-Marashi and Sammy Salama, *Iraq's Armed Forces*, 54.

were all Sunni Arabs and supported Iraq's involvement in the Arab world. The main figure in this circle was as-Sabbagh who developed the notion that army and masses should rally and unite in Iraq under the flag of Arabism.[32] He was known to be a proud soldier who fought during WWI in the Ottoman army against the British, which made him resent taking orders from British advisors in the Iraqi army.[33]

The "Seven" continued their predecessor's role in empowering the army, and by 1939, the Iraqi army had 1,426 officers and 26,345 soldiers.[34] The group also ruled from behind the scenes but could not agree on a policy regarding Iraq's foreign relations especially when WWII began, and the debate about what stance Iraq should take during the war divided the "Seven." The main question was how to approach Iraq's relationship with Britain. Hence, as-Sabbagh, Shabib, Salman and Said ousted the other three collaborators in the "Seven," thus forming the anti-British, pro-Nazi group, the "Golden Square."

Iraq faced five military coup attempts between 1936 and 1941[35] and changed seven governments during this period.[36] What destroyed the army and at that time the Golden Square was the wrong assessment regarding the ongoing military developments in Europe during WWII. In 1939 King Ghazi died in a car accident, leaving his infant Faisal II as heir to the throne, so Ghazi's first cousin Abd al-Ilah was appointed as Regent. The Golden Square and the Regent disagreed in 1941 about Iraq's foreign relations with European powers. The Golden Square were influenced by Nazi Germany and believed that it is going to win the war, so they decided to contact Germany for an arms deal,[37] while the Regent wanted to preserve ties with the British. The Golden Square then sent the army to the Regent's palace to force him to appoint their protégé Rashid Ali Gylani as Prime Minister, who was a well-known pan-Arab nationalist, associated (along with the Golden Square) with anti-British sentiments and pro-Nazi affection.[38] However, the Regent managed to flee the palace before the army appeared, so the Golden Square forced parliament to provide legitimacy to

---

32 Salah Ad-Din As-Sabbagh, *Fursan al-'Urubah: Muthakkarāt ash-Shahīd Salah ad-Din as-Sabbagh* [The Knights of Arabism: The Memoirs of the Martyr Salah Ad-Din As-Sabbagh], (Rabat: Tanit lil Nashr, 1994), 43.
33 Ibrahim al-Marashi, "Disbanding and Rebuilding the Iraqi Army: The Historical Perspective," *Middle East Review of International Affairs* 11, no. 3 (2007): 42.
34 FO 371/23217/E 2372/72.93, 28 February 1939.
35 Ibrahim al-Marashi and Sammy Salama, *Iraq's Armed Forces*, 61.
36 Ibrahim al-Marashi, "Iraq's Gulf Policy and Regime Security," 453.
37 Reeva S. Simon, *Iraq between the Two World Wars: The Creation and Implementation of a Nationalist Ideology* (New York: Columbia University Press, 1986), 147.
38 Ahmed Hashim, "Saddam Husayn and Civil-Military Relations," 15.

Gylani's government and appoint a new Regent contrary to the constitutional arrangements that required the Regent/Monarch to appoint the Prime Minister.[39] This smooth political coup was welcomed by the axis powers specially that Iraq refused Britain's request to land 2,000 soldiers in Basra (March 1941). Nevertheless, after the actions of the Golden Square and their siding with Germany, Britain neglected Iraq's rejection of British troops landing in Basra as per the 1930 Anglo-Iraqi Treaty that allowed it to deploy its troops in Iraq for security purposes.[40] The deployment of British troops in 2 May 1941 triggered the Thirty Days War, by which British troops destroyed the Iraqi army and put an end to the rule of the Golden Square.[41]

After the defeat of the Golden Square by the British, the latter purged the army from nationalist officers loyal to as-Sabbagh,[42] and also it sought to review the indoctrination process of officers in the military academy to make sure it does not emphasize Arabist ideology.[43] The aim was to depoliticize the officer corps and remove anyone who had ideological commitments to pan-Arabism. In addition, the operational units in the army were approximately 50 percent below strength, and the British recalled officers who were politically reliable and at the same time making the Iraqi army reliable on UK arms again as during the mandate period.[44] Finally, the army that Britain helped refurbish was less in numbers and consisted of three divisions rather than four.[45] This helped provide a long period of stability to Iraq until 1958 when the army overthrew the monarchy in a bloody military coup.

3 The Republic of Abdul-Karim Qassim

In the mid-1940s, graduates from the military school were overwhelmingly Sunni Arabs (70 percent), less than one third Shiite, and around 10 percent Kurds, Turcoman, Yazidi and Christians.[46] Hence, the monarchy continued to rely on the Sunni community to represent the core of the army, and the British did not object on that, but made sure to keep those officers under control

---

39 Ibrahim al-Marashi and Sammy Salama, *Iraq's Armed Forces*, 62.
40 Ibid., 63.
41 George M. Haddad, *Revolutions and Military Rule in the Middle East: The Arab States* (New York: Robert Speller and Sons, 1971), 72.
42 Ibrahim al-Marashi, "Disbanding and Rebuilding the Iraqi Army," 43.
43 Ibrahim al-Marashi and Sammy Salama, *Iraq's Armed Forces*, 65.
44 Ibid.
45 Ibid.
46 Ahmed S. Hashim, "Military Power and State Formation".

and punished them if they followed a specific ideology. The problem, however, that would intimidate the armed forces and form the basis for instability in Iraq was due to regional issues, particularly from the Palestinian cause, and the rise of Arab nationalism after the Free Officers' coup in Egypt on 23 July 1952. The monarchy's reliance on the Sunni officers to support the regime neglected the fact that those officers might seek pan-Arabist schemes, and Nasser's rise provided them with the motivation needed to embolden them against the monarchy. Also, the monarchy's inability to create an inclusive platform to accommodate the Kurdish demands of autonomy and cultural recognition meant that the Kurds were in a constant state of war against the regime, which made the Regent and his government suspicious of Kurdish elements in the army. Hence, between 30 and 40 officers from Kurdish background were removed from the army in 1944 simply because of their ethnicity.[47] Consequently, the Sunni over-represented in the army at a time when Arab nationalism was on the rise meant that if Sunni officers decided to go to war against the monarchy, the whole army would follow their lead.

Iraq participated in the first Arab-Israeli in 1948 but it did not play a leading role because the monarchy was not interested in pan-Arabist projects. Its real motive was to participate in the war to silence any possible dissent from army officers. Nevertheless, the defeat in 1948 had a severe impact on the Arab world: Arab armies began to disdain their political leadership and were convinced of the need to control the political sphere. This is what happened in Syria with Hosni al-Zaim's coup in 1949, even though it lacked a pan-Arabist ideological motivation, the Palestinian cause and the defeat in 1948 were a good cause to use a pretext to overthrow the elected government. However, with the Free Officers' Coup of 1952 and the rise of the charismatic figure of Gamal Abdul-Nasser, officers with pan-Arabist inclinations in the Arab armies began to orchestrate a move against their governments, including Iraqi officers. In 1954, the underground Iraqi Free Officers movement began to expand: it included Colonel Abdul-Karim Qassim (main figure of the 1958 revolution which ended the monarchy), along with officers from the Baath and communist parties.

The other problem related to foreign affairs was Iraq's alliances in the region that were perceived by Arab nationalist as a threat to Arabism, especially that these alliances were sponsored by the UK and the USA. The first was the Baghdad pact, a British sponsored alliance in the Middle East to contain the Soviet influence in the region in 1955. The pact included Pakistan, Iran, Iraq and Turkey, and it was a source of disdain for Arab nationalists in Iraq especially

---

47　FO 371/40028/E3302/26, 23 May 1944.

in the armed forces. The second was the Eisenhower doctrine, the US pledge to support any country in the world which was "threatened" by communism. Iraq was a strong supporter of the doctrine and played an important role in implementing it, especially that Iraq was perceived as a country that could counterbalance Nasser's Egypt.[48] Consequently, on 14 July 1958, Abdul-Karim Qassim led a military coup that resulted in the abolition of the monarchy, and the Prime Minister, Regent and Crown Prince were all executed. Qassim then aborted the Baghdad pact and Eisenhower's doctrine.

Qassim's regime, however, was not stable as the main challenge came from the officer corps divided by their ideological allegiance. What united the officers against the monarchy was their anti-imperial inclinations, but then new divisions surfaced after the revolution between communists, pan-Arabists, Baathists and Nasserists (supporters of Nasser's Egypt). However, Qassim intended to build his own patronage system within the military and subdued his rivals who initially helped him in the coup. Moreover, the Arab World apparently was small to accommodate the ego of Nasser and Qassim, so they leadership competition led to a dispute, in addition to Qassim's communist inclinations (despite purging the Iraqi Communist Party later) as opposed to Nassir's commitment to pan-Arabism.[49] In order to neutralize any threat from the army, Qassim removed 2000 competent but politically unreliable officers.[50] Simultaneously, he tried to appease the army by allocating it 40 percent of the budget, increasing the number of promotions and pay of officers, and providing them with housing compounds, schools, cinemas, swimming pools and health facilities in the Officer's city.[51]

Qassim established a firm grip over the country by a military-legal method represented through the Popular Resistance Forces and the Special Military Court. The former trained civilians to maintain domestic order and was used to eliminate political opponents, and the latter served as a legal-military court to convict royalist and officers who opposed Qassim.[52] The republic turned also to the Soviet Union to receive military support and Soviet military advisors were stationed in Iraq for training purposes.[53] Indeed, after Qassim alienated

---

48 Gregory Brew, "Our Most Dependable Allies: Iraq, Saudi Arabia, and the Eisenhower Doctrine, 1956–1958," *Mediterranean Quarterly* 26, no. 4 (2015): 90.
49 Nahla Yassine-Hamdan and Frederic S. Pearson, *Arab Approaches to Conflict Resolution: Mediation, Negotiation and Settlement of Political Disputes* (New York: Routledge, 2014), 181.
50 Mark Heller, "Politics and the Military in Iraq and Jordan," 84.
51 Ibrahim al-Marashi, "Iraq's Gulf Policy and Regime Security," 454.
52 Ibrahim al-Marashi and Sammy Salama, *Iraq's Armed Forces*, 79.
53 Ibid.

the pan-Arab officers the communist officers became stronger in the army, which forced Qassim to twist their arms, and used the Kirkuk massacre in 1959 (when the Iraqi Communist Party attacked and killed tens of Turkmen) as a pretext to subdue communists. Finally, Qassim moved on to attack the Kurds whom he used previously to suppress Communists. During the army deployment in the north, around two-thirds of the army was deployed in-and-around Iraqi Kurdistan, which increased Qassim's unpopularity in the Army.[54] Also, Kurdish officers became less influential in the army than under the monarchy, and the clash with the Kurds during Qassim's rule led to a dozens of desertion of Kurdish officers who joined the Peshmerga.[55] As for the Shiite community, the senior and middle ranking officer corps were largely unattainable to them, and community members faced subtle institutional discrimination regarding limited acceptance to cadets in the military academy, appointment to non-prestigious branches such as the infantry, and sending many of them to the northern part of the country without rotation back to the center or to the south.[56] Under such circumstances, Qassim was ousted in February 1963 allowing the pan-Arab Baath party to take power.

4   The Rise of the Baath and the Baathification of the Army

The officers who ousted Qassim were Baathists and Nasserists, and the strongman who emerged from this military coup was Abdul Salam Arif, who opted to rely on Baathists support instead of the Nasserists. The Baath party began its efforts to expand its influence and network in the military,[57] to guarantee that no other group would be able to isolate it in case of a drift among army officers in the future. The party established a militia "National Guard" (around 34,000 members),[58] used as shock troops in case of civil unrest. Nasserists and Baathists helped Arif get rid of the communist officers, before the Baathists move on to support Arif in purging the military from Nasserist elements who wanted unity with Egypt, and then Arif himself purged the military from hawkish Baathist figures. In addition, an internal drift within the Baathists emerged between a civilian and a military wing: the former wanted the army to be

---

54 Ibid., 89.
55 Ahmed S. Hashim, "Military Power and State Formation".
56 Ibid.
57 Hanna Batatu, *The Old Social Classes*, 1011.
58 Andrew Parasiliti, "Lessons Learned: The Iraqi Military in Politics," in *Iran, Iraq, and the Arab Gulf States*, ed. Joseph Kechichian, (New York: Palgrave Macmillan, 2001), 86.

under civilian control, while the latter opted for the military to rein over civilian authorities. By the end of 1968, the Baathists prevailed over the Nasserists, then in early 1970s, the civilian wing purged the military win of the Baath party.

With the Arif regime the Baath began to slowly infiltrate the military, and Arif made sure to counter the party's influence and protect his position. Arif created an elite military unit called the Republican Guard, and most of its members came from the twentieth brigade that Arif headed before the coup.[59] He recruited many others from his Arab Sunni al-Jumaila tribe.[60] The Republican Guard was led by a relative named Said Sulaibi (Colonel), and then Arif appointed his brother Abdul Rahman as Chief of General Staff. With this move, Arif consolidated his power in the military by a double tactic: special units filled with tribal nepotism and close relatives. This became the norm in civil-military affairs in Iraq even during the Baath era under Saddam.

Abudl Salam Arif died in 1966 when his plane crashed in southern Iraq, and his brother Abdul Rahman was elected as President. Nevertheless, Abdul Rahman was ousted by a Baath coup in 1968, bringing Hasan al-Bakr as President, commander-in-chief of the army and head of the Revolutionary Command Council (RCC) who enjoyed real political power control over Iraq, combining executive and legislative powers. With Bakr in power, the whole Iraqi society was subject to Baathification, and above all the armed forces. It is important to note, however, that Baathification does not mean that members who joined the party were faithful or ideologically motivated; in the case of Iraq, people joined the Baath party to have a position in the public sector as civilians or guarantee a position in the military academy and receive fast promotions. Baathification then was a synonym to a patron-client network that the party used to exercise control over the population.

5   The Army and the Baath

The Baath took full control of the system two weeks after their coup in 1968 when they undertook a second coup against non-Baathists officers who began to demand key positions in the regime as a reward for helping the Baath to takeover and eliminate the Arif regime.[61] By December 1968, around 2000

---

59   William D. Huggins, "The Republican Guards and Saddam Husein's Transformation of the Iraqi Army," *The Arab Studies Journal* 2, no. 1 (1994): 31.
60   Hanna Batatu, *The Old Social Classes*, 1027–8.
61   Ahmed Hashim, "Saddam Husayn and Civil-Military," 19.

officers were purged from the military.[62] The Baath skepticism of other officers was based on the fact that in 1963, Arif outmaneuvered everyone by swiftly and unilaterally controlling the army. Hence, it became of critical importance for the Baath leadership to centralize all aspects of power and eliminate all threats from the very beginning. The main threat of ousting the Baath came from the military, and hence new tactics were employed to prevent any future coup. First, executive and legislative power were concentrated in the RCC, but the Baath civilian wing made sure to transform this highest authority in the country into a civilian one: all RCC members were military men in 1968, only five of the 15 members were officers in 1971, and by 1979 when Saddam took over, no military members were present in the RCC.[63] Second, in the Baath Party Congress of 1974, the party's leadership decided to completely subsume the army under its control,[64] so that the military bureau of the party organized the armed forces as if the army were a party organization, not a national one. For instance, the military bureau selected cadets and organized men in uniform, and the National Security Council (NSC) controlled all intelligence and security organs in the country. Moreover, the Ministry of Defense, the Air Force and the Republican Guards (most important units and security ministries) were associated with the Baath leadership via clan (tribal belonging) or kinship,[65] something Baathists carried on from the Qassim and Arif regimes. As a result, the party became the dominant player in military affairs, and whoever controlled by party could control the armed forces.

The most important transformation in the army taking place during the Baath era was the systematic infiltration of "Tikritis" (people from Tikrit, a Sunni region in central Iraq that Saddam Hussein came from), into the armed forces, tribalizing civil-military relations in the country. The army remained controlled by the Sunni community especially with the dominant positions of Sunnis in the officer corps. However, the Shiite Arabs constituted the bulk of the infantry particularly in the commando units.[66] The Baath in general allowed for some Shiites, Kurds and other minorities to be represented in the higher ranks of the military,[67] but their presence was not a threat to the overwhelmingly dominant position of the Sunni community in general, and the Tikiritis in particular.

---

62 Ibid.
63 Faleh A. Jabar, "The Iraqi Army and Anti-Army: Some Reflections on the Role of the Military," *The Adelphi Papers* 43, no. 354 (2003): 117.
64 Ibid., 116.
65 Ibid., 117.
66 Ahmed S. Hashim, "Military Power and State Formation".
67 Ibrahim al-Marashi, "Disbanding and Rebuilding the Iraqi Army," 44–5.

The Iraqi army underwent further structural and institutional changes when Saddam Hussein became chairman of the RCC and President of Iraq on 16 July 1979. These changes were required to protect Saddam's position in the country that relied on his ability to assume full authority over the armed forces. These changes represented Saddam's strategy to coup-proof his regime. The structural changes introduced by Saddam related were to four points: expanding the Republican Guards, preventing communication between military divisions and their respective units, nepotism, and restraining commanders' freedom to take military decisions during the Iran-Iraq war without Saddam's approval. Saddam provided special treatment for the Republican Guard which developed into ten primary divisions (by 1990 before creating the Special Republican Guard),[68] and its mission was to secure Baghdad from any internal or external threat, defend the country, and protect Saddam. With this expansion, the units in the Republican Guards were organized under a corps command structure similarly to other regular army units. However, the Guards reported to the State Special Security Apparatus rather than the Ministry of Defense,[69] except in cases when it was in active duty on the front during the Iran war that it reported to the Ministry. The corps structure allowed the Guards to be part of the military but linked it to the State Special Security Apparatus that came directly under the command of Saddam Hussein as president.[70] In practice, the Republican Guards constituted a parallel army to that of the IAF because after its expansion it had more armored and mechanized brigades than the regular army,[71] making it the core of the security apparatus. Moreover, the personnel of the Republican Guards had unwavering loyalty to Saddam as he relied on them more than the regular army.[72]

A second structural characteristic of Saddam's army was the deliberate absence of communication between divisions and units in the army. Commanders were prohibited to interact with neighboring units that were not under their chain of command.[73] Also, Republican Guards and Regular Army units and their equipment were not allowed to be moved without orders from

---

68 William D. Huggins, "The Republican Guards and Saddam," 31.
69 Anthony Cordesman, *After the Storm: The Changing Military Balance in the Middle East* (Boulder: Westview Press, 1993), 458.
70 William D. Huggins, "The Republican Guards and Saddam,".33.
71 Ibid.
72 Ibid.
73 Stephen T. Hosmer, *Why the Iraqi Resistance to the Coalition Invasion was so Weak* (Santa Monica: RAND Corporation, 2007), 35.

Baghdad.[74] Finally, regular army and Republican Guard units were not allowed to enter Baghdad,[75] to make sure that commanders will not have a chance of initiating a coup against Saddam.

A third structural characteristic was the reliance on nepotism and patronage in the armed forces. Saddam appointed members of his immediate and extended family (from his Tikrit tribe) to key military positions and battlefield commands.[76] In the process of doing so, he sacrificed military experience and competency for assured loyalty to his person,[77] but it was a necessary price to be paid for preserving the survival of his regime. Moreover, Saddam used to give his senior commanders cash bonuses, new cars, Rolex watches and before the American invasion in 2003, he handed 150 generals a cash gift of 5,000 USD, and prior to that in 2001 he gave them around 20,000 USD each.[78] In principle, the combination of nepotism and patronage allowed Saddam to establish firm control over his officer corps.

The final structural characteristic in Saddam's army was the centralized decision-making process in the military, even during the Iran-Iraq war. Saddam was worried that any military success for a division or brigade that comes as a result operational independence might inflate the egos of officer corps, which would put them in conflict with the political goals stated by Saddam as a civilian leader.[79] This led to a series of setbacks and defeats during the war, especially when the Iranians began to conquer Iraqi land. Hence, complaints about Saddam's control came from within the army,[80] so he had to acquiesce to save his regime and prevent any section of the army of blaming Saddam for a possible defeat. His response to this crisis was by expanding and empowering the Republican Guard division to an extent that it became stronger than the regular army, and simultaneously giving regular army divisions the freedom of action in building, executing, and conducting military operations across armed units.

The other set of changes are related to the institutional organization of the army. To start with, Saddam created overlapping security intelligence services that were diffused and disconnected from one another. There were five main agencies that dealt with intelligence: the Special Security, the General Security,

---

74 Charles Duelfer, "Comprehensive Report of the Special Adviser to the DCI on Iraq's WMD," Vol. I, 93, 30 September 2004.
75 Stephen T. Hosmer, *Why the Iraqi Resistance Was So Weak*, 35.
76 Ibid., 33.
77 Ibid.
78 Molly Moore, "A Foe That Collapsed from Within," *Washington Post*, 20 July 2003.
79 Ahmed S. Hashim, "Military Power and State Formation," 36.
80 Faleh A. Jabar, "The Iraqi Army and Anti-Army," 117.

General Intelligence, Military Intelligence, and Military Security.[81] The agencies' jurisdiction was designed to be overlapping intentionally, to encourage competition and ensure that no agency would threaten Saddam.[82] One can add that by having several agencies with overlapping jurisdiction, it would become harder for internal dissents from the army to take action against the regime because if one agency is complicit, there is a high change that another agency would be able to infiltrate it. This is why some agencies were created to monitor the actions of other ones,[83] which created a sphere of mistrust. All security agencies reported directly to Saddam,[84] making the president in such a strong position that allowed him to control intelligence and analyze it.

Saddam's institutional manipulation of his standing army also meant that he had to balance divisions and units in a way that prevents one from being too strong, especially when it comes to legitimacy. For instance, after the end of the Iran-Iraq war, the Republican Guards emerged as a dominant and prestigious corps in the Iraqi Armed Forces. To prevent a possible action by this army against his regime, Saddam demobilized the Iraqi population (at one point, the number of soldiers in the army reached a million), and more importantly he introduced the Special Republican Guards to counterbalance the legitimacy, power and prestige of the Republican Guards. Then to provide an element of public protection for the regime, Saddam created the Quds Militia in 2001to serve as a second line of defense in case of a western invasion.[85] Even though members of the Quds militia were lightly armed and not well trained as other regular military units,[86] Saddam's intention was more likely to make it harder for any internal element in the army from taking over. This is due to the fact that the Republican Guards, Special Republican Guards, regular army and Quds Army Militia all had separate chain of commands that ended with Saddam as ultimate commander of these corps.[87]

---

81   Ibrahim al-Marashi, "Iraq's Security and Intelligence Network: A Guide and Analysis," *Middle East Review of International Affairs* 6, no. 3 (2002): 1, https://ciaotest.cc.columbia.edu/olj/meria/ali02_01.pdf, accessed 30 August 2021.
82   Ibid.
83   Ibid.
84   Sean Boyne, "Inside Iraq's Security Network," 313.
85   Rajiv Chandrasekaran, "Iraq Arms Civilians as Second Line of Defense Against U.S.," *Washington Post*, 5 February 2003, https://www.washingtonpost.com/archive/politics/2003/02/05/iraq-arms-civilians-as-second-line-of-defense-against-us/49970c19-5d7a-4ab3-968f-5bac3dc95e04/, accessed 12 July 2020.
86   Stephen T. Hosmer, *Why the Iraqi Resistance to the Coalition Invasion was so Weak*, 34.
87   Ibid.

Saddam also made sure that his army officers were kept under his firm control and prevented them from cultivating regional relations with fellow Arab commanders. Hence, one of the most critical decisions he took was to send the least number of officers abroad for training in foreign academies.[88] Iraq became the major Arab military power with the least number of officers trained abroad, a contradiction taking into account its involvement in the war with Iran and the need to empower the training of its officers. Finally, Saddam exercised direct control over military commander through his party's political officers, whose role was to Baathist to monitor the work of military commanders in different units and divisions.[89] These political officers in the army sent report back to Saddam and checked the loyalty of the commanders. They played an important role in extending Saddam's personal control over the armed forces, diminishing the capability of army commanders from taking any independent military measure.

The structural and institutional tactics that Saddam introduced in the IAF succeeded in controlling the army but hindered military professionalism. This was seen during the Iran-Iraq war when Iranian troops had the upper hand and controlled Iraqi land. Only when Saddam agreed to give operational independence to his commanders that Iraq changed the status quo, which led to the end of the war in 1988 and the survivor of his regime. With the end of the Iran war, the army had to be downsized, but it posed a threat to Saddam as the country was under heavy financial burdens and the demobilized soldiers could not be properly integrated into the labor force. Hence, one of the reasons why Saddam chose to invade Kuwait was to divert the attention of the military from taking over or posing a threat to his regime. This came after the four coup attempts between 1988 and 1990.[90]

After the heavy defeat of IAF following the invasion of Kuwait, Saddam downsized his army, and it was used to put down the Kurdish rebellion in the north and Shiite rebellion in the south. With Kurds and Shiites turning against the regime, many soldiers from these two communities at the level of rank and files deserted, making the Sunni community and the tribes close to Saddam the main elements of the IAF. The army, however, was destroyed during the 2003 invasion, and the Americans began the process of military reconstruction.

---

88   Ahmed S. Hashim, "Saddam Husayn and Civil-Military Relations," 20.
89   Stephen T. Hosmer, *Why the Iraqi Resistance to the Coalition Invasion was so Weak*, 34.
90   Ahmed S. Hashim, "Saddam Husayn and Civil-Military Relations," 20.

6 Reconstructing the IAF after the 2003 Invasion

The invasion of Iraq in 2003 led by the United States shocked the world when the Iraqi army collapsed in 26 days of major combat operations. At one stage, the IAF was believed to be the 5th strongest army in the world,[91] and many observers anticipated a prolonged battle particularly around Baghdad. However, it turned out that IAF was no match to the coalition forces which marched to a swift victory. Once Saddam was ousted, a Coalition Provisional Authority (CPA) was installed to govern Iraq until a new constitution and regime were established with popular support. The CPA was led by Paul Bremer, and it functioned from May 2003 till April 2004, when the CPA handed power to the Iraqi Interim Government. Despite the short-term rule of the CPA, its decisions had major impact on Iraqi affairs particularly on civil-military relations. In this section, I discuss the CPA decisions that had an impact on civil-military relations in Iraq, then I analyze the first reconstruction of the IAF by the Coalition forces in Iraq.

6.1 *CPA Civil-Military Decisions*

Beside the infamous CPA order no. 1 that called for a full de-baathification of Iraqi society and regime, CPA order no. 2 was by far the most outrageous policy that held the seed of Iraq's security failure. This order disbanded all security related agencies: the Ministry of Defense, Ministry of Military Affairs, the regular army and all its branches, the Republican Guard, the Special Republican Guard, all intelligence agencies, al-Quds forces, Emergency Forces, and all paramilitary forces (Fedayeen Saddam, Baath party militia, Friends of Saddam, and Saddam's Lion Cubs).[92] The order also terminated the pension payment for any person who was a senior party member in the Baath, and any soldier who held the rank of Colonel or above in Saddam's regime, or its equivalent. Moreover, CPA order no. 22 prohibited persons involved in the Baath party from joining the newly created Iraqi Army under the auspices of the CPA.[93] Effectively, it meant that soldiers who served in Saddam's army had to present

---

91 John M. Broder and Douglas Jehl, "Iraqi Army: World's 5th Largest but Full of Vital Weaknesses," *Los Angeles Times*, 13 August 1990, https://t.ly/ebyh, accessed 12 July 2020.

92 CPA Order Number 2, 23 May 2003, https://nsarchive2.gwu.edu/NSAEBB/NSAEBB418/docs/9b%20-%20Coalition%20Provisional%20Authority%20Order%20No%202%20-%208-23-03.pdf, accessed 12 July 2020.

93 CPA Order Number 22, 7 August 2003, https://govinfo.library.unt.edu/cpa-iraq/regulations/20030818_CPAORD_22_Creation_of_a_New_Iraqi_Army.pdf, accessed 12 July 2020.

proof that they were not members of the Baath, before the de-baathification committee headed by Shiite politicians Ahmad Chalabi. Consequently, the committee prevented many of the Sunni soldiers from rejoining the army, because historically the army was controlled by the Sunni community and was used in several instances against the Shiites. Therefore, while CPA Order 22 prevented soldiers from joining a political party, organization, association, or participation in any political party, the manner in which the de-baathification committee worked with respect to soldiers wishing to join the new army was politicized.

The problem with CPA orders 2 and 22 was that they created a security vacuum because Iraq now had no army to stop looting and re-establish order, especially that the police was corrupted and weak, and the CPA forces were a foreign army that had to deal with the culture shock of policing a society in which they had no knowledge about. In order to deal with these challenges, Bremer established the Iraqi Civil Defense Corps (ICDC) as a temporary institution to conduct military operations alongside the coalition forces.[94] He then moved on to create the Department of Border Enforcement and the Border Guards to ensure the transit and movement of people and goods were regulated according to law.[95] The CPA continued with its plan to create a new army for Iraq, and CPA order no. 67 established the Ministry of Defense and the IAF with all its branches: the ground army, air force, coastal defense force, reserve components, Iraqi civil defense corps, Iraqi counter-terrorism force and their associated headquarters.[96] This was followed by CPA order number 69 that established the Iraqi National Intelligence Service (INIS).[97]

Iraqi soldiers serving under Saddam perceived the manner of their dismissal and subjective recruitment to the new IAF as a humiliation, which fueled their motives for revenge. The overwhelming majority of those people were Sunnis, since Iraq's army was dominated by Sunnis at the level of officer corps and those who were refused entry to the new Iraqi army were also Sunnis, since the Shiite dominated committee of de-baathification perceived the return of those Sunni soldiers as a threat and a possible takeover of the army by Sunnis. Also, it was a chance for the Shiite community to have their revenge from the 1920s for

---

94 CPA Order Number 28, 3 September 2003, https://govinfo.library.unt.edu/cpa-iraq/regulations/20030903_CPAORD_28_Est_of_the_Iraqi_Civil_Defense_Corps.pdf, accessed 12 July 2020.
95 Ahmed S. Hashim, "Military Power and State Formation".
96 CPA Order Number 67, 21 March 2004, https://govinfo.library.unt.edu/cpa-iraq/regulations/20040321_CPAORD67_Ministry_of_Defence.pdf, accessed 12 July 2020.
97 CPA Order Number 69, 4 April 2004, https://govinfo.library.unt.edu/cpa-iraq/regulations/20040405_CPAORD68.pdf, accessed 12 July 2020.

the use of the army against the community throughout the history of Iraq. In addition, there were no plans of reintegrating those soldiers into society who were denied re-entry into the army. Hence, a large bulk of Sunni soldiers who served in Saddam's army, impoverished, humiliated, insulted by the sense of defeat, were ready to adopt terrorist measures to upset the new order.

In his defense, Bremer argued that the decision to for de-baathification was made by President Bush,[98] and Bremer considered – alongside the Department of Defense in the USA – that the Iraqi army had self-demobilized by leaving abandoning their units and going home during the invasion, and it would have been impossible to bring the soldiers back into the barracks which were destroyed by the coalition forces.[99] Moreover, he justified his decision to dissolve the army by the support he received from Jalal Talbani, leader of the Patriotic Union of Kurdistan, who viewed the dissolution of the army as a wise decision that "struck at the roots of the Arab nationalist militarism that plagued Iraq even before Saddam."[100] Bremer also stated that the Shiites were against the military,[101] an additional incentive to dissolve the army and bring the Shiites aboard to create a new Iraq. While the Shiite and Kurdish view had a legitimate claim, the intentional humiliation of the Sunnis and their marginalization turned to be a huge mistake; Bremer and many observes forgot to consider that most of the coup attempts against Saddam were led by Sunni Arab officers,[102] so the association of Sunnis and Baathism was a mistake from the first place.

The only success in civil-military relations by the CPA was that it managed to provide some sort of compensation for soldiers who served in Saddam's army. In June 2003, the CPA announced that it would pay former officers, non-Commissioned Officers (NCOs), rank and files, civilians who worked in the Ministry of Defense, cadets enrolled in Iraq's military colleges, the families of prisoners of war (POW) and those missing in action in the Iran-Iraq war, monthly stipend that reflected their military rank and prior pay.[103] Only senior Baath party members in the army, members of the Special Republican

---

98 James P. Pfiffner, "US Blunders in Iraq: Debaathification and Disbanding the Army," *Intelligence and National Security* 25, no. 1 (2010): 78.
99 Dina Badie, *After Saddam: American Foreign Policy and the Destruction of Secularism in the Middle East* (Maryland: Lexington Books, 2017), 122.
100 Ahmed S. Hashim, *Insurgency and Counter Insurgency in Iraq* (Ithaca: Cornell University Press, 2006), 94.
101 Paul Bremer, *My Year in Iraq: The Struggle to Build a Future of Hope* (New York: Simon and Schuster, 2006), 55.
102 Ibrahim al-Marashi, "Disbanding and Rebuilding the Iraqi Army," 42.
103 Dina Badie, *After Saddam*, 140.

Guard and Fedayeen Saddam were not allowed to receive stipend. The personnel arriving for payment were checked against a database of military personnel acquired by the CPA, which meant that around 280,000 people were receiving regular payment by January 2004.[104] Payment continued under successive Iraqi governments, but without paying the top four Baath party ranks who numbered around 6,000.[105] However, the International Crisis Group reported that the treatment of soldiers was humiliating and there was a complete absence of a plan to get them back to work on reconstruction and humanitarian tasks, thus alienating a large segment of the population.[106] Also, the CPA failed to introduce any program that helped reintroduce soldiers into the civilian economy.[107] This was a strong incentive to blame the tragic life of many Iraqis on the CPA.

7   The Reconstruction Framework of the Iraqi Army

The reconstruction of the Iraqi security apparatus was a threefold plan: to create an army from scratch, to establish a Ministry of Defense run by civilians, and create an intelligence institution to gather and analyze security-oriented information.

7.1   *The New IAF*

The CPA began to unfold plans to reconstruct a new Iraqi Army from mid-2003 onwards. The initial plan was to create a small force that could become the nucleus of a larger army with defensive capabilities.[108] There were several key players that dealt directly with reconstructing the Iraqi army alongside the CPA, like CENTCOM, CIA, and the Combined Joined Task Force-7 (CJTF-7),[109] which was replaced by the Multinational Security Transition Command – Iraq

---

104   Ibid., 140–1.
105   James Dobbins, Seith G. Jones, Benjamin Runkle, and Siddharth Mohandas, *Occupying Iraq: A History of the Coalition Provisional Authority* (Santa Monica: Rand Corporation, 2009), 59. https://www.rand.org/content/dam/rand/pubs/monographs/2009/RAND_MG847.pdf, accessed 12 July 2020.
106   Dina Badie, *After Saddam*, 141.
107   James Dobbins et all, *Occupying Iraq*, 60.
108   Seth G. Jones, Jeremy M. Wilson, Andrew Rathmell, K. Jack Riley, *Establishing Law and Order After Conflict* (Santa Monica: Rand Corporation, 2005), 146.
109   Andrew Rathmell, Olga Oliker, Terrence K. Kelly, David Brannan, Keith Crane, *Developing Iraq's Security Sector: The Coalition Provisional Authority's Experience* (Santa Monica: Rand Corporation, 2005), 15. https://www.rand.org/content/dam/rand/pubs/monographs/2005/RAND_MG365.pdf, accessed 12 July 2020.

(MNSTC-I) which retained responsibility for advising, organizing, equipping, training, overseeing and supporting all Iraqi armed forces.[110] The plan called for the recruitment of 40,000 personnel organized into three motorized infantry divisions by March 2005 (around 12,000 soldiers per division).[111] The first military unit created was the ICDC, later renamed the Iraqi National Guard (ING) by the Interim Iraqi Government in July 2004.[112] Initially, the ICDC was a mobilized reserve force which was lightly armed, trained for internal security missions in support of the police and coalition forces.[113] The training consisted of two-to-three week recruit training followed by on the job mentoring by the coalition forces.[114] The Americans granted the training newly recruited soldiers to a private enterprise, Vinnel Corporation, a subsidiary of Nothrop Grumman, with a 48 million one-year contract.[115] Vinnel had a good experience in training the National Guards of Saudi Arabia,[116] but it subcontracted the job of training the force to MPRI, a firm based in Virginia which had a previous experience in rebuilding military forces in Bosnia-Herzegovina and Croatia.[117] The private contractor was asked to produce nine battalions (three brigades) of Iraqi infantry within twelve months, by training Iraqi officers in Jordan at a non-commissioned officers' academy and a recruit – training academy in Kirkush.[118] The officers trained in Jordan then went back to Iraq to train new recruits, something that was heavily criticized by former Iraqi officers,[119] who perceived their army, historically, to be superior to that of the surrounding Arab countries. The new Iraqi army was officially called into being on 7 August according to CPA order no. 22.[120]

The approach to create the army was based on a bottom-up approach, which is calling for recruits to be led by foreign commanders, and on the concept of "train the trainer," who in turn will train the new recruits in following stages.

---

110 Frederick Kienle, "Creating an Iraqi Army from Scratch: Lessons for the Future," *National Security Outlook*, May 2007, 3. https://www.aei.org/wp-content/uploads/2011/10/20070525_200705NSOg.pdf, accessed 12 July 2020.
111 Walter Slocombe, "Speech - Foreign Press Center, Washington DC," 17 September 2003.
112 Seth G. Jones et all, *Establishing Law and Order After Conflict*, 147.
113 Ibid.
114 Ibid., 152.
115 Dina Badie, *After Saddam*, 142.
116 T.X. Hammes, "Raising and Mentoring Security Forces in Iraq and Afghanistan," in *Lessons Encountered: Learning from the Long War*, ed. Richard D. Hooker Jr. and Joseph J. Collins, (Washington D.C.: National Defense University, 2015), 306.
117 Dina Badie, *After Saddam*, 142.
118 Frederick Kienle, "Creating an Iraqi Army from Scratch," 2.
119 Ibrahim al-Marashi, "Disbanding and Rebuilding the Iraqi Army," 47.
120 Dina Badie, *After Saddam*, 142.

Walter Slocombe, former Under Secretary for Policy in the Clinton administration and responsible for the reconstruction of the Iraqi Ministry of Defense and the internal security forces, announced that the Pentagon's goal was to have 27 battalions ready within a year (by early 2005), with an air force and a coastal defense contingent.[121] By March 2004, Bremer issued CPA order no. 67 establishing an Iraqi counter-terrorism force (later known as Counter Terrorism Service, CTS), used for rapid deployment and with a special operation structure.[122] A month later, General Amer Bakr al-Hashimi was named Chief of Staff of the Iraqi army and a Kurdish General by the name of Babaker Zebari was named senior military advisor to the Ministry of Defense. More military personnel were also assigned by the CPA as division commanders and air force commanding general who were named just prior to the transfer of power to the Iraqi Interim Government in 2004.[123]

The CPA also tried to incorporate militias into the armed forces by stating the legal foundation in CPA order number 91. The aim of this order was to demobilize militias and empower the legitimate armed forces. A series of negotiations in 2004 resulted in an agreement with nine key parties to disband their militias and integrate them into the legal security sectors in the country; these included the Kurdish militias of the KDP and PUK, the Islamic Supreme Council of Iraq (SCIRI) which run the Badr Corps militia, the Iraqi Communist party, the Iraqi National Accord militia of Iyad Allawi, the militia of the Da'wa Party, the Iraqi National Congress militia of Ahmed Chalabi, Iraqi Hezbollah, and the Iraqi Islamic Party (Sunni). Despite this important attempt, the integration of militias faced serious issues with al-Qaeda succeeding in recruiting Sunni young men from Anbar province to fight the Coalition forces and the Iraqi army. Moreover, one main Shiite militia led by Moqatada as-Sadr fought the Americans and the Iraqi army before being defeated in 2005. Another problem was loyalty of ex-militiamen to their respective parties while serving in the security sector. An example of this is the politicization of the police force by the members of SCIRI who infiltrated its ranks and practiced unconstitutional methods to intimidate people from other sects and parties.[124]

The IAF reflected the demographic composition of the country, particularly at the level of rank and files, where 65 percent of soldiers were Shiites, 20 percent Sunnis, 18 percent Kurds, and around 2 percent for minorities, as

---

121 Ibid., 145.
122 CPA Order Number 67.
123 Dina Badie, *After Saddam*, 146.
124 Robert Perito, "Iraq's Interior Ministry: Frustrating Reform," *USIPeace Briefing*, May 2008, https://www.usip.org/sites/default/files/PB-Iraq-Interior-5-08.PDF, accessed 12 July 2020.

per art. 9 of the Iraqi constitution.¹²⁵ Army units were deployed and staffed in a manner that reflected the sectarian nature of the region into which they were present. For instance, Sunni, Shiites, and Kurds mostly served in geographic areas familiar to their ethnic groups.¹²⁶ These divisions were more noticeable at the battalion level, where commanders tended to command soldiers of their own sectarian background.¹²⁷ The National Guards became more diverse than other battalions; their ethnic and sectarian composition reflected the region they are to be deployed in.¹²⁸

Another important step taken by the CPA was to recreate the Iraqi Ministry of Defense (MoD), established by CPA order number 67. Slocombe was given the task by the Bush administration to rebuild the MoD.¹²⁹ The plan that Slocombe worked on was to model the Iraqi MoD based on the American, British and to some extent the Australian model of defense policy, acquisition and personnel.¹³⁰ The role of the MoD was to provide policy oversight of the Iraqi army (including the Counter terrorism force and the ICDC), formulate the overall defense and military policy, recruit and train military and civilian personnel in the ministry, provide acquisition, sustainment, and logistics, build infrastructure and provide intelligence analysis.¹³¹ The MoD proposes the defense budget in coordination with the Ministry of Finance, and it comes under the civilian control,¹³² a major breakaway from the Saddam era. The command and control of the army runs through the MoD's Iraqi Joint Headquarters that oversees all branches of the military.¹³³

The third and final security related involvement of the CPA in reconstructing Iraq's military sectors was related to the intelligence service. The concept of an Iraqi National Intelligence Service (INIS) was first brought up in a CPA meeting in November 2003.¹³⁴ The role of INIS was to gather and analyze domestic intelligence, assess threats to national security and advice the

---

125 Constitution of Iraq, art. 9.
126 Anthony Cordesman, "Iraq Force Development and the Challenge of Civil War," *Center for Strategic and International Studies*, 28 November 2006, 68. https://www.comw.org/warreport/fulltext/0611cordesman.pdf, accessed 12 July 2020.
127 Ibid.
128 Ibid.
129 Dina Badie, *After Saddam*, 122; Slocombe also overlooked the reconstruction of the Ministry of Interior.
130 Ibid., 138.
131 Ibid.
132 Ibid.
133 Marisa Sullivan, "Maliki's Authoritarian Regime," *Middle East Security Report*, no. 10 (2013): 10.
134 Dina Badie, *After Saddam*, 150.

Iraqi government.[135] The first INIS director was an ethnic Turkman (minority group) who headed the agency on 4 April 2004.[136] The CPA gave the CIA the role to set up the intelligence agency alongside the British intelligence,[137] and the INIS mirrored the US model of having a director of the central intelligence appointed for 5 years.[138] The INIS director reports to the Ministerial Committee on National Security, thus avoiding the possibility of one community having exclusive control over national intelligence data. INIS, however, does not have any authority to arrest,[139] another breakaway from the Saddam era, in order to keep shied civilians from the impact of the intelligence agents from interfering in their lives, and protect the political sphere from the famous *moukhabarat* (intelligence unit) that wrecked the liberties of Iraqis under Saddam.

In today's Iraq there are five more intelligence agencies beside the INIS: the Ministry of State for National Security Affairs (MSNSA), the Military Intelligence directorate (M2) within the MoD's joint Headquarters, the Director General for Intelligence and Security (DGIS) in the MoD, the National Information and Investigative Agency (NIIA) in the MoI, and the Office of Information and Security (OIS).[140] The INIS and MSNSA are rival national-level intelligence that gather and analyze data on internal and external threats, the M2 and DGIS provide operational focus on intelligence support to the security forces.[141]

Despite these security related decisions, the way the events unfolded after the Iraqi government took over the MoD and later with the American withdrawal from Iraq in 2011 actually showed that the MoD did not resemble the Western model of defense. The failure of the Iraqi government in preserving the status of the armed forces, shielding it from corruption and political interventionism, led to the downfall of the army and the rise of ISIS in 2013.

8 Problems and Challenges in the IAF

The IAF faced a set of challenges that hindered its capability to provide law and order in the country. The very fact that the IAF disintegrated when ISIS took over Mosul, forcing an international coalition to re-train the army and get involved in the fight against ISIS meant that the IAF could not overcome the

---

135   Seth G. Jones et all, *Establishing Law and Order After Conflict*, 154.
136   Dina Badie, *After Saddam*, 151.
137   Seth G. Jones et all, *Establishing Law and Order After Conflict*, 154.
138   Ibid.
139   Seth G. Jones et all, *Establishing Law and Order After Conflict*, 154.
140   Marisa Sullivan, "Maliki's Authoritarian Regime," 15.
141   Ibid.

challenges that it faced since 2006. The data in this book suggests that the IAF, which was handed to the Iraqi government by coalition in 2006, suffered from three sets of challenges: lack of professionalism and sectarianism, corruption, ambiguity in civil-military relations.

8.1 *Professionalism*

Armies pride themselves with their *esprit de corps*, that is the sense of belonging to the armed forces which creates a corporate identity. This quality is extremely important because it preserves cohesion and order in the army. Unfortunately, this characteristic is absent in the IAF, and this is manifested in the leadership and unit cohesion problem among the army's ranks.[142] There are problems in the lack of qualified officers, absenteeism, lack of cohesion and under-equipment for missions.[143] The main problem is absenteeism, which reflects a complete absence of order within the army ranks and a lack of *esprit de corps*. Absenteeism is very high in the IAF- around 25 percent of staff are absent at any given time.[144] It may be due to the long distances that soldiers need to travel back to their homes to give their families their pay, the lack of enforcement of the Iraqi Code of Military Discipline, the counting of wounded or even non-existent soldiers, and the inability to properly count number of soldiers who are on leave.[145] What makes matters worse is that the rate of absenteeism goes up to 50 percent once units are deployed for combat operations outside their usual area of deployment.[146] The problem of absenteeism dates to 2003, when the new recruits for the 1st battalion graduated in October but soldiers reporting for duty dropped from 694 to 455.[147]

Cohesion, order and fighting spirit were characteristics that the IAF lacked from its inception. The ICDC was first put to the test during the battle of Fallujah in 2004. The battalion came under fire while transiting a Shiite neighborhood in Baghdad and refused to continue, then its coalition's effort to airlift the battalion to Fallujah was aborted because of continued refusal by its personnel

---

142   Anthony Cordesman, "Iraq Force Development," 39.
143   Florence Gaub, "Building a New Military? The NATO Training Mission – Iraq," *Research Paper NATO Defense College*, no. 64 (2011): 5, https://www.files.ethz.ch/isn/128709/rp_67.pdf, accessed 12 July 2020.
144   Ibid., 6.
145   Ibid.
146   James L. Jones, "The Report of the Independent Commission on the Security Forces of Iraq," 6 September 2007, https://www.files.ethz.ch/isn/129488/2007_09_The_report_of_the_Independent.pdf, accessed 12 July 2020.
147   Dina Badie, *After Saddam*, 145.

to proceed.[148] Consequently, the coalition efforts to build a professional IAF proved to be a failure from the very beginning.

The Iraqi authorities carried on the burden of training the IAF after receiving the army from the CPA in 2006. The Iraqi National Defense College – the highest level military institute which focuses in its one-year program on strategic issues – was opened in 2006, and the following year saw the inauguration of the Military Academy in ar-Rustamiyah.[149] Moreover, the Iraqi government reopened the Iraqi Staff and Command College, conducting three Captain's Preparation courses per year, a 13 month Joint staff Course for Major as well as Command Courses for Battalion and Brigade Commanders. This was followed by the inauguration of the Iraqi War College in September 2010 which provide a one-year course for officers up to the rank of Colonel.[150]

Despite all of these institutional developments, there is still a lack of cohesion and the army has not cultivated corporate identity. For instance, during a graduate parade in the Habbaniya military base in western Baghdad, some 1,000 new soldiers protested and a number of them threw their shirts in rage when they were informed that they would be serving outside their hometowns.[151] Another example was in May 2013, when the Kurdish commander of the 16th Brigade of the 4th Division refused order to rotate his unit outside the disputed internal borders in Iraq (between the Kurdish Regional Government and the Iraqi State), eventually defecting with the rest of the Kurdish soldiers and their equipment to the Peshmerga.[152] Also, during the battle of Fallujah in 2004, the military unit that went to the city to help suppress the rebels, disbanded and sided with the rebels.[153] While it is true that that event happened around a year after the American invasion, and supposedly the IAF should have become more efficient, the disintegration of the army after the ISIS takeover of Mosul reveals that the IAF had no corporate identity and no clear military doctrine. Four of Iraq's 14 army divisions abandoned their posts, stripped off their uniforms and fled when confronted in cities such as Mosul and Tikrit by

---

148 Ibid., 147.
149 Florence Gaub, "Building a New Military?," 3.
150 Ibid., 4.
151 Ibrahim al-Marashi, "Disbanding and Rebuilding the Iraqi Army," 47.
152 Ben Van Heuvelen and Patrick Osgood, "Amid Rising Ethnic Tension, Kurdish Brigade Soldiers Stop Taking Orders from Baghdad," *Washington Post*, 11 June 2013, https://t.ly/bydQ, accessed 12 July 2020.
153 Ibrahim al-Marashi, "Disbanding and Rebuilding the Iraqi Army," 47.

ISIS.[154] The real shock is that since the US invasion in 2003 until 2013, the US spent 23 billion dollars on the IAF, in addition to the Iraqi government purchase of some F-16 fighter jets, M-1 battle tanks, Apache helicopters, hellfire missiles and other weapons.[155] The Iraqi army was in such a mess that Shiite religious leader Ayatollah Ali as-Sistani issued a Fatwa asking Shiite men to join in a Jihad against ISIS for the protection of the country. This Fatwa became the basis for the formation of the Popular Mobilization Forces (PMF).[156]

The lack of corporate identity and a clear military doctrine had a direct impact on the absence of a corporate identity that defines the essence and role of the IAF and the soldiers. This identity-oriented vacuum opened the door for sectarian and political loyalties to fill the gap. Officers are recruited on a quota basis as per art. 9 of the constitutions which states that the IAF is composed of all the components of the Iraqi people, so 60 percent are Shiites, 20 percent Sunnis, 18 percent Kurds, and the remaining are from minorities.[157] However, most officers (and NCOs) are caught up in the pressure of Iraq's ethnic and sectarian makeup,[158] so they tend to be lenient and supportive of their communities. An example could be seen in the link between Shiite militias and high-level officers in the military headquarters and government officials, where in different instances, a number of operations were cancelled in order to protect a friend or a specific neighborhood that an officer may belong to in sectarian terms.[159] Moreover, military units have been carrying Shia, Sunni, Arab or Kurdish banners and slogans,[160] as opposed to the corporate identity that army slogans should be the only banner allowed in military units. Even the prestigious Counter Terrorism Service (CTS) leaders claim that sectarian expressions are forbidden in their units, but there are proven claims that units display Shiite banners during religious holidays, and Shiite flags are flown from

---

154 Eric Schmitt and Michael R. Gordon, "The Iraqi Army Was Crumbling Long Before Its Collapse, U.S. Officials Say," *The New York Times*, 12 June 2014, https://www.nytimes.com/2014/06/13/world/middleeast/american-intelligence-officials-said-iraqi-military-had-been-in-decline.html, accessed 12 July 2020.
155 Ibid.
156 Renad Mansour, "The Popularity of the Hashd in Iraq," *Carnegie Middle East Center*, 1 February 2016, https://carnegie-mec.org/diwan/62638?lang=en/, accessed 12 July 2020.
157 Florence Gaub, "Building a New Military?," 4.
158 Anthony Cordesman, "Iraq Force Development," 39.
159 Ibid., 67.
160 Florence Gaub, "An Unhappy Marriage: Civil-Military Relations in Post-Saddam Iraq," *Carnegie Endowment for International Peace*, 13 January 2016, https://carnegieendowment.org/2016/01/13/unhappy-marriage-civil-military-relations-in-post-saddam-iraq-pub-61955, accessed 12 July 2020.

CTS vehicles during the battle of Mosul.[161] This is not only due to the lack of a corporate identity, but also because Kurds, Sunnis, and Shiites usually serve in battalions that consist largely or exclusively of their own communities.[162] Moreover, it is clear that the Shiite community became the hegemonic group in the armed forces. For instance, by 2013, 11 of the 14 army division commanders were Shiites, only one was Kurd (head of the 3rd division) and two were Sunnis. Moreover, all regional commander by that date were also Shiites, until the unrest in Anbar began with the rise of ISIS, a Sunni was appointed as regional commander.[163]

8.2 Civil-Military Ambiguity

A second problem relates to the ambiguity in the civilian control over the army. Art. 78 of the Iraqi constitution states that the Prime Minister is the commander-in-chief, and this article had been exploited by Prime Minister Nuri al-Maliki (2006–2014), especially in the absence of a legal framework to the way and extent of civilian control over the military. The daily stewardship is delegated to the Joint Operations Command (JOC) in Baghdad, which sends orders to provincial Operations Command that in turn exercises tactical control over their respective units.[164] Problems in civil-military relations and command-and-control of the army began with al-Maliki's establishment of the Office of the Commander-in-Chief in 2007, which controlled security matters in the country.[165] The office was envisioned by the American advisors as a coordinating forum between all security sector representatives and the MoI, MoD and the Prime Minister as head of the organization.[166] Al-Maliki put the entire security organization under the control of his office. Hence, according to US sources, the office became powerful enough overrule other government ministries, including the MoD and MoI.[167] This extra-constitutional body was not

---

161   David M. Witty, "Iraq's Post-2014 Counter Terrorism Service," *The Washington Institute for Near East Policy*, 2018, 23, https://www.washingtoninstitute.org/uploads/Documents/pubs/PolicyFocus157-Witty-3.pdf, accessed 12 July 2020.
162   T.X. Hammes, "Raising and Mentoring Security Forces," 64.
163   Marisa Sullivan, "Maliki's Authoritarian Regime," 18.
164   Michael Knights, "Helping Iraq Take Charge of its Command-and-Control Structure," *The Washington Institute*, 30 September 2019, https://www.washingtoninstitute.org/policy-analysis/view/helping-iraq-take-charge-of-its-command-and-control-structure, accessed 12 July 2020.
165   Marisa Sullivan, "Maliki's Authoritarian Regime," 11.
166   "Loose Ends: Iraq's Security Forces Between U.S. Drawdown and Withdrawal," *International Crisis Group*, 26 October 2010, 7, https://t.ly/LSdD, accessed 12 July 2020.
167   "Shadowy Iraq Office Accused of Sectarian Agenda," *CNN*, 1 May 2007, https://edition.cnn.com/2007/WORLD/meast/05/01/iraq.office/, accessed 12 July 2020.

subject to legislative oversight, had no legal framework to govern its existence and therefore was accountable to no one.[168] Consequently, the office bypassed the command of the MoD, the Joint Headquarters, and the Iraqi Ground Forces Command by issuing orders sometimes by cellphone to the operations commands, brigade and battalion commanders in the field.[169]

Al-Maliki then sought to expand his military powers by bringing elite units in the army under the direct control of the office of the commander in chief. For instance, the 56th brigade of the 6th Division of the Iraqi Army, known as the Baghdad Brigade (one of the best trained units in the army), was put under the direct control of the Prime Minister, bypassing the command of the 6th Iraqi army division. Then the 1st and 2nd Presidential Brigades were put directly under the control of the office of the commander in chief and used as the Prime Minister's guard force.[170] Al-Maliki went further in his intervention in the command-and-control structure of the security forces by putting the well trained and equipped CTS under the control of the office.[171] Moreover, in an attempt to put his hands on provincial security and military affairs, al-Maliki created the Regional Commands that came under the authority of the office,[172] and put under it military and police operations in the nine provinces that were hit hard by violence in 2007.[173] As a result, the Prime Minister enjoyed excessive security authorities that no one could override or oppose.

The concentration of military powers in the hands of al-Maliki meant that he could remove effective military commanders on an ethno-sectarian basis.[174] He replaced them by loyalists, like the Kurdish officers who were purged from Mosul's two army divisions and replaced by al-Maliki's loyalists,[175] in addition to Sunni officers,[176] and he began to issue orders to move troops around and

---

168   Marisa Sullivan, *Maliki's Authoritarian Regime*, 11.
169   Ibid.
170   Ibid.
171   Jim Michaels, "Chain of command concerns raised in Iraq," *USA Today*, 23 February 2009, http://usatoday30.usatoday.com/news/world/iraq/2009-02-23-maliki_N.htm, accessed 12 July 2020.
172   Marisa Sullivan, *Maliki's Authoritarian Regime*, 15.
173   Department of Defense, "Measuring Stability and Security in Iraq, Quarterly Report to Congress," May 2006, 52, https://images.derstandard.at/2008/10/01/Measuring%20Stability%20and%20Security%20in%20Iraq.pdf, accessed 30 August 2021.
174   Michael Gordon, "Bush Adviser's Memo Cites Doubts about Iraqi Leader," *The New York Times*, 29 November 2006.
175   Florence Gaub, "An Unhappy Marriage," 8.
176   Joshua Partlow, "Maliki's Office Is Seen Behind Purge in Forces," *Washington Post*, 30 April 20007, https://www.washingtonpost.com/wp-dyn/content/article/2007/04/29/AR2007042901728_pf.html, accessed 13 July 2020.

order the arrest of dissenting individuals.[177] Al-Maliki believed that political power should be manifested in military control of the army, probably something he learned from Saddam success in taming the Iraqi military. For this purpose, al-Maliki called for a new force initiative that created the following:
- three division headquarters
- the 11th division headquarters which split the span of control for battalions in Baghdad between Karkh and Rusafa
- five Brigade headquarters and 20 more battalions
- Introducing brigades to the 5th, 6th, 7th and 10th Iraqi Army Divisions
- One additional battalion to the 1st, 2nd, and 4th Brigade of the 8th Iraqi Army Division
- One battalion to the 2nd and 3rd Brigade of the 10 Iraqi Army Divisions[178]

Al-Maliki used his position as Prime Minister and Commander-in-Chief in order to alter and amend the capabilities of the Counter Terrorism Force (CTS), which was initially created by the Americans. He exploited his position as Commander-in-Chief to change the role and structure of the CTS through an executive order.[179] The CTS then became an independent military structure of command and control parallel to the armed forces. It comes under the direct control of the office of Prime Minister, but is tied to the MoD for administrative functions like salaries, management of promotions, and supply of ammunition and weapons.[180] The CTS consists of the CTS headquarters, the Counter-Terrorism Command (CTC), and three Iraqi Special Operation Forces (ISOF) brigades. The CTS headquarters was intended to be a strategy, policy and resourcing unit that provides combat operations oversight as a means to liaison with the government and control the CTS budget.[181] The CTC was the operational-level headquarters to control directly the three ISOF brigades.[182] However, the control over the operations has been disputed between the CTS headquarters and the CTC.[183] The CTS maintains a Baghdad-based national

---

177 James Hackett, *The Military Balance 2008* (London: International Institute for Strategic Studies, 2008), 229
178 Anthony Cordesman, "Iraq Force Development," 45.
179 David M. Witty, "The Iraqi Counter Terrorism Service," *Center for Middle East Policy at Brookings*, 10, https://www.brookings.edu/wp-content/uploads/2016/06/David-Witty-Paper_Final_Web.pdf, accessed 30 August 2021.
180 Anwār Kaisi, "al-Farīk ar-Rokn Abdul Ghani al-Asadi: at-Tansiq maʿ al-hashd ash-Shaʿbi wasala ila 'Auj 'Athmatihi" [Lieutenant General Abdul Ghani al-Asadi: Cooperation with the Popular Mobilization Forces Reached its Peak], *Al-Mustaqbal al-Iraqi*, 3 October 2016, http://almustakbalpaper.net/content.php?id=23048, accessed 13 July 2020.
181 David M. Witty, "The Iraqi Counter Terrorism Service," 11.
182 Ibid., 10–2.
183 David M. Witty, "Iraq's Post-2014 Counter Terrorism Service," 19.

strike force composed of the 1st Battalion (or the 36th Commando Battalion), a second battalion referred to as the Iraqi Counter-Terrorism Force (ICTF), and a Special Tactic Unit (STU) battalion, all of which operate as a nationwide force.[184] The ICTF and STU are specialized in high-end counter-terrorism missions such as hostage rescue.[185] It was in August 2016 that the CTS became an institution legalized by the Iraqi legislature. Initially the parliament eliminated the CTC but then reinstated it in March 2018.[186] Al-Maliki has used the CTS to silence opposition, whether from the Shiite community as happened in the battle of Basra against Muqatada as-Sadr, or to use it as a strike force against Sunni politicians like Rafiʿ al-Issawi and Tariq al-Hashimi.[187] After the law was passed in 2016, the CTS was charged with coordinating and directing all counter terrorism efforts in law enforcement, drawing the policy, planning and development of national counter terrorism strategy, and monitoring communications, social media sites, websites, and it can organize media campaigns to act against terrorism.[188] It has the right to ask for freeze of bank accounts subject to approval from the ministerial council.[189]

Despite this ambitious plan, the application took a twisted path because of politicization of the armed forces. For example, the Shiite dominated 8th division became influenced by Maliki's Da'wa party, the 4th division by the former Iraqi President Jalal Talibani's Patriotic Union of Kurdistan, 7th Division by the Sunni Iraqi Awakening Party, and the 5th Division by the Shiite Islamic Supreme Council of Iraq.[190] Moreover, the Iraqi National Defense College and the Iraqi War College only became operational in 2011.[191] Also, the army became top-heavy, with 1300 brigadier generals (compared with 300 in the American army), and commanders were selected based on political criteria

---

184   Ibid., 21.
185   "Tashkil Quwa Amniya Jadida li-Mukafaha Irhab fi Baghdad" [Forming a New Security Force to Fight Terrorism in Baghdad], *Rudaw*, 5 July 2015, https://www.rudaw.net/arabic/middleeast/iraq/0507201514, accessed 13 July 2020.
186   Law Number 31, 5 March 2016, see in *As-Sumariya*, https://www.alsumaria.tv/mobile/news/230991/iraq-news, accessed 13 July 2020.
187   "Iraq Confirms Arrest of Minister's Bodyguards," *Washington Post*, 21 December 2012, https://www.washingtonpost.com/world/middle_east/iraq-confirms-arrest-of-ministers-bodyguards/2012/12/21/df60b1c6-4b9f-11e2-9a42-d1ce6d0ed278_story.html, accessed 13 July 2020.
188   Law Number 31, 5 March 2016.
189   David M. Witty, "Iraq's Post-2014 Counter Terrorism Service," 25.
190   Florence Gaub, "An Unhappy Marriage," 10.
191   Ibid., 8.

rather than professional one, to an extent that many of the Iraqi soldiers that the US trained were no longer in the army.[192]

8.3 Corruption

A final challenge that has created a severe institutional and operational problem for the Iraqi army is corruption. For instance, junior offices claimed that defense officials demand a bribe of 3000 USD for a place at the Officer Training Academy, the price for promotion to General can be as much as 30,000 USD,[193] the position of battalion commander costs 50,000 USD, and that of division command 2 million USD.[194] There are several accounts of embezzlement of soldiers' food and fuel subsidies,[195] and it has been reported that soldiers in Mosul prior to June 2014 had to buy and prepare their own food.[196] To make matters worse, neither the MoD in Iraq nor the military leadership is able to count the number of active soldiers they have. Double counting of soldiers is a significant issue: in 2007, 22000 personnel had to be removed from the lists when it emerged that they had been included due to a miscount.[197] Moreover, after the fall of Mosul in 2014 and the rise of ISIS, an investigation into the IAF found that there were 50000 "ghost soldiers" in the army. Ghost soldiers refers to names of people that did not really exist but were included in the military, or soldiers who did not report for duty, either way they received their payment.[198] The commanding officers receive the payment for the name of soldiers who do not exist and share the salary of those who do not report for duty. In such circumstances, it is obvious that soldiers and military units are demoralized and fragile, facing full meltdown once subject to threats and challenges.

These problems in the civil-military relations, in addition to that in the command-and-control structure in the IAF had an important role in the marginalization of the Sunni community from the armed forces and the rise of ISIS. As commander-in-chief of the army, al-Maliki refused to incorporate the Sons of Anbar (or the Anbar Awakening), who were used by the Americans to

---

192 Linda Robinson, *Assessment of the Politico-Military Campaign to Counter ISIL and Options for Adaptation* (Santa Monica: Rand Corporation, 2016), 27.
193 Toby Dodge and Becca Wasser, "The Crisis of the Iraqi State," *Adelphi Series* 54, no. 447–448 (2014): 22.
194 Peter Van Buren, "You Too Can Command an Iraqi Division for Only $2 Million," *Reuters*, 10 December 2014, http://blogs.reuters.com/great-debate/2014/12/10/you-too-can-com-mand-an-iraqi-army-division-for-only-2-million/, accessed 13 July 2020.
195 Toby Dodge and Becca Wasser, "The Crisis of the Iraqi State," 22.
196 Ibid., 22–3.
197 Florence Gaub, "Building a New Military?," 3.
198 "Iraqi Army 'had 50,000 Ghost Troops' on Payroll," *BBC*, 30 November 2014, https://www.bbc.com/news/world-middle-east-30269343, accessed 13 July 2020.

defeat al-Qaeda in Iraq. The idea was that the Americans would train, equip and finance tribes in Anbar to fight al-Qaeda, and after that the militants would be incorporated to the Iraqi security forces. Nevertheless, al-Maliki did succeed in preventing this integration,[199] which eventually led to the radicalization of these very elements which fought al-Qaeda. To add insult to injury, the Iraqi Prime Minister then deployed army units to disperse demonstrators in Iraqi Sunni villages in Anbar as a result of the Arab Uprisings in 2011.[200] In the end, the region became fertile with the Syrian civil war to the rise of ISIS.

9 ISIS, the PMF and the Retraining of the Iraqi Military

ISIS is an offshoot of al-Qaeda in Iraq which was led by Abu Mas'ab az-Zarqawi, and took advantage of instability in Iraq and Syria to emerge as a threat to states in the Middle East.[201] The organization became famous as it succeeded in taking over Iraq's second largest city, Mosul, in three days,[202] controlling large amounts of weapons, ammunition, trucks, vehicles, military equipment, and above all, laying hands over the central bank assets in Mosul. The 30,000 Iraqi government troops in Mosul apparently were no match to the ISIS militants.[203] ISIS then fought its way to the outskirts of Baghdad, Diyala province, Anbar, then controlled Tikrit and Ramadi. ISIS stemmed from al-Qaeda in Iraq, and one expert estimated that more than 25 of the ISIS's top 40 leaders served in Saddam's army.[204] This fact shows the terrible consequences of disbanding the Iraqi army after the invasion without properly re-integrating Saddam's soldiers into society. Also, it shows the failure of the de-baathification process

---

199 "Baghdad's Misguided Crackdown on the Sons of Iraq," *Los Angeles Times*, 26 August 2008, https://www.latimes.com/world/middleeast/la-oe-brimley26-2008aug26-story.html, accessed 13 July 2020.
200 Linda Lavender, "The Re-Awakening of Anbar," *Civil-Military Fusion Centre*, April 2013, 8, https://reliefweb.int/sites/reliefweb.int/files/resources/Anbar_Province_Final%20(1).pdf, accessed 13 July 2020.
201 "Timeline: The Rise, Spread, and Fall of the Islamic State," *Wilson Center*, 28 October 2019, https://www.wilsoncenter.org/article/timeline-the-rise-spread-and-fall-the-islamic-state, accessed 13 July 2020.
202 Ned Parker, Isabel Coles and Raheem Salman, "Special Report: How Mosul fell - An Iraqi General Disputes Baghdad's Story," *Reuters*, 14 October 2014, https://www.reuters.com/article/us-mideast-crisis-gharawi-special-report/special-report-how-mosul-fell-an-iraqi-general-disputes-baghdads-story-idUSKCN0I30Z820141014, accessed 13 July 2020.
203 Dan Kedmey, "Iraq is 'Run by al-Qaeda': Appalling Carnage Shows Terror Group's Resurgence," *Time*, 14 October 2013, http://world.time.com/2013/10/14/this-is-qaedacountry-blasts-and-prison-breakserode-iraqi-sovereignty/, accessed 13 July 2020.
204 Mark Thompson, "How Disbanding the Iraqi Army Fueled ISIS," *Time*, 28 May 2015, https://time.com/3900753/isis-iraq-syria-army-united-states-military/, accessed 13 May 2020.

that turned out to be a tool to oppress the Sunni community and wrongfully blame them for Saddam's atrocities, as if they were not victims themselves of Saddam's rule.

Haidar al-Abadi, successor of al-Maliki as Prime Minister, took an important decision in civil-military relations by disbanding the Office of the Commander-in-Chief,[205] allowing the JOC to take over military decisions.[206] He then moved to depart from Maliki's sectarian practices in appointing military commanders, and named two Sunni Generals, Tawfiq and al-Juburi, as commanders of Iraqi Ground Forces and Ninewa Operations Commander, respectively.[207]

The response of the Iraqi authorities was to concentrate what was left of their army around Baghdad to protect the capital. Due to this existential threat, the most reverent Shiite religious authority, Ayatollah Ali as-Sistani, issued a Fatwa, calling for defending the country, and it this Fatwa was the basis for the creation of the PMF. The Iranians welcomed this call, as it now could find its way to infiltrate the security apparatus of Iraq by sponsoring a large coalition of Shiite militias who are bound together by a religious ruling. Hence, Iran supplied the Iraqi government with intelligence and provided the PMF with training and new weapons.[208] After the creation of the PMF, the Iraqi army's role changed from being the sole military organization that defended the country from threats to its sovereignty, into supporting and assisting the Shia militias.[209] Moreover, the PMF received legal status from the Iraqi Parliament in November 2016, transforming it into "an independent military formation as part of the Iraqi armed forces and linked to the Commander-in-Chief."[210] In practice, this meant that the PMF became attached to the National Security Council.[211] The NSC is a civilian institution that conducts civilian oversight

---

205 Kenneth M. Pollack, "Iraq's Mr. Abadi comes to Washington," *Brookings*, 13 April 2015, https://www.brookings.edu/blog/markaz/2015/04/13/iraqs-mr-abadi-comes-to-washington/, accessed 13 July 2020.

206 Jessa Rose Dury-Agri, Omer Kassim, and Patrick Martin, "Iraqi Security Forces and Popular Mobilization Forces Orders of Battle," *Institute for the Study of War*, 2017, 10, http://www.understandingwar.org/sites/default/files/Iraq%20-%20ISF%20PMF%20Orders%20of%20Battle_0_0.pdf, accessed 13 July 2020.

207 Ibid.

208 Kardo Rached and Ahmed Omar Bali, "Post-ISIS and the Shia Armed Groups," *Central European Journal of International & Security Studies* 13, no. 1 (2019): 129.

209 Ibid.

210 Renad Mansour, "More than Militias: Iraq's Popular Mobilization Forces are Here to Stay," *War on the Rocks*, 3 April 2018, https://warontherocks.com/2018/04/more-than-militias-iraqs-popular-mobilization-forces-are-here-to-stay/, accessed 13 July 2020.

211 Ibid.

of security agencies, but provides the PMF with greater maneuverability and autonomy.[212] For instance, PMF may keep the identities of its militias, flags, symbols, leaders,[213] and participate as a security organization in political life. The parliament voted to match the PMF salaries to those of the other members of the security forces in the 2018 federal budget.[214] Consequently, it got 1.63 billion USD from the government in 2017, which exceeded the 683 million allotted to the CTS.[215] As a result, the security apparatus in Iraq had been "Iranianized," which is a new armed organization bound by a Shiite religious doctrine has become stronger, and more influential, than the army itself. This echoes the Revolutionary Guards of Iran which is superior to the Iranian army.

The PMF is aggressively expanding its presence and legitimacy in Iraq in order to take over the role of the IAF. It provides medical care and rehabilitation assistance to its fighters, with a specialized directorate which oversees provision of administrative and financial assistance to wounded fighters and their families as well as the families of the deceased fighters.[216] Moreover, the PMF has established a lobbying arm in the government to advocate for favorable laws, regulations and budgetary increase to its members, along a media directorate that serves as an official source to all PMF related activities.[217] They are also engaged in reconstruction of areas destroyed by the fight against ISIS.[218] Regarding the hierarchy, the PMF is put directly under the Prime Minister, but because PMF leaders are already politicians, according to al-Maliki,[219] and are in control of civilian and military wings,[220] that does not mean necessarily that they are under the full control of the Iraqi state. Hence, in theory, the PMF formally reports to the Prime Minister's office, but the largest and strongest PMF groups had a reputation for being responsive to their own leaders rather than to Iraqi forces and officials.[221] It is hard to imagine that the Badr Organization, Asā'ib Ahl al-Haq, or Peace Brigades of Muqatada as-Sadr, will abandon their

---

212 Ibid.
213 Ibid.
214 Jessa Rose Dury-Agri, Omer Kassim, and Patrick Martin, "Iraqi Security Forces," 29.
215 Ibid.
216 Ibid., 30.
217 Ibid.
218 "Iraq's Paramilitary Groups: The Challenge of Rebuilding a Functioning State," *International Crisis Group*, no. 188, 30 July 2018, 11.
219 "The Law of the Popular Mobilisation Units Commission Number 40 for the Year 2016", Ministry of Justice, 5 January 2017.
220 Iraq's Paramilitary Groups,", 7.
221 Erica Gaston and András Derzsi-Horváth, "Iraq After ISIL: Sub-State Actors, Local Forces, and the Micro-Politics of Control," *Global Public Policy Institute*, March 2008, 20–1, https://www.gppi.net/media/Gaston_Derzsi-Horvath_Iraq_After_ISIL.pdf, accessed 13 July 2020.

leaders' order to follow that of the government. When finance, weapons and training come from Iran, it means that the Iranians hold the real power in the PMF. This explains the parallel and informal chain of command in the PMF which responds to the Iranian Revolution Guards' Quds Force.

The PMF is made up of three main groups: the strongest group include militias loyal to Ayatollah Khamenei of Iran, which includes Saraya Khurasani, Abul Fadl al-Abbas Brigade, Badr Organization, and Asā'ib Ahl al-Haq; The second group includes loyalists to Ayatollah Ali as-Sistani, Saraya al-Ataba al-Abbasiya, Saraya al-Ataba al-Hussainiya, Saraya al-Ataba al-Alawiya, and Liwa 'Ali al-Akbar, Saraya el-Jihad, Saraya el-'Aqida, and Saraya 'Ashura; finally, the third group consists of the Sadrists faction (loyal to Moqatada as-Sadr), like the Peace Regiments (Saraya as-Salam).[222] The PMF, then, is not a cohesive unit, but rather a forum of Shiite militias contesting among different political groups in Iraq. The problem is that these groups do not necessarily abide by government directives. Hence, the relationship between PMF groups and the IAF is not smooth and there is a sense of animosity between them. At one point, Iraqi Shia militias in Basra expelled the 9th Iraqi Army Armored Division deployed by Prime Minister Abadi to suppress crime and tribal violence in January 2016.[223] More recently, it has been the case that PMF units have been shelling the Green Zone in Baghdad, coordinating their attacks with IRGC. This led Prime Minister Mustafa al-Kadhimi to order the CTS to raid a Hezbollah-Iraq base where they found militants preparing to stockpiling Katyusha rockets and planning to shell the Green Zone.

As the Americans felt that the formation of the PMF – even without a legal framework at the beginning – was a move that provided Iran with greater leverage in Iraq, and due to the fact that the US had withdrew its army from Iraq in 2011 after spending 25 billion dollars on the country's security sector (in 8 years),[224] it was important for the Americans to call for an international coalition to retrain the Iraqi army after the fall of Mosul. The training of the Iraqi security forces included basic combat skills, demining operations and combat lifesaver training, training of 18000 members of Iraq's CTS force, equipping and training the Iraqi air force, in addition to providing Iraq with more than

---

222 Renad Mansour and Faleh A. Jabar, "The Popular Mobilization Forces and Iraq's Future," *Carnegie Middle East Center*, 28 April 2017, https://carnegie-mec.org/2017/04/28/popular-mobilization-forces-and-iraq-s-future-pub-68810, accessed 13 July 2020.
223 Jessa Rose Dury-Agri, Omer Kassim, and Patrick Martin, "Iraqi Security Forces," 31–2.
224 Heath Druzin, "Retraining Iraq's Fractured Army: Will it Work this Time?," *Stars and Stripes*, 11 September 2014, https://www.stripes.com/news/middle-east/retraining-iraq-s-fractured-army-will-it-work-this-time-1.302407, accessed 13 July 2020.

2 billion dollars' worth of military equipment.[225] For instance, 17 Iraqi army brigades were provided with initial equipment sets, including equipment, small arms, ammunition, around 1000 non tactical vehicles and 1100 armored vehicles. The coalition also provided additional equipment to federal police and border force brigades, beside 400 explosive detection and demining kits to assist in the detection and removal of improvised explosive devices.[226] The Americans have also provided small arms and heavy weapons, night-vision goggles, vehicle maintenance support, spare parts, and training to CTS units.[227] They have also provided body armor, AT-4 antitank rockets, Humvees, armored bulldozers, mine-resistant ambush-protected vehicles (MRAP), in addition to 194 million USD in 2019.

Despite the success of the IAF, Peshmerga and the PMF, supported by the Americans in the fight against ISIS, the way these security organizations dealt with civilians was disturbing and to some extent, dangerous for the legitimacy of Iraqi security forces. The Human Rights Watch (HRW) reported that Iraqi and Peshmerga units screened suspects from the ISIS dominated regions violently, inhumanely, detaining suspects without notifying their families and with no access to a lawyer throughout interrogations.[228] Moreover, security forces carried out serious abuses like torture, execution of captured militants, bombarding civilian objects targets like homes and hospitals, in addition to densely populated areas.[229] According to HRW, "it is likely that Iraqi and coalition forces have killed many thousands of civilians in the course of their military operations against ISIS."[230] During the fight to take Fallujah, PMF units committed serious atrocities and crimes against Sunni civilians,[231] and in the Sunni village of Qaim, the PMF prevented the farmers from taking care of their cultivated fields.[232] All these violations and the state's incapability of

---

225 Jim Garamone, "Coalition Trainers in Iraq Helping 'Make a Good Force Better'," *Department of Defense*, 22 May 2018, https://www.defense.gov/Explore/News/Article/Article/1528637/coalition-trainers-in-iraq-helping-make-a-good-force-better/, accessed 13 July 2020.
226 Ibid.
227 David M. Witty, "Iraq's Post-2014 Counter Terrorism Service," 27.
228 Human Rights Watch, *World Report 2018 - Iraq*, 18 January 2018, https://www.refworld.org/docid/5a61ee64a.html, accessed 13 July 2020.
229 Ibid.
230 Ibid.
231 Human Rights Watch, *Iraq: Fallujah Abuses Inquiry Mired in Secrecy*, 7 July 2016, https://www.hrw.org/news/2016/07/07/iraq-fallujah-abuses-inquiry-mired-secrecy, accessed 13 July 2020.
232 Tamer El-Ghobashy and Mustafa Salim, "As Iraq's Shiite Militias Expand Their Reach, Concerns About an ISIS Revival Grow," *Washington Post*, 19 January 2019, https://t.ly/KEnZ, accessed 13 July 2020.

controlling the now legal PMF, means that in the long run the Sunnis will be further radicalized and the legitimacy of the security forces will be hindered.

10 Conclusion

The IAF has had a history of construction, destruction and reconstruction. External actors played a critical role in construction and reconstruction, the British in 1920s and the Americans post-2033 invasion. The army, however, has been suffering from politicization and disintegration. During WWII the army had to be reconstructed in order to avoid ideological politicization, but after 1958, the army became a tool for political consolidation, which meant that it played an important role in socio-political control for the dominant group.

The Baath subsumed the army and transformed it into something similar to a party militia. Hence, there was no separation between army and politics, but the army was not part of society; it was rather a body within the whole Baath party apparatus. Saddam and his predecessors utilized nepotism and familialism as tools to consolidate control over the army, beside party ideology. The end result was that the army became Saddam's militia, a tool to achieve domestic political goals. The end of Saddam's era and the post-2003 invasion, however, did not elevate the army into a national, impartial and professional one. Hence, after spending more than 25 billion USD on the new IAF by the Americans, the army eventually disintegrated in 2014 after the ISIS attack. Also, the army was used by al-Maliki to suppress opposition. Under such circumstances, we can see that the IAF requires further restructuring that would tackle the sectarian composition of the units and battalions, the method of training, the tactics used to conduct military operations, and above all a full control over the newly created PMF to prevent military infiltration by neighboring countries.

CHAPTER 6

The National Defense Force of Burundi

The Burundian military is a case of interest for researchers studying multi-ethnic armies. Its army was established by the Belgian colonial administration to serve the interest of the mandate in preserving law and order, basically a similar story replicated almost in all the colonized parts of the world. The army was not involved in politics during the mandate period. The trajectory of the rise of the army shows that it moved from a passive stance in domestic affairs into one of hegemony in political affairs. The hegemonic status of the army stayed until the Arusha agreement in 2000. Afterwards, the army moved back to barracks, but its vital role is still present, he who controls the army controls Burundi.

    This chapter talks about the role of the army in Burundian politics. I begin by a brief history of the establishment of the country during the union with Rwanda. Then, I move on to discuss the domestic context that led the army to intervene and dominate the politics of the country. From its inception until the Arusha Agreement, the army, and the state in general, was controlled by the Tutsi minority while the Hutu majority was marginalized. When the Arsuah agreement was signed and the country transitioned to a power sharing democratic system, the army had a smooth transition into a professional institution with ethnic equilibrium, but events after 2015 led to the politicization of the army and the control of the CNDD-FDD over the institution. I intend to explain this shift, and what led to the de-professionalism and re-politicization of the army. I emphasize on specific loopholes in the Arusha Agreement, where negotiators equated between parity in the army and power sharing while the problem remains that an ethnically balanced army still requires consensus to avoid politicizing it, and its exploitation in domestic politics. This explicitly reveals that the army under the control of the president, as in the case of Burundi, leads to its politicization and exploitation in deeply divided societies.

1 Burundi: The Colonial Period and Independence

Burundi's territory stabilized in its current borders during the 1850s before becoming part of the German East Africa in 1890.[1] Nine years later, Germany established its first military district of Rwanda and Burundi, known at that time as Ruanda-Urundi.[2] The German rule was indirect through the King and local chiefs. Since that time, the Europeans reported that the population of Burundi consisted of the Hutu who represented the majority of the population, the Tutsi as the minority, one percent of the population were known as the Twa, and a separate ethnic group, the Ganwa, that formed the royal family.[3] The army of the King was composed mainly of Tutsis and Ganwas.[4] These pre-colonial ethnic categories were not rigid and most importantly were still apolitical, and changes in identity from Hutu to Tutsi and vice-versa was possible.[5] There were commercial, social, and familial interactions between Tutsis and Hutus, making ethnic classification questionable,[6] especially by following a mythical-stereotypical concept that Tutsis and Ganwas are tall, have a lighter color and long noses while Hutus are short and stocky with flat noses.[7] However, ethnic identities slowly became a main political feature in colonial Burundi that institutionalized the politics of identity after independence.

After WWI, Ruanda-Urundi became a Belgian colony, and they institutionalized identity politics in the territory by favoring Tutsis over Hutus in a genuine colonial policy of divide and rule. For instance, the Belgians gave more positions to Tutsis and left Hutus with the task of tilling the soil or looking after the Tutsi's cattle.[8] The colonial authorities stripped Hutu landowners and religious leaders from their privileges.[9] Then, to manage identity politics and keep it under the control of the colonial authorities, the Belgians introduced identity

---

1 Nigel Watt, *Burundi: The Biography of a Small African Country* (London: Hurst Publishers, 2008), 23.
2 Richard Cornwell and Hannelie de Beer, "Burundi: The Politics of Intolerance," *Africa Watch* 8, no. 6 (1999): 84
3 Nigel Watt, *Burundi*, 24.
4 Ibid., 25.
5 Alexandre W. Raffoul, "The Politics of Association: Power Sharing and the De-Politicization of Ethnicity in Post-War Burundi," *Ethnopolitics* 19, no. 1 (2020): 10.
6 Robert Krueger and Kathleen Tobin Krueger, *From Bloodshed to Hope in Burundi: Our Embassy Years during Genocide* (Texas: University of Texas Press, 2007), 25.
7 For further details on the physical distinction between Hutus and Tutsis, see Jean-Pierre Chretien, *The Great Lakes of Africa* (New York: Zone Books, 2003), 74–83.
8 Robert Krueger and Kathleen Tobin Krueger, *From Bloodshed to Hope*, 26.
9 Ibid.

cards indicating ethnic origin which deepened ethnic enmity.[10] In addition to the Hutu-Tutsi divide, there was also an internal clan struggle within the Tutsi community, where Tutsis from Muramvya saw themselves as superior to those from Bururi.[11] This intra-Tutsi struggle was a vehicle for oppression used by the Bururi to dominate the system and put the Muramvya in a secondary position in the state. Nevertheless, the status of the Muramvya, was much better than that of the Hutu during Tutsi rule.

The Belgian rule in Burundi began to wane by the late 1950s with the rise of the anti-colonial movement all over the world. Hence, the local elite reached an agreement with the mandatory power (Belgium) to grant Burundi independence and transfer of power in early 1960s. To prepare for independence, Belgium created the Territorial Guard in 1960 marked a new chapter in military affairs in Burundi, and it became the embryonic unit of the national army.[12] Recruits received training by the Belgian military authority, and when the country became independent in 1962, a defense ministry was established and announced the creation of the *Forces Armées du Burundi* (FAB, until 2005 when its name was changed). Nevertheless, because of the colonial practices of favoring the Tutsis over the Hutus, the FAB was overwhelmingly composed of Tutsi elements.

The political involvement of the army began after the assassination of Prince Louis Rwagasore, the founder of the nationalist multi-ethnic party *Union Pour le Progrès National*, UPRONA. Rwagasore was assassinated shortly after his electoral victory in September 1961, leading to a state of chaos in the country. Few months later in January 1962, Tutsi militants from UPRONA youth wing attacked a number of Hutu trade unionists and supporters of the People's Party, leading to a split in UPRONA along ethnic lines.[13] The King stepped in to fill the political vacuum but could not provide any stability to a deeply divided and wounded country. In less than four years, there were five prime ministers none of whom could govern for more than two years.[14] As a result, the monarch had no option but to rely on the army for support. Once the army became

---

10   Nigel Watt, *Burundi*, 29.
11   Ibid., 27.
12   Ministère de la Défense Nationale et des Anciens Combattants, http://mdnac.bi/?q=content/historique-du-mdnac, accessed 20 January 2021.
13   Rene Lemarchand, *Burundi: Ethnic Conflict and Genocide* (Cambridge: Cambridge University Press, 1994), 62–8.
14   Patrick Hajayandi, "Wounded Memories: Perceptions of Past Violence in Burundi and Perspectives for Reconciliation, *The Institute for Justice and Reconciliation* (2019): 23; https://media.africaportal.org/documents/IJR-Burundi_Wounded-memories-WEB.pdf, accessed 20 January 2021.

involved in politics, it seemed impossible to return them to the barracks and depoliticize them. To add insult to injury, another political figure who followed Rwagasore's path in bridging the gap between Tutsis and Hutus, Pierre Ngendandumwe (a Hutu married to a Tutsi), was killed by a Tutsi refugee,[15] unleashing an era of chaos and violence that sealed the army's domination over political affairs until 2005. In October 1965, Hutu elements in the army and police initiated a revolt that was brutally crushed by the Tutsis, leading to a complete exclusion of Hutus from the army and political power.[16] One can see how the royal interest at this moment coincided with that of the Tutsi community: the Tutsis preserved their hegemonic status in the state by using the army to prevent the Hutus from gaining power, in the name of protecting the monarchy, despite the fact that the Hutu gained a parliamentary majority up until 1965. The monarchy preserved its grip on the country through the armed forces, but it was incapable to act without the latter. Moreover, the monarchy no longer played a unifying role in the country, so the army exploited the situation for its corporate and ethnic interests. Captain Michel Micombero, a young Tutsi officer from Bururi who was recently appointed by King Ntare V as Prime Minister, took over power by a coup, abolished the monarchy and established a republic. The era of the Tutsi-controlled-army began as the only dominant institution in the country.

2 The Army in Power

From 1966 until 2005 – with the exception of a short rule by a democratically elected Hutu President, Melchior Ndadaye in 1993 – the army was the source of political power in the country. The FAB reign was led by the Tutsi-Hima clan from Bururi which provided the three Presidents who ruled Burundi during this period: Michel Micombero (1966–76), Jean-Baptiste Bagaza (1976–87) and Pierre Buyoya (1987–93, 1996–2003).[17]

2.1 *Micombero*
Like most dictators from the armed forces in the last century, Micombero created a dictatorship by abolishing parliament and installing instead the

---

15 Nigel Watt, *Burundi*, 31.
16 Rene Lemarchand, *Rwanda and Burundi* (New York: Praeger Publishers, 1970), 297, 416–17.
17 Peter Uvin, *Life After Violence: A People's Story of Burundi* (London: Zed Books in association with International African Institute, Royal African Institute and Social Science Research Council, 2009), 9.

National Revolutionary Council (NRC),[18] a junta which functioned until 1968. He exploited the official visit of the King to Congo to stage a bloodless coup and threatened the King that he will be treated like a common criminal if he returns to Burundi.[19] Next, Micombero abolished the monarchy and established a republic on 28 November 1966, making the army as the pillar of domestic politics. Micombero ruled through the NRC which consisted of 12 members – all of whom were army officers – with himself as chairman. He also became President of the Republic, Prime Minister, Minister of Defense and President of UPRONA,[20] thus creating a crucial political link between the army, the masses (through the party), and the civilian authority. He politicized the army with its affiliation with UPRONA, and as president, he integrated the gendarmerie into the army,[21] thus circumventing the possibility of a Hutu revolt which could begin from the gendarmerie, especially after the revolt that happened in 1965 which the army violently crushed.

Micombero could not prevent Hutu rebellions despite the fact that all security forces were under his direct control. Nevertheless, when Hutus rebelled the army would violently respond by massacring Hutu population. The most violent response was in April 1972, as a result of Hutu uprising, the army responded by slaughtering up to 3000 Hutus overwhelmingly from the educated class.[22] The events of 1972 were so important in the country that those who joined the rebellion of the 1990s were relatives to the victims. For instance, among the Hutu victims of 1972 were the father of President Pierre Nkurunziza, who happened to be a member of parliament.[23] Intriguingly, the end of Micombero came from within the institution that he promoted as the arbiter of politics in the country, the army. In 1976, Micombero was ousted by Major Jean-Baptiste Bagaza, another Tutsi from Bururi to run the country relying on the armed forces.

2.2 *Bagaza*

Major Bagaza was a ruthless military dictator who implemented harsh policies that widened the gap between Hutus and Tutsis. In order to continue his predecessor's extermination of the educated Hutu class, he set out a policy to prevent Hutus from going to school or succeeding in exams.[24] The aim of this policy was to guarantee that the Hutu community would never develop an elite

---

18 Nigel Watt, *Burundi*, 33.
19 Rene Lemarchand, *Rwanda and Burundi*, 433.
20 Richard Cornwell and Hannelie de Beer, "Burundi: The Politics of Intolerance," 86.
21 Rene Lemarchand, *Rwanda and Burundi*, 462.
22 Richard Cornwell and Hannelie de Beer, "Burundi: The Politics of Intolerance," 86.
23 Nigel Watt, *Burundi*, 37.
24 Ibid., 40.

of its own capable of participating in government.[25] For those who worked their way and became educated, Bugaza made it extremely hard for qualified Hutus to get a job.[26] Moreover, only Tutsis were allowed to serve as the regional and cantonal inspectors who were responsible to determine which students should proceed to secondary education.[27] The examiners classified examination papers with an *i* for Tutsi students and a *u* for Hutu,[28] to make sure that examiners know whom to pass and whom to fail. Moreover, 10 percent of the teachers in the National University and 20 percent of its students were Hutu, with 89 percent of managers in public corporations being Tutsis.[29]

Regarding the political system, Bagaza's government consisted at best of 5 Hutu ministers (out of 18), less than one-third of MPs were Hutu, UPRONA's Central Committee had only 2 Hutu members out of 52, only 1 ambassador of Hutu origins out of 22 and 2 Hutu provincial governors out of 15. Moreover, only one Hutu worked in the office of the president out of 99, one hospital director out of 20, one court president out of 8, and 5 magistrates out of 97.[30] To make matters worse, there sectors that had no high-ranking Hutu official, like in the ministerial permanent secretaries, embassy diplomats, and justice prosecutors.[31] In the army, the Hutus had only two high-ranking officers, with 30 sergeants and privates, while Tutsis had 398 and 11970 respectively. Moreover, there were no army barracks commanders or judiciary police officers and inspectors from the Hutu community.[32] Under such circumstances, the Hutu were not only marginalized, but their presence in the country was threatened because of the institutional and structural discrimination against them. Despite this systematic attempt to drive the Hutu out of the country, the threat on Bagaza's reign, again, came not from the Hutu but rather from the army itself. In 1987, the army initiated another bloodless coup, overthrew Bagaza,

---

25 Robert Krueger and Kathleen Tobin Krueger, *From Bloodshed to Hope*, 30.
26 "Burundi: Targeting Students, Teachers and Clerics in the Fight for Supremacy," *Amnesty International*, 31 August 1995, https://www.amnesty.org/download/Documents/176000/afr160141995en.pdf, accessed 20 January 2021.
27 Robert Krueger and Kathleen Tobin Krueger, *From Bloodshed to Hope*, 30.
28 Tony Jackson, "Equal Access to Education: A Peace Imperative for Burundi," *International Alert*, June (2000): 26, https://www.international-alert.org/sites/default/files/publications/equal_access_to_education.pdf, accessed 20 January 2021.
29 Peter Uvin, *Life After Violence*, 10.
30 Raphael Ntibazonkiza, *Au Royaume des Seigneurs de la Lance : Une Approche Historique de la Question Ethnique au Burundi* (Brussels: Bruxelles droits de l'homme, 1993); Janvier Nkurunziza and Floribert Ngaruko, "Explaining Growth in Burundi: 1960–2000," (2004), *Centre for the Study of African Economies*, 22.
31 Janvier Nkurunziza and Floribert Ngaruko, "Explaining Growth in Burundi," 22.
32 Ibid.

and the new 31-member Military Committee of National Salvation appointed Pierre Buyoya president.[33]

2.3 Buyoya

Buyoya's era can be divided into two parts: prior to the 1993 democratic elections and afterwards with the military coup that ended the short-lived democratic experience until the free and fair elections that happened in 2005. In the first phase, Buyoya engaged in a political experiment to try to integrate the Hutu community to the political landscape, but the essence of his policies was cosmetic. The Tutsi continued their domination over all public institutions. For instance, the Tutsi community represented 99 percent of the officer corps, 95 percent of the judiciary, 88 percent of the faculty at the University of Bujumbura, and above all, all members of the MCNS who had final authority over all national issues, were Tutsis.[34]

In 1988, there was an outbreak of violence in Ntega and Marangara on the Rwandan borders, which led to the killing of 300 Tutsis. The army responded with a massive retaliation that killed thousands of Hutus and used Napalm bombs against civilians.[35] Buyoya refused to condemn the army or hold it responsible, and instead launched the "Ubumwe," known as the Charter of Unity which was approved in a referendum in 1991. This charter designed a special unity flag and anthem,[36] and with Buyoya's openness to the Hutu community, they began to be seen on television, got new jobs, received education, and political parties were allowed to function, including the *Burundi Democratic Front* (Frodebu) led by Melchior Ndadaye.[37]

Buyoya capitalized on his openness to the Hutu and accepted to hold free and fair elections in June 1993. However, he failed to realize that allowing the Hutu to hold rallies, talk on TV, and compete in elections were by no means a full reconciliation of the genocides that happened in the past decades. Hence, the first democratic elections took place since decades and led to the victory of Ndadaye, even though Buyoya was confident during the campaign of his victory as he decreed that political parties had to move mixed-ethnic membership to be eligible for elections.[38] Nevertheless, after Buyoya's defeat, the army

---

33 Richard Cornwell and Hannelie de Beer, "Burundi: The Politics of Intolerance," 87.
34 Robert Krueger and Kathleen Tobin Krueger, *From Bloodshed to Hope*, 31.
35 Kate Hunt, "Burundi Rejects Outside Investigation of Massacres," *The Christian Science Monitor*, 30 August 1988
36 Andrea Purdekova, *Making Ubumwe: Power, State and Camps in Rwanda's Unity-Building Project* (New York: Berghahn Books, 2015), 16.
37 Nigel Watt, *Burundi*, 42.
38 Ibid., 43.

rejected the new era which threatened its loss of political dominance and its Tutsi identity. Hence, in October, it launched a coup – believed to be supported from behind the scenes by Buyoya – killing the president, speaker, and deputy speaker of the National Assembly. The army ruled directly for three years until they re-installed Buyoya back in power.[39] In the second phase of Buyoya's rule, the Arusha talks were initiated and a long process of deliberation and discussion between the Tutsi and Hutu parties led to the Arusha agreement signed between the state and rebels on different occasions between 2000 and 2003.

A very interesting event happened on the eve of the coup, whereby the army only kept Burui Tutsis on duty, allowing non-Bururis to take a leave. This shows the deep mistrust that Bururis' have towards their co-ethnic non-Bururis, and the deep divisions that exist within the community. Nevertheless, the Bururi domination in the army had always been lenient to the non-Bururis, unlike their treatment of the Hutu community. Despite that, the Hutu community showed severe resistance to the Tutsi domination throughout the whole period, and fought to retain their status in the country.

3   The Hutu Response

The first political movement to emerge among the Hutu was the *Mouvement des Etudiants Progressistes du Burundi* (MEPROBA), among exiled Hutu students in Belgium in the 1970s.[40] This political movement galvanized the massacres against the Hutu in 1965, 1969, and 1972 to gain political support. Later on, the movement split into different groups and the new ones overshadowed MEPROBA as the first political grouping among the Hutus. Another party founded in 1980 with a radical Hutu nationalism was the *Parti pour la libération du peuple Hutu* (PALIPEHUTU) and established its armed wing the *Forces Nationales de Liberation* (FNL) in 1985, hence the PALEPEHUTU-FNL. A strong representative of the Hutu community was the FRODEBU, a progressive and moderate party found by Melchior Ndadaye, who was the democratically elected President of Burundi in June 1993, only to be killed during the military coup in October same year. After the erosion of the influence of the FRODEBU by the military, Léonard Nyangoma, a Hutu minister and member of the FRODEBU, broke away from the party and established the *Conseil National*

---

39   Ibid., 61.
40   Katrin Wittig, "Politics in the Shadow of the Gun: Revisiting the Literature on 'Rebel-to-Party Transformations' through the Case of Burundi," *Civil Wars* 18, no. 2 (2016): 145.

Pour la Défense de la Démocratie (CNDD), with an armed wing *Forces pour la Défense de la Démocratie* (FDD), hence the CNDD-FDD.

Despite the emergence of these political parties with armed wings who shared the same goal of achieving a fair representation for the Hutu in Burundi, these groups did not cooperate or gather under one coalition-led political platform. At best, these parties and their armed wings managed to avoid direct confrontation, and very rarely did they coordinate attacks against the Tutsi regime. They were involved in heavy fighting amongst themselves in several instances during the rebellion period. For example, CNDD-FDD launched joint military operations with the FAB against PALIPEHUTU-FNL strongholds in the early 2000s.[41] Moreover, just like the regime massacred Hutus, these rebel parties themselves also got engaged in gross-acts against humanity, targeting the Tutsis. By the end of 1999, the rebellion was at its height, with CNDD-FDD being the major actor in majority of provinces, while the PALIPEHUTU-FNL restricted to western areas but was the main threat to the roads leading out of the capital Bujumbura.[42] It is important to note here that all Hutu rebel groups were also implicated in gross acts against humanity in a similar manner like the FAB.

The success of Hutu rebel parties in exercising maximum pressure on the Tutsi regime forced the army to enter into talks with the Hutu community. Hence, the Arusha talks sponsored by Tanzania began in the late 1990s, followed by the Pretoria talks in South Africa that sealed a power sharing deal between the two communities with the blessings of Nelson Mandela.

4   Arusha and Pretoria

By the end of the 1990s, eighty percent of the rural population in Burundi lived in absolute poverty.[43] Economic growth was extremely low and sometimes negative, with real GDP growth averaging 1.3 percent between 1998–2011.[44] The years of upheaval and instability in Burundi that followed the elimination of the FRODEBU from power led to a regional initiative to resolve the Burundian crisis. The initiative was first led by the President of Tanzania, Julius Nyerere in 1998 who invited the Burundian leaders to negotiate a peace resolution in

---

41   Ibid., 148.
42   Nigel Watt, *Burundi*, 66.
43   Rene Lemarchand, "Consociationalism and Power Sharing in Africa: Rwanda, Burundi, and the Democratic Republic of the Congo," *African Affairs* 106, no. 422 (2007): 11.
44   Ibid., 12.

Arusha. However, Nyerere passed away a year later, and the mediator for the conflict was Nelson Mandela, who reluctantly accepted to mediate between the warring parties.

Proper negotiations started in Arusha on 15 June 1998, with 17 delegations taking part of the process including tiny Tutsi parties, which Mandela sarcastically commented that the members of these small parties could fit into a telephone kiosk.[45] Representatives from the military participated as part of UPRONA or as consultants to the government in one of the four committees.[46] From the Hutu side, the main rebel party, CNDD-FDD was excluded at the beginning of the talks,[47] but was included few years later, while the PALIPEHUTU-FNL refused to negotiate with the authorities, insisting that power sharing arrangements were a disguise for UPRONA's rule.[48] Eventually, the PALIPEHUTU-FNL became the last rebel group to sign the Arusha agreement. During the negotiation process, five committees were created to discuss broad areas of concern: nature of the conflict, democracy and good governance, peace and security, reconstruction and development, and finally guarantees of implementation of the agreement.[49] Mandela's most important breakthrough was in June 2000 when he persuaded President Buyoya to close the apartheid-like-camps in Bujumbura, and agree on ethnic parity in the army (which Buyoya did).[50]

The official declaration, of the signing of the Arusha agreement, however, was tiresome. The plan was to have the parties sign at noon, but the delegations stalled the process, forcing everyone to wait until 9 pm, by which 13 out of the 19 parties signed amid government reservations on some security issues.[51] Three more small parties signed within a few days, and the Arusha process began to attract regional and international support that encouraged

---

45 Nigel Watt, *Burundi*, 67.
46 Patricia Daley, "The Burundi Peace Negotiations: An African Experience of Peace-Making," *Review of African Political Economy* 34, no. 112 (2007): 341.
47 Richard Barltrop, "The Negotiation of Security Issues in the Burundi Peace Talks," *Centre for Humanitarian Dialogue*, no. 1 (2008): 17, https://www.files.ethz.ch/isn/95072/HD%20Centre%20NegDis%20Burundi%20Country%20Study%20PDF.pdf, accessed 21 January 2021.
48 Jessica Piombo, "Peacemaking in Burundi: Conflict Resolution versus Conflict Management Strategies," *African Security* 3, no. 4 (2010): 262.
49 Patricia Daley, "The Burundi Peace Negotiations, 343.
50 "Regroupment Camps in Burundi Condemned: Tens of Thousands of Civilians Still Held in Squalid Conditions," *Human Rights Watch*, 19 July 2000, https://reliefweb.int/report/burundi/regroupment-camps-burundi-condemned-tens-thousands-civilians-still-held-squalid, accessed 21 January 2021.
51 Nigel Watt, *Burundi*, 71.

the CNDD-FDD to change its stance and join the negotiations. By doing this, it eventually outmaneuvered its competitor, PALIPEHUTU-FNL by benefitting from the need of the Tutsi-led government to sign the Arusha agreement with a main Hutu rebel party for the purpose of legitimizing the peace agreement. The CNDD-FDD maneuver led it to capture the lion's share in the army and public institutions at the expense of the PALIPEHUTU-FNL, which joined the peace process on 26 May 2008. This allowed the party's leader, Agathon Rwasa to return for the time to Burundi since 1988.[52] In return of recognition and political participation, it agreed to integrate some of its militants into the security force and surrendering its weapons, but they secretly kept some of the weapons they previously owned.[53]

Even after the signing of Arusha, Buyoya, as President and representative of the Tutsi-led army and its interests, faced some difficulties at home. There were two coup attempts in April and July 2001, with the second attempt being very serious as junior officers joined university students in a demonstration followed by an attack on the army headquarters, the Mpimba prison, and the homes of senior officials.[54] Consequently, Buyoya agreed in the second round of negotiations on a transitional period to start on the 1st of November 2001, with himself as president for the first 18 months, and Domitien Ndayizeye (Hutu) from FRODEBU as Vice President, after which Ndayizeye would become president for 18 months,[55] and Alphonse-Marie Kadege from Uprona (Tutsi) would be vice president. In order to guarantee security and protection for the Hutu politicians, South African troops were invited as personal bodyguards for them, and these forces later became the nucleus of the African Union peacekeeping force.[56] The third round of negotiations was on 8 October 2003, known as the Pretoria Protocol, signed by the government of Burundi, Tutsi parties, Hutu parties, and most importantly the CNDD-FDD, but without the PALIPEHUTU-FNL that still refused to negotiate at that time. It was this round that imposed significant institutional and structural changes in the armed forces, culminating in the establishing of a whole new army with a proper procedure to integrate rebel combatants. The final round in Pretoria

---

52 Carla Schraml, *The Dilemma of Recognition: Experienced Reality of Ethnicised Politics in Rwanda and Burundi* (Marburg: Springer VS, 2011), 55.
53 "Burundi: To Integrate the FNL Successfully," *International Crisis Group*, 30 July 2009, https://www.crisisgroup.org/africa/central-africa/burundi/burundi-integrate-fnl-successfully, accessed 21 January 2021.
54 Nigel Watt, *Burundi*, 72–5.
55 "Burundi: IRIN Update on Coup Attempt/Transition Accord," *The New Humanitarian*, 24 July 2001.
56 Nigel Watt, *Burundi*, 75.

in August 2004 led to a new constitution that was approved by the parliament in October, and it was approved in a referendum on 28 February 2005 by 90 percent.[57] This meant that the PALIPEHUTU-FNL signed a peace treaty this time with the CNDD-FDD led government in Tanzania on 18 June 2006,[58] and not with UPRONA or the Tutsis.

In political and security terms, the Arusha Protocol emphasized and acknowledged the ethnic nature of the conflict in Burundi. The agreement called for two vice-presidents, a Hutu from a party to whom the President is not a member of, and another for the Tutsi community. The constitutional amendment in 2018, which eliminated one of the two positions of the vice-president, mainly as an attempt by the CNDD-FDD to prohibit another Hutu party from taking this post. When the CNDD-FDD signed the Arusha agreement in Pretoria, October 2003, its leader Nkurunziza became Minister of State for good governance, and was to be consulted on key matters in the government, and his party gained four ministers, two officers, 15 members in the National Assembly, three provincial governors, two ambassadors, and 20 percent of the leading posts in the public administration.[59] As for changes in the political system, the agreement stipulated that parity was to be established in the Senate while in Parliament and the executive Hutus would represent 60 percent and Tutsis 40 percent. Most importantly, the army incorporated the Hutu community and parity became the norm in the military.[60]

5   Institutional and Structural Changes in the Armed Forces

The Arusha and Pretoria Protocols formed the essence of the new constitution of Burundi adopted in February 2005. This meant that the army underwent radical changes in its outlook, form, capacity, ethnic belonging, hierarchy, and

---

57   Constance Johnson, "Burundi: Constitutional Referendum Planned," *Global Legal Monitor*, 20 December 2017, https://www.loc.gov/law/foreign-news/article/burundi-constitutional-referendum-planned/, accessed 21 January 2021.

58   "PSC Demands Total Peace Deal in Burundi," *Pan African News Agency*, 29 June 2006, https://reliefweb.int/report/burundi/psc-demands-total-peace-deal-burundi, accessed 21 January 2021.

59   "The Pretoria Protocol on Outstanding Political, Defence and Security Power Sharing Issues in Burundi," (known as Pretoria Protocol), 2 November 2003, https://www.peaceagreements.org/viewmasterdocument/584, accessed 21 January 2021.

60   "Arusha Peace and Reconciliation Agreement for Burundi," (known as Arusha agreement), 28 August 2000, https://peacemaker.un.org/sites/peacemaker.un.org/files/BI_000828_Arusha%20Peace%20and%20Reconciliation%20Agreement%20for%20Burundi.pdf, accessed 21 January 2021.

decision making. Accordingly, this section highlights these changes into two categories: Institutional and Structural.

5.1 Institutional Reforms

At the institutional level, it was important to reflect on the history of the army in politics and its involvement in aggression against civilians, mainly from the Hutu community. As a result, the *Forces Armées Burundaises* (FAB) was transformed into the *Force de Défense Nationale* (FDN, or the National Defense Force), in an attempt to break away from the past after integrating rebel combatants into its ranks. In the post-conflict environment, the new army became a legitimate security force, representative of the Burundian people, professional and impartial. This remained the case at least until 2015 with the coup attempt and the suppression of the opposition.

According to the constitution, the president of Burundi is the supreme commander of the army,[61] enjoying a wide range of military privileges. The army is led by a chief of general staff, referred to as the Chief of the FDN, who is assisted with a deputy commander.[62] Initially, the position of chief of general staff was occupied by a Hutu (mainly from CNDD-FDD or other related Hutu rebel party) and the deputy chief from the ex-FAB (basically a Tutsi), but after the attempted coup in 2015, the CNDD-FDD government ended this arrangement and controlled both positions.[63] The MoD as an institution is responsible for running the day to day business of the security sector, but the minister has to report to the President. The constitution has also defined the mission of the armed force, outlined in several points with specific roles. The army's role accordingly is to protect the integrity and sovereignty of the country, combat armed aggression against the country's institutions, preserve public order when authorized by the civilian authorities, participate in assistance activities during natural disasters, and contribute to the development of the country.[64] To achieve this role, army personnel are prohibited from joining political parties and must preserve their neutrality in public affairs.[65] Moreover, the constitution prohibited the presence of any militia or organized armed force outside of the military institution.[66] Hence, militias that came under the "self-defense" program, financed by the government of Buyoya, and which

---

61 Art 10, organic law no. 1/04 of 20 February 2017.
62 Art 19 and 20, organic law no. 1/04 of 20 February 2017.
63 "Burundi: The Army in Crisis," *International Crisis Group*, 5 April 2017, https://www.crisisgroup .org/africa/central-africa/burundi/247-burundi-army-crisis, accessed 21 January 2021.
64 Art. 12, Arusha Agreement.
65 Art. 82, 250, Constitution of Burundi.
66 Art. 246, Constitution of Burundi.

included Hutu militia such as Guardians of the Peace, and other Tutsi groups, were disbanded.[67]

There were no new military institutions established to run the armed forces, and so the institutional reforms were extremely limited to cosmetic changes in the army. Nevertheless, more changes were introduced at the structural level aimed at enhancing the status of the army.

5.2 Structural Reforms

To start with the structural reforms, the most important element in the Arusha agreement was related to the role of the president in civil-military affairs. Critical military and security decisions rest in the hands of the president. According to the constitution, the president has the right to deploy the army in defense of the state, in restoring public order, and in discharge of international obligations.[68] He is only obliged to give a notice to the parliament and senate about the nature, extent, and reasons for the use of the army within 7 days, but the legislature or the government has no right to overturn the president's decision. Moreover, the commander of the army and his deputy are appointed by the president but required a confirmation from the senate.[69] As for the other important high ranking officers, he has the exclusive right in naming them: the chief of services of the army, commanders of land, air and maritime forces, commanders of divisions, commander of the higher military school, and commander of the general staff.[70] The chief of intelligence, his deputy, and the chief of staff are appointed by the president.[71] This makes the presidency an extremely powerful tool in managing civil-military relations in such a deeply divided society, even though the constitution stated that the army is subjected to the authority of the government and the control of the parliament.[72] In practice, however, real military power lies in the presidency, as the president is more powerful than the Minister of Defense (appointed by the president with senate confirmation but with the right of the former to dismiss him) and the Chief of the General Staff of the army.

The chain of command begins with the president as the commander-in-chief with extensive security prerogatives, leaving the MoD with duties related to

---

67   "To Protect the People: The Government-Sponsored "Self-Defense" Program in Burundi," *Human Rights Watch*, 14 December 2001, https://www.hrw.org/report/2001/12/14/protect-people/government-sponsored-self-defense-program-burundi, accessed 21 January 2021.
68   Art. 255, Constitution of Burundi.
69   Art. 10 and 92 of law no. 1/022 of 31 December 2004.
70   Art. 60 of organic law no. 1/04 of 20 February 2017.
71   Art. 21, organic law no. 1/17 of 11 July 2019.
72   Art. 248, 252, 255, 256, 260, Constitution of Burundi.

the day-to-day business of the army. The minister is assisted by the Chief of General Staff of the army, who in turn is assisted by a deputy chief, who overlooks the work of the Inspector General, the training institutions, commanders of specialized units, commanders of military regions, air and maritime wings, as seen in Figure 1. For the sake of ethnic balance in security affairs, the constitution states that the Minister of Defense and the Minister of Police should belong to different ethnic communities.[73] In this context, the role of the ministry of defense is to design and execute the national defense policy, strengthen the operational and institutional capabilities of the army, and assure the respect of Burundi's military commitments at the international level.[74] The ministry summarizes its values as follows as RETAIN:

"*R*espect for human rights: In its mission, the MDNAC refers to universal principles. By his example, he inspires the gentle force which reassures and protects the strong and the weak.

*E*fficiency: The discipline imposed by MDNAC is bearing fruit. The professionalism of the FDN is confirmed through missions outside national borders.

*T*ransparence: Democratic assurance is reflected in institutions that reflect the image of its people. Ethnic differences are at the heart of MDNAC's exemplary transparency.

*E*quity: Respect for each member of society is based on the unique value of each. The MDNAC constantly demonstrates that legitimate force is at the service of all.

*N*eutrality: The MDNAC is a republican institution. His concern for serving his people prevents him from serving partisan interests.

*I*ntegrity: MDNAC is at the service of the people. In turn, integrity is the condition of his trust.

*R*edevability: Democratic legitimacy implies accountability to the people. It is to him and to his representatives that MDNAC is indebted."[75]

The intelligence service is also mentioned in the Arusha agreement. Accordingly, the mission of the service is to seek out and utilize all information to protect the state and institutions, detect threats as early as possible, prevent the manipulation of ethnic or regionalist sentiments, or any other threat that hinders constitutional order.[76] Moreover, it is entitled to protect the country's

---

73   Art. 135, Constitution of Burundi.
74   Ministère de la Défense Nationale et des Anciens Combattants, http://mdnac.bi/?q=content/mission, accessed 21 January 2021.
75   Ministère de la Défense Nationale et des Anciens Combattants, http://mdnac.bi/?q=content/valeurs-du-mdnac, accessed 21 January 2021.
76   Arusha Agreement.

ecological environment, fight terrorism, drug trafficking, criminal organizations, and detect cases of misappropriation of funds within the state's public agencies.[77] Since the intelligence service enjoys widespread powers and is tasked with protecting the vital interests of the state, the Arusha agreement acknowledged its special status and allowed it to function beyond the paradigm of ethnic parity. Moreover, intelligence sector cooperates with the public prosecutor for law enforcement but reports directly to the president.[78] Hence, the president enjoys an additional tool in Burundian security affairs with his capability to have access to intelligence and sensitive information that no other politician has.

Another important structural reform is the DDR process that paved the way for creating an ethnically balanced military. The DDR program started in December 2004 by the initiative of the World Bank, as part of the Central African Multi-Country Demobilization and Disarmament Program (MDRP).[79] The program was implemented by several NGOs and they were assisted by the National Ceasefire Commission.[80] Around 84.4 million USD was invested in the program aimed at demobilizing some 70,000 combatants by giving them direct monetary payments which varied according to rank. It ranged from 500 USD for ordinary ranks to 3,000 USD for generals.[81] Between 2004 and 2005, some 14,000 soldiers were demobilized: 5,000 from the FAB and 9,000 from the rebel forces. By 2005–2006, the newly created FDN was trimmed to include 25,000 soldiers. In the army, the first wave of mobilization in 2004 was voluntary, and from 2005 onwards, the demobilization of soldiers in the FAB was involuntary, based on renewed application of soldiers from 45 years of age and retirement threshold.[82] The process, however, was slow and at one point many demobilized ex-combatants protested for not being paid.[83] Nevertheless, DDR paved the way for a transition from a Tutsi-dominated military into an ethnically balanced military.

Military integration required harmonization and re-indoctrination of both elements of the new army. At first, some 26,000 members of the rebel armies were put in cantonments with 7,000 CNDD-FDD militants immediately merging into the 40,000 strong FAB. This was the first phase and it lasted from 2004

---

77 Ibid.
78 Art. 36 of Law no. 1/17 of 11 July 2019.
79 Patricia Daley, "The Burundi Peace Negotiations, 348.
80 Ibid.
81 Ibid.
82 Cyrus Samii, "Perils or Promise of Ethnic Integration Evidence from a Hard Case in Burundi," *The American Political Science Review* 107, no. 3 (2013): 561.
83 Patricia Daley, "The Burundi Peace Negotiations," 348.

till mid-2005.[84] The second phase that began in late 2005 rationalized the integration by bridging training of rebel combatants and mixing them with FAB army members.[85] Later, when the PALIPEHUTU-FNL signed the peace treaty with the CNDD-FDD government, some 3,500 militants were integrated into the defense and security forces while the DDR program offered assistance to 5,000 combatants.[86] Thus, the FDN was the production of physical merging, retraining, and re-indoctrination of ex-rebels with ex-FAB soldiers.

The Pretoria protocol between the government and the CNDD-FDD as the largest Hutu rebel group, allowed for absorbing Hutu militants into the army. The agreement created an army that respected parity between Hutus and Tutsis, and later the MoD was charged to maintain this parity in the army.[87] In order to begin with unification of the army, a joint General Staff from the FAB and the CNDD-FDD was created to identify combatants and harmonize the ranking system.[88] Also, the officer corps of the new army absorbed 60 percent of the ex-FAB and 40 percent from the CNDD-FDD within the general framework of ethnic parity.[89] In the intelligence sector, 35 percent of the new apparatus came from the CNDD-FDD and the remaining from the ex-FAB.[90] The intelligence sector, however, was left out of the parity paradigm due to its sensitive security nature. Moreover, the Pretoria protocol allowed the CNDD-FDD to get two of the five regional military commanders, and it filled the position of the Chief of Police.[91]

6   From Success to Failure: CNDD-FDD Hegemony in Security Affairs

By all standards, the transformation of the Burundian army from a Tutsi-dominated military into one that is representative of the Burundian society was a success after Arusha. Soldiers from FAB and the rebel groups formed a new army that received international, regional, and domestic

---

84   Cyrus Samii, "Perils or Promise of Ethnic Integration," 561.
85   Ibid.
86   Stef Vandeginste, "Power-Sharing, Conflict and Transition in Burundi: Twenty Years of Trial and Error," *Africa Spectrum* 44, no. 3 (2009): 80.
87   Art. 60, organic law no. 1/04 of 20 February 2017.
88   Willy Nindorera, "The CNDD-FDD in Burundi: The Path from Armed to Political Struggle," *Berghof Transitions Series*, no. 10 (2012): 25.
89   Nina Wilen, "From Foe to Friend? Army Integration after War in Burundi, Rwanda and the Congo," *International Peacekeeping* 23, no. 1 (2016): 83.
90   Pow Stef Vandeginste, "Power-Sharing, Conflict and Transition in Burundi," 78.
91   Pretoria Protocol.

recognition for its legitimacy. At the international level, the government established the Burundi-Netherlands Security Sector Development program (SSD) to implement democratic and accountable governance of the security sector in Burundi.[92] The military itself was extremely interested in professionalizing its forces and rebuilding its reputation.[93] The program consisted of three pillars: defense, public security, and governance, and the Burundians played an increasingly greater role in the management of the program.[94] An interesting approach of the program was its flexible problem-solving approach by which it re-evaluated its progress and adjusted accordingly every two years.[95]

The army also benefitted from the UN Security Council resolution 1545 that established the United Nations Operation in Burundi (ONUB), that functioned from 2004 till 2006.[96] The resolution allowed ONUB "to carry out institutional reforms as well as the constitution of the integrated national defense and internal security forces."[97] After the end of the ONUB mandate, the UN established the United Nations Integrated Office in Burundi (BINUB) by resolution 1719 (2006), to help support the demobilization and reintegration, combat the proliferation of small arms and light weapons, in addition to support for the development of security sector reform with respect to the professionalization of the army.[98] BINUB was later on replaced with the United Nations Office in Burundi (BNUB) on 1 January 2011in order to consolidate peace before ending its mandate in 2014.

The professionalization of the army was reflected in its participation in the UNSRC 2372 that established the African Union Mission in Somalia (AMISOM). Burundi joined AMISOM in 2007, and at one point its forces in Somalia is the second largest contingent.[99] The army benefits from this mission to enhance its status and legitimacy domestically. Also, it benefits financially by receiving payments for its soldiers from donor states who fund the AMISON. In addition to that, the army receives training of its personnel and new weapons. However,

---

92 Nicole Ball, "Lessons from Burundi's Security Sector Reform Process," *Africa Security Brief*, no. 29 (2014): 2.
93 Ibid., 3.
94 Ibid.
95 Ibid., 4.
96 UNSRC 1545, 21 May 2004, https://www.un.org/press/en/2004/sc8101.doc.htm, accessed 21 January 2021.
97 Ibid.
98 UNSRC 1719, 25 October 2006, http://unscr.com/en/resolutions/doc/1719, accessed 21 January 2021.
99 African Union Mission in Somalia (AMISON), https://amisom-au.org/burundi/, accessed 21 January 2021.

the African Union is reconsidering Burundian participation in AMISOM because of the role of the army in repressing opponents to the CNDD-FDD government. The party's activities in the military are threating the successful process of legitimization of the Burundian army.

7 CNDD-FDD Hegemony in the Army

In August 2005, former rebel leader of CNDD-FDD, Pierre Nkurunziza (Hutu), became the new president of Burundi. This marked the culmination of almost a decade of ceasefires, peace agreement and protocols, a transitional government and democratic elections.[100] During this period of peace building, the army was successfully being rebuilt on integrative basis. However, CNDD-FDD and Nkurunziza exploited the wide security-military prerogatives that the president enjoyed in the constitution to use the intelligence and the army to silent opposition to his rule, whether Hutu or Tutsi. In this context, the CNDD-FDD had worked on three levels to achieve its hegemony in the armed forces: preferential status of FDD soldiers at the expense of other rebels and ex-FAB personnel in the new army, establishing a parallel chain of command and a militia (contrary to the constitutional prohibition on creating militias), and abusing constitutional prerogatives related to the intelligence service. Consequently, the CNDD-FDD had worked to transform the army into an armed wing of the party by infiltrating and controlling the military.

7.1 *FDD Preferentialism and Elimination of Opponents*

The main problem that emerged in the way that the CNDD-FDD practiced its civilian-led authority over the military began after the 2015, when president Nkurunziza campaigned for a third presidential term and pressured the constitutional council to legitimize his argument of third term. Consequently, he campaigned for a third term and won in 2015, but his plan was met by fierce resistance from the military, particularly elements of the ex-FAB and others who did not accept this break-away from the Arusha agreement. Nkurunziza's stubborn stance for a third term re-politicized the army, and officers found themselves dragged into the political quagmire of Burundian domestic affairs.[101] In May 2015, a month before the projected presidential elections, a coup attempt was organized by Major General Godefroid Niyombare (Hutu), Major General Cyrille Ndayirukiye (Tutsi), and 28 other high commanding

---

100 Patricia Daley, "The Burundi Peace Negotiations," 333.
101 "Burundi: The Army in Crisis," 2.

officers in the army. Niyombare was a former rebel commander of the CNDD-FDD and a popular figure in the party who occupied important military positions like Chief of Staff and head of military intelligence while Ndayirukiye was minister of defense when Burundi was still governed by the Tutsis. The coup attempt took place when Nkurunziza was attending a summit in Tanzania. The army, however, fought the mutineers and successfully quelled the coup, forcing Niyombare to flee the country while Ndayirukiye was captured. Consequently, an organized purification of the military began by the CNDD-FDD.

After the coup attempt, the government abandoned the principle of parity when appointing officers at the highest level of the military. Moreover, the government halted the appointment of Tutsis in the army to replace ex-FAB soldiers who retired,[102] and with these policies the CNDD-FDD circumscribed the role of the Tutsi community in the army. What followed was a series of assassinations targeting high ranking military officials loyal to the CNDD-FDD, from the Tutsi and Hutu communities alike, like the former head of the national intelligence General Adolphe Nshimirimana, Colonel Jean Bikomagu, General Athansae Kararuza, Major Didier Muhimpundu (prominent members of the FAB), and General Prime Niyongabo (army officer not from the CNDD-FDD).[103] Other officers in the army and NCOs who rejected Nkurunziza's third term bid were arrested or killed, regardless whether they were FAB members or Hutus.[104] In other cases, retired personnel and FAB members serving in Somalia were arrested upon return from their mission abroad by the national intelligence,[105] as the CNDD-FDD government was suspicious of their loyalty. This led to a wave of desertion in the army, between 600 and 2000 soldiers deserted since the crisis began (including senior officers).[106]

The CNDD-FDD carried a purge policy to purify the army from elements that might pose a threat to its rule. This allowed the party to tighten its grip over the military and make a coup-proof system. In addition, CNDD-FDD created a patron client network in the army to secure the loyalty of army personnel. For instance, former rebels in the CNDD-FDD were prioritized for training opportunities abroad or deployment in peacekeeping missions.[107] Tutsi officers

---

102   Ibid., 10.
103   Ibid., 3.
104   Katrin Wittig, "Politics in the Shadow of the Gun," 144.
105   "Burundi: The Army in Crisis," 4–5.
106   Ibid., 5.
107   Thierry Vircoulon, "Insights from the Burundian Crisis (I): An Army Divided and Losing its Way," *International Crisis Group*, 2 October 2015, https://www.crisisgroup.org/africa/central-africa/burundi/insights-burundian-crisis-i-army-divided-and-losing-its-way, accessed 21 January 2021.

were removed from their command posts and redeployed to remote areas,[108] particularly if they happen to be ex-FAB. Moreover, the government discriminated against ex-FAB members by giving them a rifle and one magazine once they came from their mission abroad, while Hutus were given two or three magazines along with their rifle.[109] Officers were also subjected to abuse by policemen, so if an officer happened to be an ex-FAB, the police would search everything in the house, if he were a former member of the rebel group, they would not bother to search.[110] The national intelligence service from its part, played a role in silencing any opposition to the CNDD-FDD from the military. Hence, they used to kidnap officers from the Para-commando camp and the logistic Brigade under the suspicion that they were planning another coup (they were killed or threatened).[111] The message that the government intended to send was that the job security, wellbeing, security, and promotion in the army depends on the loyalty of army personnel to the CNDD-FDD. It was a major setback that transformed the army from a professional military institution into one that was subjected to patron-client network and the politics of preferentialism. This policy by the CNDD-FDD was reinforced through an alternative chain of command and the establishment of a youth organization that was a disguise of a militia, the Imbonerakure.

7.2   Alternative Chain of Command and the Imbonerakure

The CNDD-FDD has moved to transform the army from a national institution into a party organ. For this purpose, they created an alternative chain of command, a shadowy structure to substitute the real chain of command. Consequently, the legitimate one has become a structure that rubber stamped decisions of the alternative one. To understand the impact of this alternative chain, after the re-election of Nkurunziza in July 2015, around 400,000 Burundians have fled the country,[112] mainly because of repression and violence by the security apparatus.

The alternative chain of command is often referred to as the "Committee of Generals," which includes the president, minister of public security,

---

108   Ibid.
109   Ibid.
110   Ibid.
111   Ibid.
112   "Burundi Risks becoming a Forgotten Refugee Crisis without Support," *United Nations High Commissioner for Refugees*, 6 February 2018, https://www.unhcr.org/news/briefing/2018/2/5a79676a4/burundi-risks-becoming-forgotten-refugee-crisis-support.html#:~:text=Since%202015%2C%20more%20than%20400%2C000,and%20the%20related%20humanitarian%20crisis., accessed 21 January 2021.

the administrator-general of the national intelligence service, head of police affairs, and the secretary-general of the CNDD-FDD.[113] The mixture of state officials and party member means that those who hold critical and important positions are party loyalists. The committee takes political and security decisions, transmit the orders to a parallel hierarchy and shadowy chain of commands that is based on a network of loyalists in state institutions.[114] The result is that soldiers who work in this chain of command treat the official ones with disdain, allowing them to take advantage of the system and force the legal institutions to take illegal measures, like manipulating grades in favor of partisans, promoting supporters, and denying access to training for soldiers whose loyalties are not secured to the party.[115] This structure empowers the existing patron-client network in the armed forces and allows the president to bypass the framework of power sharing as established by the Arusha agreement.[116]

The alternative chain of command is empowered by the presence of CNDD-FDD's youth organization that plays the role of an unofficial militia, the Imbonerakure, "those who see from afar." The organization was created during the civil war by the CNDD-FDD to monitor the movement of the government and other rebel groups.[117] After the war it was integrated into the official party youth movement,[118] and from 2014 it played an important role in security committees at local levels, working on behalf or alongside the police and the national intelligence service.[119] They are used by the official security apparatus to carry out arbitrary arrests and abuses,[120] by their own initiative or on behalf the police and the national intelligence service.[121] To make matters worse, individuals in the Imbonerakure sometimes wear same uniforms and carry same weapons as the defense and security forces.[122] It was a powerful tool to suppress opposition to Nkurunziza's third term and force voters to support the

---

113 "Report of the Commission of Inquiry on Burundi," *Human Rights Council 39th Session*, 8 August 2018, https://www.ohchr.org/Documents/HRBodies/HRCouncil/CoIBurundi/ReportHRC39/A_HRC_39_63_EN.pdf, accessed 21 January 2021.
114 Ibid.
115 "Burundi: The Army in Crisis," 8–9.
116 Ibid., 9.
117 Katrin Wittig, "Politics in the Shadow of the Gun," 149.
118 Ibid.
119 "Explainer: 10 Things Burundi's New Government can do to Improve Human Rights," *Amnesty International*, 11 August 2020, https://www.amnesty.org/en/latest/news/2020/08/explainer-10-things-burundis-new-government-can-do-to-improve-human-rights/, accessed 21 January 2021.
120 Ibid.
121 "Report of the Commission of Inquiry on Burundi," 6, 9.
122 Ibid., 6.

constitutional referendum of 2018.[123] Consequently, Imbonerakure acts as if it is an official security apparatus to do the dirty job against suspects. This is a huge setback for the legitimacy of the security institution, as the Imbonerakure may become more powerful and maybe one day it will be the apparatus that orders the police, intelligence, and even the army to take specific actions, as the case of Baath militias during Saddam's era or today with Iraq's PMF. The Imbonerakure may be used, also, to monitor the action of the army or some of its personnel if the CNDD-FDD finds that there is a growing dissident within the ranks. The party's firm security grip over the army is not complete without controlling the national intelligence service.

7.3 The National Intelligence Service (SNR) and the CNDD-FDD

The SNR is responsible for internal security in Burundi along with the national police.[124] The SNR is run by a general administrator and a deputy, nominated by the president and approved by the Senate, and they enjoy the status of ministers.[125] The general administrator reports directly to the president,[126] making the presidency an important pillar in intelligence affairs since he also appoints these two high ranking officials by decree, so analysts tend to refer to the SNR as the "presidential police."[127] The SNR has the right to investigate a broad range of unlawful acts, from terrorism threats to problems related to the environment.[128] Moreover, the SNR is exempt from the ethnic quotas applied to other security apparatuses, and the fact that the CNDD-FDD controls the presidency along with the influence the president has on the SNR, politicization of this unit has become inevitable. The CNDD-FDD uses the SNR in a clientelistic approach, using the institution to pay for its former combatants to deliver information or for other security services occasionally.[129]

On paper, the SNR is subjected to control by the National Assembly and is forced to cooperate with a prosecutor,[130] who is charged with directing agents of the SNR for judicial matters.[131] However, this is confronted with the reality that SNR agents enjoy a wide range of prerogatives since the law states that

---

123 Ibid., 4–5.
124 "BTI 2020 Country Report: Burundi," *Bertelsmann Stiftung's Transformation Index*, (2020): 12, https://www.bti-project.org/content/en/downloads/reports/country_report_2020_BDI.pdf, accessed 21 January 2021.
125 Art. 4, 21, Organic Law no. 1/17 of 11 July 2019 and art. 192 of the Constitution.
126 Art. 36, Organic Law no. 1/17 of 11 July 2019.
127 "We Flee When We See them," *Human Rights Watch* 19, no. 9(2006): 8–9.
128 Art. 17–18, Organic Law no. 1/17 of 11 July 2019.
129 "We Flee When We See them," 9.
130 Ibid., 10–1.
131 Ibid., 11.

they have powers to take all legal measures to pursuit their mission, and they have competences of officers of the judicial police, meaning that they can investigate crimes, submit evidence to prosecutors, make arrests, and carry out warrants of the prosecutor.[132] Moreover, Human Rights Watch reports that the prosecutor of Bujumbura, who is charged with directing SNR agents to pursuit specific judicial matters, stated that the prosecutor rarely works with the agents except if there is an accused person whom they are unable to find.[133] Thus, the work of the SNR is not really kept under checks and balances.

The Commission of Inquiry on Burundi found that several members of the SNR have committed human rights violations (in 2017 and 2018).[134] For instance, SNR agents have been accused (along with Imbonerakure) of arbitrary and extrajudicial killing, disappearance of people, extortion and asking for ransom in return of realizing detainees, and torture of people.[135] It was also reported that independent monitors were not allowed to visit secret facilities used by the SNR to detain and interrogate suspects.[136] As the president enjoys wide prerogatives over the SNR, the agency has mainly been directed to harass opposition groups, politicians, and their supporters, and the SNR was used as an effective tool to force citizens to support the CNDD-FDD sponsored constitutional referendum.[137] No agent from the SNR has ever been held accountable, and instead, the CNDD-FDD government has actually rewarded the SNR instead of putting together a stricter system of checks and balances. A new law passed in 2019 expanded the role of the SNR to include all current and potential threats to the security of the state, in addition to modernizing and professionalizing the agency.[138] Above all, the new law rewarded staff members with financial incentives and guarantees to their career.[139]

The CNDD-FDD hegemony in the army has transformed the army and national intelligence service into a party organ, used to suppress opposition,

---

132   Ibid., 10.
133   Ibid., 11.
134   "Report of the Commission of Inquiry on Burundi," 5.
135   "Country Report on Human Rights Practices 2018 – Burundi," *US Department of State*, document no. 2004140, https://www.ecoi.net/en/document/2004140.html, 2018, accessed 21 January 2021.
136   Ibid.
137   Burundi on the Brink: Looking Back on Two Years of Terror, *International Federation of Human Rights*, 2017, https://www.fidh.org/IMG/pdf/burundi_jointreport_june2017_eng_final.pdf, accessed 21 January 2021.
138   "Burundi MPs Debate on the Re-Organization of the National Intelligence Body," *Region Week*, 29 May 2019, https://regionweek.com/burundi-mps-debate-on-the-re-organization-of-the-national-intelligence-body/, accessed 22 January 2021.
139   Ibid.

whether Hutu or Tutsi in a brutal manner. The CNDD-FDD has also made use of the president's prerogatives to exploit the powers of the national intelligence service for narrow political gains, and make it look more like a presidential police, rather than a national institution. In addition, the presence of the Imbonerakure as a security apparatus in disguise of a youth organization for the CNDD-FDD, which is capable of carrying out arrests and detention on behalf of the state, means that it has become a state-sponsored militia under party command. As such, Burundi is witnessing a return to the scenario of re-politicization of the security apparatuses, particularly the armed forces.

8 The Dangers of CNDD-FDD Politicization of the Army

The Arusha Accord stated that power sharing in the military was to be guaranteed by creating parity between Hutus and Tutsis in the army.[140] Accordingly, Tutsis and other Hutu groups that were smaller and weaker than the CNDD-FDD felt that this clause would protect the army from politicization. The truth is that proportionality between ethnic groups in an institution creates a balance of power between them, but it does not suffice to protect it from politicization. The issue that negotiators missed during the Arusha talks was that military power sharing requires a division of power rather than concentration of military prerogatives in one executive office. According to the Arusha agreement, two main security prerogatives give the president excessive power in civil-military relations: his ability to deploy the army for peace and order within Burundi, and his control over the national intelligence service. As such, no matter how the officer corps, rank, and files of the army are divided ethnically or politically between groups, the party that controls the presidency will always have the upper hand in security affairs.

Politicization and hegemony of the army by the CNDD-FDD means that other groups will resort to violence against the security forces. For instance, in July 2015, the army engaged in fierce fighting against rebels in the north of the country in response to rebel attacks inside Burundi.[141] On 2 August 2015, Lieutenant-General Adolphe Nshimirimana, a very close ally to Nkurunziza and head of internal security, was killed in an attack on his car by armed men

---

140 Arusha Agreement.
141 Gerard Nzohabona, "Burundi Military: 31 Suspected Rebels Killed in Fighting," *Associated Press*, 13 July 2015, https://apnews.com/article/3b43504f76aa49f29c484ac9c0a1dbfd, accessed 22 January 2021.

in military uniforms.¹⁴² This was followed by an assassination attempt on the life of General Prime Niyongabo, chief of staff of the Burundian army.¹⁴³ Later in December 2015 few months after the re-election of Nkurunziza, rebels unleashed three coordinated attacks against army barracks in the country.¹⁴⁴ In March 2016, Lieutenant-Colonel Darius Ikurakure, head of the Combat Engineering Battalion (CEB), a central figure the repression of the opposition to Nkurunziza, was killed by an unidentified man in military uniform right inside army headquarters.¹⁴⁵ In April the same year, unidentified attackers used rockets and gunfire to kill Brigadier General Athanase Kararuza, a military advisor in the office of the vice president.¹⁴⁶ The UNSC reported on 24 October 2019 that several attacks took place against a group of police officers and Imbonerakure on patrol, in addition to attacks against the office of the chief of staff of the army, and an Imbonerakure leader living in Gisagara commune.¹⁴⁷

The examples above explain that the politicization of the army is so severe that opposition began to implement violent strategies and organize as rebel groups, just like during the crisis that began when Hutu organized to rebel against Tutsis post-independence. In 2011, Resistance to the Rule of Law in Burundi (RED-Tabara) was created. Colonel Edward Nshimirimana, a former officer in the army established the Republican Forces of Burundi (FOREBU) in December 2015, and some elements from the FNL have returned to their military activities as well since 2010.¹⁴⁸ It is important to note that these groups are not only Tutsis, but include large number of Hutus and some are Hutu

---

142 Drazen Jorgic, "Gunmen in Uniform Kill Ally of Burundi President Nkurunziza," *Reuters*, 2 August 2015, https://www.reuters.com/article/us-burundi-attacks-idUSKCN0Q70AL20150802, accessed 22 January 2021.

143 "Burundi Army Chief Escapes Assassination Attempt," *France 24*, 11 September 2015, https://www.france24.com/en/20150911-burundi-army-chief-assassination-attempt-attack-niyongabo, accessed 22 January 2021.

144 "Burundi Crisis: Military Bases Attacked in Bujumbura," *BBC*, 11 December 2015, https://www.bbc.com/news/world-africa-35070154, accessed 22 January 2021.

145 "Burundi Rebel Group Says Behind Killing of Senior Army Officer," *Reuters*, 26 March 2016, https://www.reuters.com/article/us-burundi-security-idUSKCN0WS0GB, accessed 22 January 2021.

146 "Burundi President Condemns Killing of General Amid Rising Violence," *Reuters*, 26 April 2016 http://mobile.reuters.com/article/idUSKCN0XN0FA, accessed 22 January 2021.

147 UNSC, "The Situation in Burundi: Report of Secretary General," 24 October 2019, https://www.securitycouncilreport.org/atf/cf/%7B65BFCF9B-6D27-4E9C-8CD3-CF6E4FF96FF9%7D/s_2019_837.pdf, 10, accessed 22 January 2021.

148 "Burundi Crisis Year One," *Armed Conflict Location and Event Data Project 2016*, May 2016; see also "Repression and Genocidal Dynamics in Burundi," *International Federation for Human Rights*, no. 685a, November 2016, 148–9, https://www.fidh.org/IMG/pdf/burundi_report_english-2.pdf, accessed 22 January 2021.

dominated, which means that the security crisis today emboldens the claim that the forthcoming civil unrest will take place mainly between Hutu groups.

9 Conclusion

The colonial practices in Burundi established a destructive custom which put the Tutsi minority to govern a country with a Hutu majority. German, and later Belgian colonialism instigated ethnic animosity between the two ethnic communities, whether in Rwanda or in Burundi. Hence, when Hutus rebelled in Rwanda against Tutsi rule, Burundian Tutsis were on alert to avoid a similar fate as their brethren in the neighboring country. This meant that the Tutsi community would fight fiercely for their socio-political and military privileges in the country.

After the assassination of prince Louis Rwagasore, the founder of the cross-ethnic national political party UPRONA, politics in Burundi became heavily communalized. The army allied itself with the monarchy and presented itself as the protector of the royal family and the arbitrator of domestic affairs. Hence, when Micombero saw that the royalty had become fully on the armed forces in the early 1960s, he ousted the monarchy in a military coup and established a republic that institutionalized the role of the army as the source of (in)stability in the country.

The army's iron fist in domestic affairs and systematic exclusion of Hutus until the Arusha agreement in 2000 left no option for the Hutu community but to rebel. Successive Hutu revolts in 1965, 1972, 1988, 1991, and 1995 were met with brutality and genocidal response by the army.[149] Hutu rebellion against Tutsis ended with the implementation of the Arusha agreement and Pretoria protocol that led the largest Hutu rebel group, CNDD-FDD to take power in 2005. The army was then recreated by integrating the rebels with the FAB, boosting the legitimacy of the FDN. However, its reintegration was a short-lived success as the CNDD-FDD re-politicized the army, exploiting the prerogatives of the president and his authority over the FDN and the national intelligence service. The result was that the essence of the conflict became mainly within the Hutu community.

The main source of political instability in Burundi was related to the attempted coup in response to Nkurunziza's third term that was believed to be against the spirit of Arusha. By seeking a third term, CNDD-FDD drifted away

---

149 J. 'Bayo Adekanye, "Rwanda/Burundi: 'Uni-ethnic' Dominance and the Cycle of Armed Ethnic Formations," *Social Identities* 2, no. 1 (1996): 47.

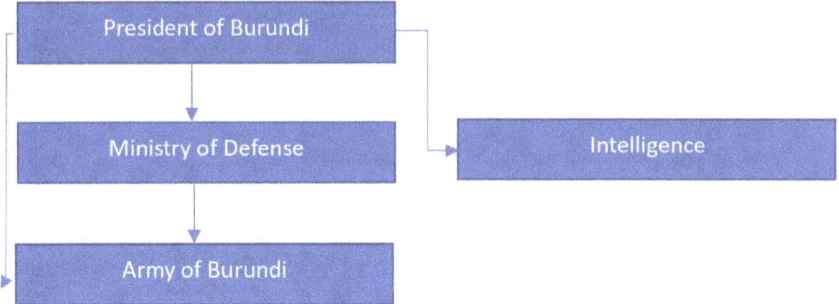

FIGURE 4   Chain of Command of the Army of Burundi

from Arusha, and the constitutional amendment in 2018 that abolished the Hutu vice-presidential position was meant to circumvent competition to the CNDD-FDD by any Hutu dominated political party. Besides the abuse of presidential prerogatives to purge the army from non CNDD-FDD elements, the party has established an alternative chain of command to preserve its hegemony over the armed forces. Consequently, the army has lost its credentials which were hard gained after the civil war, and international reports are condemning the army for its genocidal tendencies against the opposition. Needless to say, the national intelligence service and the Imbonerakure are in the same category, believed to be instruments of oppression against dissidents. Under such conditions, it is highly likely that the army will have to undergo another round of reforms to make it professional and impartial.

CHAPTER 7

Armies in Consociational, Semi-Consociational, and Post-Conflict Societies: The Quest for Stability

The case studies of Lebanon, Iraq, Bosnia-Herzegovina, and Burundi entail that armies in divided societies function in different ways, depending on the prevailing power sharing arrangements. The trajectory and development of armies in these societies show many things in common, especially in relation to the civil authorities and in policing communities to provide stability. The power sharing nature of the political systems in these case studies provide important insights on civil military relations (CMR) and the function of armies in divided societies. The analysis allows us to theorize on the relationship of armies and civil authorities in divided societies within the framework of power sharing, particularly when discussing the role of armed forces in full and semi-consociations. Moreover, the study of these four cases allows political scientists to move forward with a new theoretical approach based on recreating armies after a post-conflict environment.

This chapter is divided into four parts. In the first part I discuss the problems of armed forces in societies deeply divided and ruled by an authoritarian, non-democratic government. I scrutinize Burundi prior to the Arusha agreement and Iraq before the invasion to draw on the problems that emerge from such cases. The second part deals with armed forces in semi-consociational systems, which emphasizes the case of Burundi after the Arusha agreement, post-invasion Iraq, and prewar Lebanon. In the third part I study the consociational arrangements and CMR from the Lebanese case after the Taif agreement and Bosnia-Herzegovina. Finally, the fourth part establishes a theoretical framework for structuring armed forces in divided societies, based on lessons learned from the case studies.

1 Armies, Deeply Divided Societies and Non-Democratic Systems

Authoritarian systems heavily rely on the security apparatus to police their people. The main aim is to protect the political system from internal revolt by using the army. In the cases of Burundi and Iraq, the colonial powers had an important role in promoting Tutsi and Sunni minorities respectively to positions of power in the army, in an attempt to divide and rule over the population. As time passed, these communities institutionalized their control over the army, the strongest military institution in Burundi and Iraq. After independence, elites in the two countries failed to create a democratic system – for various reasons – and the result was a new system that heavily relied on the army. As the Tutsis and Sunnis controlled the army, the two communities eventually politicized the armed forces and used the military to establish their communal hegemony over the country. In the absence of democratic and civilian oversight of the military, acts of aggression, genocides, and ethnic cleansing became the norm in these societies. The hegemonic status of the minorities meant that other groups (Hutus in Burundi, Shiites and Kurds in Iraq), were excluded from power. As such, the military became an important factor that hampered ethnurgy in these countries, sharpening identities and widening the gap between communities, thus making the country more divided on ethnic lines. In Yugoslavia, the Serbian community represented the nucleus of the Yugoslav army and later the community became the dominant group in the military. While in Iraq and Burundi the minorities dominated the army, in Yugoslavia, the Serbs represented the largest single community in the federation, but not the majority of the population of Yugoslavia. This fact made the Serbian community the dominant group in military affairs in the country. When violence broke out in the 1990s, the Serbs had an advantage over other communities in military affairs for this particular reason. It took the Croats and Bosnians many years to be able to repel the Serbian attack.

The question is then how could minorities (Tutsi and Sunnis), or a single largest community in a multi-communal society (Serbs), control the army for so long? The answer is through mass party politics, by which the sole party played the role of vetting new recruits, whether at the level of the officer corps or the rank and files. In Burundi, the nationalist UPRONA party played the role of indoctrinating a new generation of Tutsis to preserve their dominant status, and made sure to allow only trust-worthy Tutsis to be recruited in the army. In higher ranks, emphasis was on members who came from the Bururi region. Hence, the successive Hutu revolts in 1965, 1972, 1988, 1991, 1993, and 1995,[1] were crushed by the Tutsi-controlled army, but the setback was that the army became a manifestation of Tutsi militancy and had no legitimacy beyond the Tutsi community. The army was always ruthless in dealing with Hutu rebellions, and it had been reported that the army's response accounted to acts of

---

1 J. 'Bayo Adekanye, "Rwanda/Burundi: 'Uni-ethnic' Dominance and the Cycle of Armed Ethnic Formations," *Social Identities* 2, no. 1 (1996): 47.

genocide,[2] not to mention that in 1988 that army used napalm bombs against Hutus.[3] It also played a role in widening the political gap, sharpening the political identity of both communities, and further empowering the mistrust between Tutsis and Hutus. Therefore, a political settlement definitely required a new process that reconstructed the whole army from scratch.

In Iraq, the Baath party was an Arab nationalist mass party that recruited members across ethnic lines, but when it came to the army recruits, the emphasis was on Shiites in rank and files, and Sunnis for the officer corps. Additionally, Saddam made sure to promote officers from his region, Tikrit, as to preserve the tribal control of his army in case other Sunnis had ambitions of overthrowing Saddam. Hence, when Iraq was first established in 1921, the army came under the control of the Sunni community. After the rise of the Baath party and its control of the system, the army was "tribalized," with tribes from Tikrit (Saddam's hometown in Anbar) playing a central role in the army.[4] In a similar manner to the army of Burundi, Saddam's military used chemical weapons against the Kurds in Halabja, and committed mass atrocities against them and the Shiites in the south of the country in the early 1990s. These acts had a lasting impact on the de-legitimization of the army and hence the need to reconstruct it after the American invasion in 2003. Communal identities, then, were sharpened not only because of political marginalization, but also due to attempts at exterminating entire communities in the country.

In Yugoslavia, the League of Communists controlled all aspects of recruitment and promotion of the military, allowing the Serbs to preserve an iron grip over the officer corps of the JNA. Even under Tito's leadership, Croats could not hold back their demand for further autonomy and in the 1970s Tito had to use the army to purge Croat nationalists and re-establish the hegemonic status of the League of Communists. The politicization of the JNA and domination of the Serbs were an incentive for Croats, Bosnians, and other ethnic groups to break away from Yugoslavia and establish their own states. The JNA's support of the Serbian militias during the Balkan war completely destroyed what was left of the Yugoslav period of coexistence. It also sharpened communal identities and convinced communities to create and preserve their standing armies

---

2 Lemarchand Rene, "The Burundi Killings of 1992," *Mass Violence and Resistance – Research Network*, 27 June 2008, https://www.sciencespo.fr/mass-violence-war-massacre-resistance/en/document/burundi-killings-1972.html, accessed 24 March 2021.

3 Nigel Watt, *Burundi: The Biography of a Small African Country* (London: Hurst and Company, 2008), 41.

4 Ibrahim al-Marashi, "The Family, Clan, and Tribal Dynamics of Saddam's Security and Intelligence Network," *International Journal of Intelligence and CounterIntelligence* 16, no. 2 (2003): 202.

once the war was over. The atrocities of the war in the 1990s made it hard to create a unified Bosnian army and the country had to wait for nearly a decade to unify the three armies in its territory.

Consequently, nationalist and communist ideologies were exploited to preserve the dominant status of minorities or communities with a plural majority in some deeply divided societies with an authoritarian system. This had allowed dictatorships based on ethnic exclusion or control to survive for decades, despite several rebellions that took place in Iraq and Burundi.[5] In these two cases, the army went as far as to use chemical weapons and napalm bombs against civilian population. While the armies succeeded in quelling rebellion, they eventually lost legitimacy in the eyes of the population. Hence, it became a priority for excluded communities to demand a restructuring of the armed forces.

Authoritarian systems in Burundi, Iraq, and Yugoslavia played an important role in the politics of ethnurgy and the rise of politicized ethnic communities. Moreover, these ethnic communities perceived the other as the ultimate enemy, distrusted one another and paved the way for the rise of radical leaders who always dreamt of subduing or terminating the "other" within the state. In such cases, it was hard to arrange CMR and create a legitimate army that could cast away the burden of military intervention during civil wars. In this context, post-civil war Burundi and Iraq established a semi-consociational system that tried to manage CMR. However, these systems failed to preserve the professionalism and neutrality of the armies in their societies. In Lebanon post-independence, the semi-consociational nature of the system was exploited to use the army against the Lebanese National Movement and the Muslim community.

2   CMR and Semi-Consociationalism

There are many problems detected in the way civilians act in semi-consociational systems, and in the fragile status and legitimacy of armies in these systems. In semi-consociations, the head of the executive is usually the supreme commander or commander-in-chief of the army, with extensive security powers, above all the exclusive right to deploy the army during times of unrest. In Lebanon during the semi-consociational period, the president was the supreme commander and had the exclusive right to order the army to deploy in the

---

5 See chapters 4 and 6 respectively.

country.[6] The constitution did not mention any restriction on the president's side with respect to deployment of the army. In Iraq, the president of the republic is the "High Command of the armed force for ceremonial and honorary purposes,"[7] but the prime minister is in charge of army deployment.[8] In Burundi, the president is the supreme commander and also has the exclusive right to deploy the army, but he is obliged to inform the parliament of the duration, causes, and region of deployment.[9]

These arrangements are normal in majoritarian democracies since the head of the executive is commander in chief of the armed forces. The threat is that in deeply divided places, like in the semi-consociational democracies of prewar Lebanon, post-invasion Iraq and Burundi, exclusive control of army deployment by the head of the executive is an invitation to instability. The corporate arrangement in these cases means that Maronites, Shiites, and Hutu are to head the executive and control decision of army deployment in Lebanon, Iraq, and Burundi respectively. In practice, these communities become the hegemon in the army, and once they feel that their personal or communal interest is threatened, the army is deployed to protect these interests. There are many examples that explain this exploitation of power. In prewar Lebanon, president Bchara al-Khouri ordered the army to end the general strike in 1952 that opposed his rule. In 1958, president Kamil Shamoun ordered the army to deploy and crush the cross-sectarian rebellion that demanded Shamoun to relinquish his support for the Eisenhower doctrine and Baghdad pact. It was the prudent leadership of Fouad Shihab that saved the cohesion and legitimacy of the army since he feared that getting involved in this political quagmire would lead to the disintegration of the army into confessional warring parties, each supporting its respective community.[10] According to Shihab, the crises in both cases were political, and the solution cannot be by the use of force, so he confined his role to the protection of public institutions, the airport, presidential palace, government building, and other vital locations. However, in 1975, president Suleiman Franjiyeh ordered the army to intervene against the Lebanese National Movement (LNM) and their Palestinian allies, by bombarding Aramoun which hosted a conference of Muslim leaders and other mobilizing the army to fight in other fronts against the LNM. Then, the inevitable happened

---

6   Pre-Taif Constitution of Lebanon.
7   Constitution of Iraq, art. 73(9).
8   Ibid., art. 78.
9   Constitution of Burundi, art. 258.
10 Eduardo Wassim Aboultaif, "The Lebanese Army: Saviour of the Republic?," *The Royal United Service Institute Journal* 161, no. 1 (2016): 72–3.

and the army disintegrated into confessional ones like Ahmad al-Khatib's Lebanese Arab Army and Colonel Aziz al-Ahdab's coup attempt in 1976.[11] In 1952 and 1958, the presidents Khouri and Shamoun ordered the army to deploy in order to protect their waning presidency. In 1975, Franjiyah used the army to protect the interest of the Maronite community and their allies.

A similar trend is seen in post-invasion Iraq. After the Americans reconstructed the army from scratch and transferred it to the authority of the democratically elected government of Iraq in 2005, the army was deployed in several instances to protect the interest of those in power, and at other times to protect the interest of the Shiite community. During the era of al-Maliki, his staff was involved in the deployment of the army and police units to target suspected Sunni militants, based on flimsy evidence.[12] Al-Maliki also sacked some intelligent officers because they targeted Shiite militants.[13] Most importantly, during the wave of Arab uprisings, many areas in Iraq mobilized and began their own protests and demonstrations against al-Maliki, who used the security forces to break up protests by Shiites loyal to Moqtada as-Sadr in Baghdad, as well as many other protests in Sunni regions (particularly in Anbar), where hundreds of demonstrators were detained and government troops raided groups suspected of organizing demonstrations.[14] In Sunni cities around Baghdad, al-Maliki deployed troops that surrounded protestors from a distance.[15] His powers as commander in chief at a time when the state was rebuilding its armed forces allowed him to build a personal power base in the security establishment, by appointing personal allies to important positions,[16] while dismissing others with questionable loyalty to al-Maliki.[17] The result was that the army lost its legitimacy in the eyes of the general public. To make matters worse, the army lacked military professionalism and proper training because politicians like al-Maliki prioritized loyalty to merits. Hence, when ISIS attacked the army, it disintegrated, thus ceding the west and north-west of the country under the occupation of ISIS militants for few years.

---

11   Oren Barak, *The Lebanese Army: A National Institution in a Divided Society* (New York: State University of New York Press, 2009), 103.
12   Joel Rayburn, *Iraq After America: Strongmen, Sectarians, Resistance* (Stanford: Hoover Institution Press, 2014), 89.
13   Ibid.
14   Ibid., 216–18.
15   Ibid., 237.
16   Nussaibah Younis, "Set up to Fail: Consociational Political Structures in post-war Iraq," *Contemporary Arab Affairs* 4, no. 1 (2011): 5–8.
17   Zaid al-Ali, *The Struggle for Iraq's Future: How Corruption, Incompetence and Sectarianism have Undermined Democracy* (New Haven: Yale University Press, 2014), 128.

The army of Burundi is in a similar situation to that of the Iraq and the prewar Lebanon, with the main difference is that it has not been used extensively in deployment missions. The reconstruction of the Burundian army hailed as a success in the first few years after the Pretoria Agreement since creating a new army by bringing previous antagonists into power, mainly the ex-FAB and the CNDD-FDD was no easy task to do. However, Nkurunziza's persistence on a third term contrary to the spirit of the Arusha Protocol destroyed all the previous success. First, there was an attempted coup in mid-2015, and it was followed by a series of assassinations conducted by ex-FAB and CNDD-FDD members in the army.[18] In the end, CNDD-FDD had the upper hand and purged the new army from ex-FAB members, exercising total control over the army and politicizing the whole institution.

The Burundian army has rarely been deployed in the country, probably the main one was during the attempted coup. However, the CNDD-FDD government has established an alternative chain of command and used the Imbonerakure against Hutu and Tutsi opposition groups. This new structure was built around the president, the minister of state security, the Director General of National Intelligence, the CNDD-FDD Secretary General, and the chiefs of staff of the presidency's civil cabinet, police Affairs, and military Affairs.[19] This alternative chain of command ran through a network of loyalties dating back to the Burundi's ethnically driven civil war (1993–2005).[20] In Iraq, the alternative chain of command was in place during al-Maliki's era, who undermined the chain of command by tying senior army commanders and paramilitary units to him personally.[21] He would issue orders directly to the commanders through phone calls and direct communication, thus circumventing the chain of command and making those units personally answerable to him.[22]

A final characteristic of CMR in semi-consociational systems, drawing from Iraq and Burundi relates to the role of militias. Both countries have a history of using militias as security tools to suppress the population: during 1993–2005, the *Gardiens de la Paix* (Guardians of Peace), were a pro-government militia used to monitor the population in Burundi, while the Baath's *al-Jaish al-Sha'bi* (The People's Army), was used to collect intelligence on all sectors of population, and to fight in the Iraq-Iraq war. Both militias were cross-ethnic, and their

---

18   Paul Nantulya, "Post-Nkurunziza Burundi: The Rise of the Generals," *Africa Center for Strategic Studies*, 22 June 2020, https://africacenter.org/spotlight/post-nkurunziza-burundi-the-rise-of-the-generals/, accessed 24 March 2021.
19   Ibid.
20   Ibid.
21   Toby Dodge, *Iraq: From War to New Authoritarianism* (London: Routledge, 2013), 126.
22   Zaid al-Ali, *The Struggle for Iraq's Future*, 131.

role ended with the establishment of a semi-consociational system. However, because such systems are influenced by the hegemonic status of one community, there is always an argument to provide a parallel military force to that of the army, either because the army is integrative and has substantive numbers of non-hegemonic groups, or the army has disintegrated and there is a need to fill the gap. In Burundi, the government has legalized the status of the Imbonerakure, and this youth militia sponsored by the CNDD-FDD provided ample support to the police and military. The Imbonerakure has been involved in violence against civilians, carried arrests without warrants, and broke up political gatherings of opposition groups. They functioned alone or sometimes alongside the police force, and sometimes they wore police uniforms. It has been accused by a UN report of committing human rights violations against Burundians fleeing or returning to the country.[23] They have been doing these acts with complete immunity from the state.[24] A similar trend is found in Iraq, where the *Hashd ash-Sha'bi* (Popular Mobilization Forces, hence PMF), a coalition of Shiite militant groups sponsored by Iran have become legal in 2016.[25] According to the law, the PMF is put under the authority of the prime minister as he is commander in chief of the army.[26] However, the PMF do not take orders from the prime minister and instead have their own political-military agenda, even though they are paid by the state. Also, the most important elements in the PMF enjoy training, equipment, and financial support from Iran. The most important figure, Abu Mahdi al-Muhandis, deputy chairman of the PMF, was killed alongside Qassem Soleimani, head of the Iranian Revolutionary Guards, in 2020 by the orders from Trump. To have al-Muhandis and Soleimani together in the same convoy implies deep connections between both organizations. The PMF took orders from the latter during the campaign against ISIS, and was found violating human rights in many Sunni regions in Anbar.[27] Also, during

---

23   Human Rights Council, "Report on the Commission of Inquiry on Burundi," *United Nations General Assembly*, 8 August 2018, https://www.ohchr.org/Documents/HRBodies/HRCouncil/CoIBurundi/ReportHRC39/A_HRC_39_63_EN.pdf, 5–6, accessed 24 March 2021.
24   "Burundi: Abductions, Killings, Spread Fear," *Human Rights Watch*, 25 February 2016, https://www.refworld.org/docid/56ceac814.html, accessed 24 March 2021.
25   "Iraq's Shi'ite Militias Formally Inducted Into Security Forces," *Reuters*, 8 March 2018, https://www.reuters.com/article/us-mideast-crisis-iraq-militias-idUSKCN1GK354, accessed 24 March 2021.
26   "Ta'arraf 'ala Kānūn Hai'at al-Hashd ash-Sha'bi" [Know the Law of the Popular Mobilization Forces], *al-Jazeera*, 27 November 2016, https://t.ly/cJnt, accessed 24 March 2021.
27   Eric Gaston and Andras Derzsi-Horvath, *Iraq After ISIL: Sub-State Actors, Local Forces, and the Micro-Politics of Control* (Berlin: Global Public Policy Institute, 2018), 46 https://reliefweb.int/sites/reliefweb.int/files/resources/Gaston_Derzsi-Horvath_2018_Iraq_After_ISIL.pdf, accessed 24 March 2021.

the demonstrations against corruption by the Iraqi youth in Shiite regions in Baghdad and the southern provinces, the PMF was mobilized to do dirty work, like shooting civilians, kidnapping, torturing, and assassinations.[28] The presence of such militias in semi-consociations provide hegemonic communities and their affiliated parties with impunity to attack civilians, control the security apparatus, and eliminate competition from opposition groups.

The way CMR works in semi-consociational systems is extremely flawed. Probably only prewar Lebanon had a well-established and professional army that only lost legitimacy and disintegration because of wrong political calculations. However, in the case of Burundi and Iraq, the semi-consociational system appears to rely on militias to establish control and insight fear among civilians. The aim is to control the population, rather than providing security and order. Consequently, the hegemonic community in power tries to tighten its grip over the army, and its notion of de-politicizing the army is to create a politicized militia that does the dirty work on its behalf. Powerful parties within the hegemonic community benefit most from such systems, as in the case of the CNDD-FDD in Burundi and the PMF militias and their political parties in Iraq. On the contrary, it is important to note that in full consociations, CMR relations function with the best level of accommodation and cooperation between civilian and military authorities.

3   CMR in Full Consociations

Consociational democracies enjoy a better quality of CMR than semi-consociations. Systems that are classified as full consociational democracies, like post-war Lebanon and Bosnia-Herzegovina (BiH), require some sort of consensus in the government (Lebanon) or collective presidency (BiH) to deploy the army, in addition to specific arrangements within the army to guarantee cooperation among ethnic groups in decision making. This is what Hoodie and Hartzell refer to as military power sharing, and it is best presented in consociational systems.

Post-war Lebanon and Bosnia-Herzegovina (BiH) are the case studies that show the efficiency, professionalism, and healthy relations between the civilian government and military authorities. The analysis of those two cases shows that there has not been an exploitation of the military prowess to suppress the

---

28 "Iraq: The Protest Movement and Treatment of Protesters and Activists," *European Asylum Support Office* EUSO, 1 November 2019, https://www.easo.europa.eu/sites/default/files/publications/10_2020_EASO_COI_Report_Iraq_The_protest_movement_and_treatment_of_protesters.pdf, accessed 24 March 2021.

population or any of its ethnic groups. This is because the system relies heavily on consensus for the deployment of troops. In BiH, the government, with pressure from NATO and the EU, has unified the Serbian, Bosnian, and Croatian army under one command, and created one ministry of defense to oversee this new army. The army comes under the control of the collective presidency where decisions are taken by consensus. In Lebanon, critical decisions – including security related issues – are taken by more than a two-third vote in the government in case there is an absence of consensus. In the two cases, this has provided a safety net against the use of the military internally to suppress specific ethnic communities or the opposition. Also, it has been a very important tool to preserve the impartial status of the army in domestic political affairs and its cohesion.

Despite the fact that in BiH the army was created by integrating three-previously-enemy forces during the Balkan war (the Croatian, Bosnian, and Serbian militaries), the AFBiH has not been involved in any sort of action against the civilian population. The two-time deployment of the AFBiH was in December 2010[29] and May 2014,[30] when several towns were flooded and the collective presidency had to ask the army to deploy and help civilians. The humanitarian nature of the mission gave a boost for the legitimacy of the AFBiH. The army is now trained by the NATO and the EUFOR, it has a decent proportionality representation of its ethnic constituents, and the use of force is guaranteed by the unanimous decision in the collective presidency, and since unification, the army has not been a scene of any scandal. This has guaranteed the legitimacy of the AFBiH in a country that is deeply divided.

The Lebanese army has been used more than its Bosnian counterpart because the police force is weak and undermanned, so the army is needed to help preserve law and order. Nevertheless, it has not been mobilized against the opposition. For instance, in 2005, 2019, and 2020, the army was asked by presidents Emile Lahoud (2005) and Michel Aoun (2019 and 2020) to use force against peaceful demonstrators, an unconstitutional request as that right is reserved to the council of ministers, but the army commanders at that time Michel Soleiman (2005) and Joseph Aoun (2019 and 2020) declined the presidents' request. Moreover, the army has been involved in successful campaigns against terror groups, like that of Takfir wal-Hejra (2000), Fateh al-Islam (2007),

---

29   "Bosnia and Herzegovina: Floods," *International Federation of Red Cross and Red Crescent Societies*, 13 December 2010, https://www.ifrc.org/docs/appeals/10/MDRBA006do.pdf, accessed 24 March 2021.

30   Elvira M. Jukic, "Bosnia Deploys Army to Rescue Flood Victims," *Balkan Insight*, 15 May 2014, https://balkaninsight.com/2014/05/15/hundreds-need-evacuation-from-floods-in-bosnia/, accessed 24 March 2021.

ISIS and an-Nusrah (2018). The LAF, then, is aware of the dangers of using the army in a deeply divided society and the repercussions that might occur, and at the same time takes its role to protect the country from terror groups very seriously. Hence, it perceives its role paramount in preserving the unity and cohesion of its rank and files while fighting terrorism and protecting the state as well.

Another important characteristic in CMR in consociational democracies is the administrative status of the ministry of defense. The ministry's main job is to liaison between the government and the army. It overlooks the implementation of the executive orders and the legality of the military activities of the armed forces, and at the same time works alongside the army to improve it weapons, logistics, and personnel. Therefore, there is no advantage to any community that occupies the position of minister of defense. Above all, the position is not reserved for any community, unlike in semi-consociational Iraq where the seat is reserved for the Sunni community, or in Burundi where the minister of police and that of defense cannot belong to the same community.

With respect to intelligence, consociational systems seem to demand that intelligence reports be shared in the council of ministers where all communities are represented. In this way, even if the top intelligence commander belongs permanently to a specific community, the intelligence report and analysis is shared with all ethnic groups regardless of their status as minority or majority. Also, the president, prime minister, or other important ministerial portfolios do not have any sort of hegemony or monopoly in the intelligence sector. This provides a guarantee that all communities are sharing equal power, and that the intelligence data is not manipulated against any other community. In contrast to full consociational democracies, semi-consociations establish a direct link between it and the head of the executive (prime minister as in Iraq or president as in Burundi). Consequently, the intelligence apparatus reports to the head of executive, who then takes action or shares the information he wants with the council of ministers.

A final characteristic of CMR in consociational democracies relates authority and the chain of command. In these systems, critical security decisions are left for a collective decision-making body: the government in postwar Lebanon and the collective presidency in Bosnia-Herzegovina. In the former, decisions are to be taken unanimously, if not, then a two-third majority is needed, while in the latter, decisions are taken by consensus. This puts the government and collective presidency as the real supreme commanders with real military authority over the armed forces in postwar Lebanon and Bosnia-Herzegovina respectively. Again, this is very important to provide real military power sharing, protect the army from politicization, empower security in the country, and prevent the use of the army by one community against the other. Consequently, the armed forces do not have an alternative chain of command that includes party members and military loyalists to the commander in chief who bypass the formal institutions, as in Iraq during al-Maliki's era and Burundi under the CNDD. The triumph of the alternative chain of command means that the army will be reduced into a mere illegitimate tool under partisan control to suppress the opposition or other ethnic communities.

The armies in full consociations are superior to those in semi-consocational democracies. The question, then, is how to build an army in a post-conflict environment that implements genuine military power sharing provisions.

4   Post-Conflict Armies and Military Power Sharing

From the analysis of the four case studies of the creation of armies in post-conflict environment, with societies that are deeply divided along ethnic or sectarian lines, it is important to outline three broad principles utilized in the making of new armed forces. These points are: military missions and values that include cohesion, neutrality, and professionalism; decision making and the structure of the army; power dividing and proportionality. Every new institution requires a mission to explain its role and the aim of its existence, especially if it is an institution that monopolizes the use of force. Armed forces in post-conflict environment have to present a national mission by indoctrinating soldiers and preparing them to sacrifice for the nation, and also to give a glimpse of the military rationale for people to endorse this national institution. Once the mission is outlined, it is important that elites agree on military power sharing and reflect that in the CMR and structure of the army. Military power sharing in the army means that main communities are represented in the different military institutions, particularly in the upper level. This is what researchers refer to proportionality, but it is not enough to achieve genuine military power sharing. Military proportionality requires that the community agrees by consensus on the use of force – that is deployment of the army – for domestic purposes. In this way there is a guarantee that the deployment of armed forces is done for preserving law and order, not to dominate opposition groups or marginalize communities. This balance of power is represented in the structure of the armed forces.

4.1   *Military Mission*
In post-conflict environment, military mission, values and guidelines of an army aim at safeguarding the long-term fears of any community that was previously engaged in military activities against other domestic foes. Because

the indoctrination process may transform a peasant or a militiaman into a national soldier, dedicating his life to defend the integrity of his/her country, the military mission plays an important role in transcending the previously illegitimate army, or a non-existent one, to a national unifying force in a deeply divided society.

In the four case studies in this book, the military mission of the newly created armies concentrates on protecting the integrity of the country, preserving the apolitical and impartial status of the army, and respecting the rule of law (human rights for example). In postwar Lebanon, the army's mission is outlined as defending the country against its enemy state (Israel) and terrorism, protecting the borders, and provide national security;[31] in BiH, the army's role is to protect the country, assist civilian authorities in cases of disaster and fulfil international obligations;[32] in Burundi, articles 12, 13, 14, 16, and 17 of organic law no. 1/04 of 20 February 2017 specify the role and mission of the FDNB as protecting the borders, respecting international obligations, fighting terrorism, and delivering security; finally in Iraq, the military's role is to defend the nation, preserve its neutrality and prevent intervention in domestic affairs, and accept the superiority of the civilian authority.[33]

The recreation of the armed forces in these cases shows emphasis on the mission statement, particularly regarding the defense of the state borders, protection from terrorist attacks, and prohibiting any intervention in domestic affairs. It is clear that armies in post-conflict environment try to break away with the previous activities of institution. Hence, the superiority of the civilian government in CMR is clearly stated in all mission statements of the four armies.

The armies in the post-conflict environment are protected by their mission statement that aims at neutralizing the politicization of the officer corps or its rank and file. In all cases, it is prohibited for a soldier to join a political party or show any sort of support or inclination for a political grouping. Hence, we see that the Huntingtonian method is used to make the army impartial and professional. It is important to note that soldiers follow political development and may have dissimulative support for a political group or party, but in practice

---

31 Lebanese Armed Forces Website, https://www.lebarmy.gov.lb/ar/content/%D9%85%D9%87%D9%85%D8%A7%D8%AA-%D8%A7%D9%84%D8%AC%D9%8A%D8%B4, accessed 24 March 2021.

32 Ministry of Defense, Bosnia and Herzegovina, http://www.mod.gov.ba/OS_BIH/nadleznosti/?id=21874, accessed 24 March 2021.

33 "Coalition Provisional Authority Order Number 22," 7 August 2003, https://govinfo.library.unt.edu/cpa-iraq/regulations/20030818_CPAORD_22_Creation_of_a_New_Iraqi_Army.pdf, accessed 24 March 2021.

the mission statement prohibits them from taking any action under the threat of expulsion or punishment. Moreover, the Huntingtonian method is lucid in the independent status of the army to run its internal affairs regardless of the political aims of the civilian authorities. In this context, the armies prepare their budget, though it is up to the civilian authority to accept or amend it, and the military itself develops its own programs, internal policies, development at the level of training and equipment, educational strategy, and military strategy to protect the nation.

4.2 *Collective Decision Making and Military Power Sharing*

An important step in rebuilding armies after civil wars lies in the decision-making process and power sharing in the military between different communities. Once the army has a clear mission statement that defines its doctrine, goal, and existence, parties have to agree on who should take critical security decisions. As we know by now, the ministry of defense usually guides the day-to-day business of the army, but important decisions are left to the civilian authorities. In the four case studies, postwar Lebanon and BiH which are full consociations have a consensus-oriented military power sharing system, while the semi-consociational systems of Burundi and Iraq enjoy a centralized military decision making process which lies in the office of the head of executive: the president of Burundi and the prime minister of Iraq respectively.

The two different methods have severe implications on CMR and the role of the army in hampering stability in the country. In full consociations, a collective body has to take important security and military oriented decisions by consensus or special majority, like declaring war or deploying the army. In postwar Lebanon, the army responds to the government, which should take decisions by consensus and if not, then a two-third majority vote is needed to take action.[34] In this way, it is guaranteed that all communities share in military and security decisions. In addition to that, in order to break away with the prewar obsession that the army was a Christian army since it is led by a Maronite army commander, the army hierarchy functions in the form of collective bodies, represented in the army command and the military council, both of which consists of military officers, and the Higher Defense Council, a mixture of civilian and military officers. The army command consists of the army commander, chief of staff and vice chief of staff, and those high-ranking officers are equally divided between Christians and Muslims. The military

---

34   Constitution of Lebanon.

council is also equally divided between both communities and among its main tasks is to oversee promotion and composition of brigades and battalions.[35] The Higher Defense Council consists of the president, prime minister, along with the ministers of defense, foreign affairs, economy, finance, interior, and high-ranking military commanders. Its role is to oversee the process of general mobilization and overlook the civilian-military cooperation in the times of war. Deliberations and minutes are kept secret from the public.[36]

In the Bosnian case, the collective presidency, which includes a president representing each ethnic community and whose decisions should by consensus, has the exclusive right to declare war, peace, state of emergency, and deploy the army.[37] Also, it appoints the general officers in the army, including those of the joint staff (those in the joint staff are named after the ministry of defense proposes the names, and they await a parliamentary confirmation within 45 days), and promote general officers in the army. This is similar to what the Lebanese government in Lebanon deals with regarding the armed forces. However, the Bosnian case only has one important collective body within the military with equal ethnic representation, which is the joint staff. It consists of the Chief of the Joint Staff, a deputy for operations and another for resources.[38] Its main task is to implement the security decisions of the collective presidency; hence it is similar in its nature to the role of the military council in Lebanon. The other body that had an important role in CMR and enjoyed a collective representation of each ethnic community is the Standing Committee on Military Matters (SCMM) before transferring its powers to the newly created ministry of defense. This body was similar to the Higher Defense Council in Lebanon, but its members were all civilians: members of the Presidency, the chair of the Council of Ministers, the minister of foreign Affairs, the President/Vice-President of each Federation of BiH, and the President/Vice-President of Republika Srpska. These members enjoy voting rights, and the members of the presidency may select other members of the Committee, and each ethnic community has to be represented by at least two members.[39] The chairman of the

---

35   Lebanese National Defense Law.
36   Ibid.
37   Law on Defense of Bosnia and Herzegovina, http://www.ohr.int/ohr-dept/legal/laws-of
     -bih/pdf/014%20-%20ARMY%20LEGISLATION/BH%20Law%20on%20Defence%20of
     %20Bosnia%20and%20Herzegovina%2088-05.pdf, accessed 24 March 2021.
38   Ibid.
39   "Bosnia and Herzegovina - State Level Sigma Public Management Profiles, No. 16 (2004),
     OECD Publishing, https://www.oecd-ilibrary.org/governance/bosnia-and-herzegovina
     -state-level_5kmk17zq70r8-en;jsessionid=osANqlzlC-g4X2fv8ofueZra.ip-10-240-5-119,
     accessed 24 March 2021.

Parliamentary Defense and Security Committees of the state and of each entity along with military advisors to the members of the Presidency, are members of the Standing Committee with an advisory role.[40] The SCMM coordinates relations between civilian and military authorities, and among the three armies of each ethnic community before unifying them into one national army. Iraq has the Iraqi National Security Council that includes the prime minister, ministers of defense, interior, foreign affairs, justice and finance.[41] The council's role is to coordinate between different ministries to implement the security decisions of the government and develop security strategies to protect the state.[42] This is basically identical to the Higher Defense Council in Lebanon, albeit with less responsibilities with its Lebanese counterpart.

In contrast to full consociational democracies, semi-consociational systems are similar to the presidential system of the USA with respect to the CMR and civilian authority over the army. To start with, the head of the executive (president of Burundi and prime minister of Iraq) are the commanders in chief of the army, with extensive powers. They can name and dismiss military commanders (in some cases it requires approval of the parliament), they have the right to mobilize and deploy the army, the military reports to the prime minister, and above all, the heads of the executive have exclusive access to all national intelligences in the country. With such powers, the army can become a tool in the hands of the president. In prewar Lebanon, the President as head of the executive enjoyed similar powers, and used the army in 1975 with the start of the civil war that eventually ended in its disintegration. In Iraq, al-Maliki's extensive reliance upon the army and the counter-terrorism unit that reported directly to him, bypassing the chain of command, was an important factor in the army's disintegration in 2014 with the rise of ISIS. Al-Maliki used the army to suppress Sunni opposition. In Burundi, the CNDD-FDD had been using the army and intelligence units to attack peaceful opposition to the government, leading to a mass wave of exile, in addition to systematic purge of ex-FAB soldiers, and now the president has established an alternative chain of command that is stronger than the official one. Consequently, the army has become a tool to implement the CNDD-FDD policies by force and it has become a military wing for the party.

---

40   Ibid.
41   "Coalition Provisional Authority Order Number 68," 4 April 2004, https://nsa.gov.iq/page/2/incorporation-law, accessed 24 March 2021.
42   Ibid.

4.3 *Proportionality*

The concept of proportionality in the army is very important in post-conflict environments as it provides a sense of trust to the communities with respect to the army. Communities in divided societies may feel threatened by an army that resembles an unbalanced representation across communal groups. Hence, the concept of proportionality becomes central in the thinking of communities and their leaders when it comes to re-creating armies after civil wars. The concept is applied in all four case studies, however in different ways. For instance, the Lebanese and Burundian army are established according to the principle of parity between Muslims and Christians in the former, Tutsi and Hutu in the latter. Nevertheless, because the Christians are not strictly half of the population and the number of Christians willing to be involved in the army is diminishing, the army has a higher representation of Muslims in its rank and files, but strictly adheres to parity at the level of officer corps. The overall parity in Lebanon is proportional within each sect according to the proportion of the sub-communities (Sunni, Shiites, and Druze in the Muslim sect Maronite, Orthodox, Armenians and Catholics in the Christian sect). In Burundi, the integration of the ex-FAB with the militants of the Hutu community was based on parity according to the Arusha agreement, but ceased to be applied after the purge of ex-FAB soldiers by the CNDD-FDD led government. The party has made it clear that they want to abolish parity as the Tutsi represent only around 20 percent of the population. In BiH, the army relies on strict ethnic proportionality without any form of parity: 50 percent for Bosnians, 30 percent for Serbs, 15 percent for Croats, and 4 percent for other minorities.[43] Brigades in BiH are heterogeneous but each battalion is made up of an exclusive ethnic group. The anomaly of the proportionality quota in the four case studies is Iraq, particularly in the officer corps. For example, in the joint command, the percentage of Shiites is 90, that of Kurds is 6, and Sunni with other minorities are 4.[44] The officer corps in general respect the demography of the country, but

---

43   "Rezultati popisa stanovništva: U BiH živi 50,11% Bošnjaka, 15,43% Hrvata te Srba 30,78%" [Census results: 50.11% of Bosniaks, 15.43% of Croats and 30.78% of Serbs live in BiH], *Vecernij*, 30 June 2016, https://www.vecernji.hr/vijesti/cekalo-se-25-godine-na-objavu-rezultata-popisa-stanovnistva-u-bih-ovo-su-prvi-sluzbeni-podaci-nakon-25-godina-1095916, accessed 24 March 2021.

44   Mohammed Salman Al-Tai, "Ethnic Balance in the Ministry of Defence (Iraqi Army – Counter Terrorism Service)," *The Center of Making Policies for International and Strategic Studies*, 13 July 2018, https://www.makingpolicies.org/en/posts/ethnicbalance.english.php, accessed 24 March 2021.

at the level of rank and files, 75 percent of them are Shiites.[45] These numbers are skewed in favor of Shiites who make up 60 percent of the population, followed by 20 percent Sunnis and 18 percent Kurds.

The proportionality question is important but should not be seen as the main element that protects ethnic balances in the army. The cases of Burundi and Iraq illustrate that even if a minority like the Tutsi receives a much higher quota than its proportion of the population, or if proportionality is well established in the officer corps, there is not a guarantee that the army would not be used against them. Proportionality is a supportive element that helps create a balanced army in post-conflict divided societies, but in the absence of proper power sharing mechanisms in the army, politicians can easily outmaneuver military proportionality by using the army against specific communities, and the semi-consociational cases in this book show that. The Burundian elites, particularly from the Tutsi community fell in the trap of proportionality by mistakenly equating military power sharing and proportionality. Without power sharing at the highest level in the army, particularly when it comes to war and peace, as well as deployment in the domestic arena, there is no point in applying proportionality.

The construction of armies in divided societies after civil wars with power sharing systems show that there are two trajectories: one related to the full consociational systems where the military represent a legitimate national institution, and semi-consociational democracies were the army lacks legitimacy and national endorsement across ethnic groups. Despite these two parallel trajectories, there is something important in common (with the exception of BiH): the presence of militias. Only in BiH can we see an absence of militias, probably because of the heavy hand of NATO in implementing the Dayton agreement. In Iraq, Lebanon, and Burundi, militias have been re-created (Iraq and Burundi) or temporary legitimized (Lebanon), but the presence of these militias have had severe implications on these countries.

5   Anomalies in Lebanon, Iraq, and Burundi: Militias

It is very interesting to see a salient and silent characteristic that emerges with time in post-conflict divided societies, and that is the rise of militias parallel to the construction of national armies in three out of the four cases under study

---

45   Florence Gaub, "An Unhappy Marriage: Civil-Military Relations in Post-Saddam Iraq," *Carnegie*, 13 January 2016, https://carnegieeurope.eu/2016/01/13/unhappy-marriage-civil-military-relations-in-post-saddam-iraq-pub-61955, accessed 24 March 2021.

in this book: Lebanon, Iraq, and Burundi. In this section, I study the characteristics of these militias, how they managed to preserve their extra-constitutional status, and their current divisive nature in these countries. The militias under study are Hezbollah in Lebanon, the PMF in Iraq, and the Imbonerakure in Burundi.

In Lebanon, Hezbollah was established due to a local need by the Lebanese, particularly the Shiite community to resist Israeli occupation, and it coincided in 1982 with the rise of the Islamic Republic of Iran and its Velayat-e-Faqih doctrine of exporting the religious revolution. The Iranians supported a splintered group of the Shiite Amal Movement which was religiously captivated and influenced by Imam Khomeini. The agreement was that this group – later known as Hezbollah – would fight Israel, adopt Khoemini's doctrine of Velyat-e-Faiqh, and in return receive financial, political, and military support from Iran. When the civil war in Lebanon ended in 1990–1991, militias relinquished their armed struggle and decommissioned their weapons to the Lebanese state or the Syrian army, it was agreed that Hezbollah would preserve its arsenal in order to continue the struggle to fight Israel, as 12 percent of Lebanon (the southern region) was under Israeli occupation. There was, however, a loophole, as it can be argued that no politician expected Israel to withdraw at any point (which happened in 2000), so the question of Hezbollah's military activities was never discussed, and no party demanded a promise of what to do with the weapons in case of a grand bargain that would end the Arab-Israeli conflict or if the Israeli withdrew from Lebanon. Consequently, there was national endorsement for Hezbollah's activities after the civil war until the Israeli withdrawal in 2000. The issue, however, became a source of political contestation and divisions slowly after the Israeli withdrawal, particularly in 2005 after the assassination of prime minister Rafik Hariri and Hezbollah's political participation in Lebanese domestic affairs. Prior to 2005, Hezbollah's participation in Lebanese politics was shy, but they became the core of political mobilization in support to Syria, Iran, and against anything related to American interests in the region. As a result, Hezbollah became the strongest political-military religious party in the region, with the capability to coerce the state and other political parties to impose the party's agenda, at the expense of national interest. For instance, Hezbollah has expropriated from the government the decision of war and peace, when it launched an attack against Israel in 2006 that led to the July war. It rebelled against the Lebanese government in May 2008 when the pro-American Fouad Seniora's government passed a resolution to confiscate the private military communication network of the party, leading to clashes between Hezbollah and supporters of the government. Also, the party unilaterally intervened in the Syrian civil war since 2011 supporting Assad's army, against the will of the government that opted for a de-association policy. Finally, Hezbollah is taking part of the Iranian political campaign against Saudi Arabia, which has led to diplomatic tensions between the latter and the Lebanese authorities.

Hezbollah as a political-military party enjoys enormous military and financial support from Iran. The salaries of its employees, fighters, institutions, and cadets all come from Iran,[46] bypassing the Lebanese state. In this context, the Lebanese army finds itself in a difficult position: it cannot end by force Hezbollah's military activities because the party represents a religious orientation for many Lebanese Shiite who believe in the doctrine of Velayat-e-Faqih. Moreover, the army's intervention against a party that is supported by large numbers of Lebanese Shiites may lead to the disintegration of the army along sectarian lines. Consequently, the army is cautious in how it approaches Hezbollah. Its policy seems to be one of support against Israel, perceived as the enemy of Lebanon according to the military doctrine,[47] but rejects any support of cooperation in internal security affairs or border protection, as seen in the army's attack against ISIS Front in north-east of the country in 2018, in operation Dawn of the Outskirts.[48] To complicate things, the army is fully depended upon military support from the USA, which irritates Hezbollah, especially that the equipment the army has is suitable for border defense and guerrilla warfare. Hezbollah sees this as an attempt to empower the army and push it into a conflict with Hezbollah while the army looks at this support as essential to protect the country and assume in the future its full military defense of country without Hezbollah.

In post-invasion Iraq, the Americans did the deadliest mistake in the history of military invasions when they disbanded the Iraqi army. Thus, a huge number of soldiers were left out without jobs, and the provisional authority prevented many of them from working in government sponsored jobs because of their previous affiliation to the Baath party. Consequently, the coalition forces faced several insurrections from Sunni militias under the banner of al-Qaeda, like Abu Mus'ab az-Zarqawi's al-Qaeda in Iraq (AQI), which evolved later after its defeat into ISIS. The main militias, however, that I am referring to in this

---

46 Majid Rafizadeh, "In First, Hezbollah Confirms all Financial Support Comes from Iran," al-Arabiya, 25 June 2016, https://english.alarabiya.net/features/2016/06/25/In-first-Hezbollah-s-Nasrallah-confirms-all-financial-support-comes-from-Iran, accessed 24 March 2021.

47 "Kā'id aj-Jaish fi 'Amr al-Yaum" [Army Commander in the Order of the Day], *Annahar*, 31 July 2018.

48 "aj-Jaish al-Lubnāni Yabda' Amaliyat Fajr al-Jurūd dud Dā'esh" [The Lebanese Army Begins its Operations Against Daesh], *DW*, 19 August 2017.

study are those that emerged after the rise of ISIS and the fatwa of Shiite Grand Marjaʿ Ali as-Sistani,[49] who called for the mobilization of the Shiite community to fight ISIS. Consequently, Shiite militias gathered under the PMF, and it receives support from the Iraqi state as its status has been legitimized in 2016,[50] but the bulk of military and financial support for some of these militias come from Iran. In official terms, they are part of the Iraqi security apparatus and fall under the jurisdiction of the office of prime minister. Nevertheless, PMF militias are loyal to Iran, and so they are emerging as a source of nuisance with the audacity to defy the Iraqi government.

The PMF managed to emerge after the fall of the Iraqi army. After the international community helped rebuild a new Iraqi army post-2014 which defeated ISIS with the support of PMF, the militias were not incorporated into the existing battalions of the army, nor it was disbanded or provided new opportunities for the militants to integrate into the market. Instead, the Iraqi parliament, under pressure from Iran, legitimized the status of the PMF as a fighting force independent of the army. The authority of the office of the prime minister is ceremonial because the PMF has its own agenda domestically and regionally with Iran's acquiescent. Consequently, what emerged to be a temporary fighting force to fill the gap of the downfall of the Iraqi army became a permanent-legal reality with the power to defy the government. For instance, militants from the PMF defy orders during deployment, sometime entering into Sunni or Kurdish regions without the consent of the population or the government. They have committed crimes against humanity and against civilians in the campaign against ISIS, believing that all the people who lived under ISIS rule are suspects. Recently, after the series of protests in Shiite regions against corruption by Shiite dominant political parties, these militias began to suppress the peaceful protestors,[51] on their own without orders from the government. Moreover, they were about to engage in violence against the army in several instances. At one point, the PMF was about to engage in clashes against the army that was protecting the peaceful demonstrators. In another instance,

---

49 Omar Ahmed, "Pro-Sistani Factions Leave Shia Forces, But Iraq's PM Signal they are Here to Stay," *Middle East Monitor*, 18 May 2020, https://www.middleeastmonitor.com/20200518-pro-sistani-factions-leave-shia-forces-but-iraqs-pm-signals-they-are-here-to-stay/, accessed 24 March 2021.

50 "Iraqi Parliament Passes Contested Law on Shi'ite Paramilitaries," *Reuters*, 26 November 2016, https://www.reuters.com/article/us-mideast-crisis-iraq-military-idUSKBN13L0IE, accessed 24 March 2021.

51 "Iraq: Investigate Abuses in Hawija Operation," *Human Rights Watch*, 28 September 2017, https://www.hrw.org/news/2017/09/28/iraq-investigate-abuses-hawija-operation, accessed 24 March 2021.

the PMF refused to hand in suspects believed to be firing rockets that targeted the American embassy and interests in the country.[52] These are signs that the coexistence between the army and the PMF may not last long. To end this competition, either the army will have to tame the PMF, or the latter will become stronger than the army, following the footsteps of its Iranian counterpart the Revolutionary Guards.

The main difference between the militias in Iraq and Lebanon with that of Burundi is that the Imbonerakure is that the formers rely on regional sponsorship, while the latter is dependent on the Burundian state. Indeed, the Imbonerakure is a state sponsored militia that is an organ of the ruling CNDD-FDD party. This youth militia is part of an alternative chain of command that includes the president, security officers and party members. Its role is to conduct surveillance over the population, act as a police force and sometimes do the dirty job that security institutions prefer not to do for legal reasons. The Imbonerakure activities are to carry arbitrary arrest, run unofficial prisons, torture people suspects, extort the public to influence political behavior, and threaten opponents. The rise of the Imbonerakure came after the attempted coup in 2015 that led to a series of assassinations between ex-FAB members and pro CNDD-FDD officers in the newly unified army. The CNDD-FDD heavily invested in the Imbonerakure during the third presidential campaign of president Nkurunziza that was seen as illegal and opposed to the Arusha agreement by his opponents. Today, the CNDD-FDD transformed the Imbonerakure into a semi-official security tool, whose members receive salaries and benefits from the state but answer to order from the party. The Imbonerakure militia was established by the dominant CNDD-FDD party to target opposition, whether from the Hutu or Tutsi community. The Arusha agreement and the constitution prohibit the establishment of any militia or armed organization in the country, but the CNDD-FDD's control over all the organs of the state leaves no room for accountability. As a result, opposition groups are following suit and establishing armed groups to fight the state. Hence, even though the recreation of the Burundian army was seen as a success until Nkurunziza's third term campaign in 2015, the success turned into failure afterwards with the systematic purge of ex-FAB members in addition to Hutu soldiers whose loyalty was wavering.

It seems that the present situation in Burundi is one where the Imbonerakure militia might grow strong enough to compete with the national army,

---

52 Crispin Smith, "Iraq's Legal Responsibility for Militia Attacks on U.S. Forces: Paths Forward," *Just Security*, 10 March 2021, https://www.justsecurity.org/75232/iraqs-legal-responsibility-for-militia-attacks-on-u-s-forces-paths-forward/, accessed 24 March 2021.

in case that the CNDD-FDD sees that the army becomes a threat to its rule. The alternative chain of command established alongside the official one is a setback to the democratic control of armed forces in Burundi, with negative consequences on CMR. In fact, there is no CMR, but rather party control over the whole security apparatus, including the national army.

6 Conclusion

Recreating armies after civil wars requires integration of warring forces into new units, battalions, brigades, and a set of new CMR related institutions to achieve military power sharing. The case studies of Iraq and Burundi show that in semi-consociational models, the army is subject to politicization by a ruling party (CNDD-FDD in Burundi) or a strongman (al-Maliki in Iraq). It is also there to serve the interest of the dominant-hegemonic community (Hutus in Burundi and Shiites in Iraq), with almost complete disregard to the interest of minorities. Military power sharing in semi-consociational systems is cosmetic, with minimal proportionality in the army but centralization of decision making with the hegemonic communities. Consequently, armies in these states can quickly disintegrate because of the lack of minimal professionalism, heavy politicization, and weak legitimacy. The case of Iraq in 2014 explicitly supports this argument, and the Burundian army today has come under the control of the CNDD-FDD rather than the state. Also, it appears that in semi-consociational systems it is easy to establish an alternative chain of command, empowered by party officials or a political strongman which is aimed at weakening the authority of professional officers to serve narrow interests.

Full consociations are better than their semi-counterparts in CMR, this is attributed to a well-established and balanced strategy to implement military power sharing. Besides proportionality and representation of ethnic communities, the use of armed forces for domestic purposes requires consensus. Hence, the army is not under the control of one ethnic group. Moreover, the officer corps of BiH and Lebanon are characterized as professional and impartial, which means that they follow the official chain of command and avoid politicization. With the army coming under the control of official institutions, and with the practice of military power sharing among ethnic communities, armed forces in BiH and Lebanon have a safety net against the threat of disintegration. They also enjoy endorsement from the people that boosts the army's legitimacy, making these institutions among the best functioning ones in their respective countries.

CHAPTER 8

Conclusion

This book has aimed at establishing a new paradigm in the study of deeply divided societies to shed light on the importance of armed forces. Armies in these kinds of societies are crucial in maintaining order and stability, but the literature of power sharing institutions particularly in post-conflict environments has largely neglected this side of arrangement. Consequently, there is no surprise that this is the first book that deals exclusively with the topic of armies and power sharing in pre- and post-conflict environments.

The important work on military power sharing lays a strong theoretical foundation for the book, however it is important to explain to the reader how to create this kind of power sharing, and in which system. This is the main reason that the author of these lines emphasized the study of a small *n*, with a detailed explanation and analysis of the transformation of civil-military relations and military institutions before and after the conflict. The four case studies, Lebanon, Bosnia-Herzegovina (BiH), Iraq, and Burundi perfectly fit the framework of the research and help the method of analysis to reach important conclusions on how to govern armies in divided societies.

There are important conclusions reached from this work. First, the classical theories of CMR dominated by Samuel Huntington's objective approach and Morris Janowitz's subjective approach cannot be applied in deeply divided societies, particularly in post-conflict environments. Rather than looking at the debate whether armies should be part left in a separate bubble from socio-political developments of integrated into society, we need to study the power dynamics and political context of deeply divided societies to be able to come up with a functional approach for CMR. The term "civilian control of armed forces" is very vague and dangerous to use in deeply divided societies. An army can come under the full authority of the head of executive, be it president or prime minister, with extensive legislative oversight, but due to internal frictions and divisions along sectarian or ethnic lines, armies could become tools of oppression used by politicians to suppress opposition within the same community or against others. This is the very essence of the loophole in the Huntingtonian and Janwitzian approach to CMR, rendering their theories obsolete for deeply divided societies. The emphasis should be on consensus to use the army for domestic security. Moreover, there is a need to differentiate between the status and the function of armies in post-conflict societies under full consociations versus semi-consociations. Armies in these two cases function in different ways and it is a critical matter to consider the use and possible abuse of armies: the use of army for domestic purposes needs consensus to avoid an abuse of power by politicians in power. Second, post-conflict societies need to differentiate between proportionality in armed forces and provisions that provide military power sharing. It is wrong to equate between both as communal representation in the army does not guarantee power sharing in military decision making. If the army commander or head of executive has extensive military provisions vis-à-vis other political leaders, then whatever proportionality there is in the army is no guarantee for military power sharing. Third, recreating armies in post-conflict deeply divided societies requires a strategy that goes beyond demobilization, disarmament and reintegration (DDR), and security sector reform (SSR). It is critical to look at the balance of power between communal groups and establish a mechanism that prevents a party or community from taking over the armed forces.

1   Armies and Consociationalism

The structure of full and semi-consociational systems differ in veto mechanisms built in political institutions. Full consociations provide veto powers for ethnic communities in the executive and the legislative, while semi-consociations guarantee representation in government and parliament/senate but without a clear veto power. These institutional frameworks have their effects on civil-military relations, the governing of armies (especially after civil wars), and military power sharing. In full consociations, the strategic use of the army for domestic order by deployment of troops require consensus. This is what we see in Bosnia-Herzegovina and Lebanon, with the constitutional requirement to deploy the army by consensus in the collective presidency of Bosnia and a special majority of two-third in the Lebanese government. As such, the threat of politicizing the army or using it against a specific community is neutralized by constitutional arrangements related to full consociations. In semi-consociations, the use of the army is up to the head of the executive, like the president of Burundi or prime minister of Iraq. Consequently, consensus is not required to use the army for domestic purposes, and in both cases, we have seen how heads of executive used the army to subdue opposition and other communities.

The impact of such political structures is great on civil-military relations. The absence of consensus in a deeply divided society with respect to the use of the army for domestic law and order means that armed forces may be politicized. Consequently, this may hinder the professionalism of the army, which would definitely destroy its legitimacy and popular endorsement. No army can succeed in providing law and order in deeply divided societies without popular support and legitimacy. The failure of the army of Burundi in providing law and order is due to its politicization and loss of legitimacy, which means that rebel groups are on the rise. Similarly, the politicization of the newly created Iraqi army after the American invasion in 2003 played an important role in the rise of al-Qaeda and ISIS, leading to the army's disintegration. Consensus on the use of the army, then, is of critical importance to protect the unity and professionalism of national armies in divided societies. This is why the Lebanese and Bosnian armies have succeeded in preserving their unity and improving their legitimacy, in deeply divided societies, and overcoming security challenges, whether domestic or regional.

2 Post-Conflict Military Reconstruction

It is better for militaries reconstructed in post-conflict environment, as this book has shown, to take into consideration the context of deep divisions present in such cases. DDR and SSR are mechanisms that have important contribution to achieve stability in the long term, but their achievements could be undone if the army plays a role in subduing part of the population. Hence, post-conflict military reconstruction requires a complete reproduction of the armed forces, beginning from its mission statement, into its composition, and ending in the power sharing mechanism that is embedded in the political system.

It is vital for armies to specify the aim of their existence in order to create a military framework that legitimizes their existence. When armies say that they exist to protect borders, fight terrorism, and provide domestic order, it means that the resonance of their activity is security oriented. This means that the army is set up with no political role and is put under civilian authority, but its internal hierarchy and communal balance has to be defined. The mission statement is a useful tool to indoctrinate army personnel about their role, and it is a very important mechanism that helps to create *esprit de corps*. After that, military institutions have to create institutions that govern military personnel in their professional life, like promotion, education, and rotation. It is advised that a balanced way of doing that is through a military institution that is representable of ethnic communities, rather than centralized in an office that comes under the command of one military personnel. In this way decisions will not be interpreted to be directed against one group, and instead there will be little room for politicians to intervene in military affairs.

Another point in reconstructing armies is related to proportionality. The best way to apply this concept is by representing communities in the army at all levels, instead of calculating proportionality in the army as a whole. For instance, if parity is applied in the army of Burundi between Tutsis and Hutus, calculating parity in the army as a whole could mean that all officers and military commanders may belong to one ethnic group, while the rank and file is mixed between the two ethnic groups. This means that the army is commanded by the community that controls the officer corps, and so proportionality does not serve its intended role. However, if proportionality is applied at the level of officer corps, rank, and file, it means that military power sharing within the army between communities is applied and no ethnic group will have an advantage over the other.

3   Recommendation

The main challenges of armies in deeply divided societies as shown from the case studies are institutional and economic. With respect to the institutional challenge, it relates to the cohesion and legitimacy of the army. An army that is neutral and professional in a deeply divided society can gain the confidence and support of the population by staying outside the political quagmire. Politics in deeply divided societies is a dirty business, and if the army falls to the trap of politicization, it will function in a similar manner to a militia. Politicization of the army may lead to its disintegration, as soldiers of ethnic communities will desert to join their ethnic militias in case of civil war, or will exploit their power to use force against "the other" communities. Hence, to avoid this scenario, it is highly recommended that politicians keep the army outside the sphere of politicization. Moreover, military commanders ought to work to preserve the independent status of their organization and abstain from taking sides at all costs.

Another threat to the cohesion and professionalism of these armies is the financial challenges that they face. The economies of these countries are under severe pressure, either salaries are very low as in Burundi and BiH, or there is inflation due to the loss in the value of national currencies, as in Lebanon and Iraq. This indicates that a lower number of potential recruits will be encouraged to join the army, or if they join, they might desert at one point if the value of their salaries is diminished due to currency devaluation. This is a challenge that goes beyond the army as an institution and requires the government to find a solution for these economic challenges. Moreover, because governments in deeply divided societies have financial problems and suffer from long term economic recession, they need to find regional and international sponsors to equip the army for protection of borders and to provide domestic law and order. Burundi has previously received this kind of support from South Africa and Europe while Lebanon, Iraq, and BiH have received large sums of military equipment from the United States and Europe.

A final note relates to the reconstruction of armies in divided societies. Policymakers ought to remember that armies in divided societies are highly influenced by what happens in the political and social sphere. In order to shield the army from politics, a balance between communities by ethnic representation and sharing power in decision making is imperative and a prerequisite to create a strong, professional, and legitimate army in a post-conflict environment. This is why the small n analysis of the four case studies gives a better understanding of the framework of the recreation and function of armies in divided societies and in post-conflict environments. Hence, the conclusions of this book are applicable to cases in Libya, Myanmar, Syria, and other countries which will have to deal with the reconstruction of their national armies at some point in the future.

Bibliography

Aboultaif, Eduardo Wassim. 2019. *Power Sharing in Lebanon: Consociationalism since 1820*. London: Routledge.

Aboultaif, Eduardo Wassim. 2020. "Revisiting the Semi-Consociational Model: Democratic Failure in Prewar Lebanon and Post-Invasion Iraq." *International Political Science Review* 41 (1): 108–123.

Aboultaif, Eduardo Wassim. 2016. "The Lebanese Army: Saviour of the Republic?" *The Royal United Service Institute Journal* 161 (1): 70–78.

Adekanye, J. 'Bayo. 1996. "Rwanda/Burundi: 'Uni-ethnic' Dominance and the Cycle of Armed Ethnic Formations." *Social Identities* 2 (1): 37–72.

Ahmed, Omar. 2020. "Pro-Sistani Factions Leave Shia Forces, But Iraq's PM Signal they are Here to Stay." *Middle East Monitor*, May 18. https://www.middleeastmonitor.com/20200518-pro-sistani-factions-leave-shia-forces-but-iraqs-pm-signals-they-are-here-to-stay/.

al-Ali, Zaid. 2014. *The Struggle for Iraq's Future: How Corruption, Incompetence and Sectarianism Have Undermined Democracy*. New Haven: Yale University Press.

al-Barrak, Fadel. 1987. *Daur aj-Jaish al-'Iraqi fi Hukūmat ad-Difā' al-Watani wal-Harb ma' Britaniya 'ām 1941* [*The Role of the Iraqi Army in the Government of Defense and the War on Britain in Year 1941*]. Beirut: ad-Dār al-Arabiya lil Mausū'āt.

Alden, Chris, Monika Thakur, and Matthew Arnold. 2011. *Militias and the Challenges of Post-Conflict Peace: Silencing the Guns*. London: Zed Books.

al-Jazeera. 2016. "Ta'arraf 'ala Kānūn Hai'at al-Hashd ash-Sha'bi [Know the Law of the Popular Mobilization Forces]." November 27. https://t.ly/cJnt.

Allou, Ahmad. 2018. *Tatawor Binā' aj-Jaish al-Lubnāni Bain 1945 wa 1975,"* [*The Development of the Construction of the Lebanese Army between 1945 and 1975*]. Majallat aj-Jaish [The Army's Magazine]. https://t.ly/nV73.

al-Marashi, Ibrahim. 2007. "Disbanding and Rebuilding the Iraqi Army: The Historical Perspective." *Middle East Review of International Affairs* 11 (3): 42–53.

al-Marashi, Ibrahim. 2009. "Iraq's Gulf Policy and Regime Security from the Monarchy to the Post-Baathist Era." *British Journal of Middle Eastern Studies* 36 (3): 449–461.

al-Marashi, Ibrahim. 2002. "Iraq's Security and Intelligence Network: A Guide and Analysis." *Middle East Review of International Affairs* 6 (3): 1–13. https://ciaotest.cc.columbia.edu/olj/meria/ali02_01.pdf.

al-Marashi, Ibrahim. 2003. "The Family, Clan, and Tribal Dynamics of Saddam's Security and Intelligence Network." *International Journal of Intelligence and Counter Intelligence* 16 (2): 202–211.

al-Marashi, Ibrahim, and Sammy Sammy Salama. 2008. *Iraq's Armed Forces: An Analytical History*. New York: Routledge.

al-Samir, Faisal. 1984. "The Military as an Agent of Social Change." In *Political Perspectives on the Muslim World*, by Asaf Husain, 35–43. London: Palgrave Macmillan.

al-Tai, Mohammed Salman. 2018. *Ethnic Balance in the Ministry of Defence (Iraqi Army – Counter Terrorism Service)*. The Center of Making Policies for International and Strategic Studies. https://www.makingpolicies.org/en/posts/ethnicbalance.english.php.

Annahar. 2018. "Kā'id aj-Jaish fi 'Amr al-Yaum" [Army Commander in the Order of the Day]." July 31.

Aoun, Fouad. 1976. *Ma'sāt aj-Jaish al-Lubnāni* [*The Tragedy of the Lebanese Army*]. Beirut.

Arakji, Dina. 2019. *Females in the Ranks.* Carnegie Middle East Center.

Badie, Dina. 2017. *After Saddam: American Foreign Policy and the Destruction of Secularism in the Middle East.* Maryland: Lexington Books.

Ball, Nicole. 2014. "Lessons from Burundi's Security Sector Reform Process." *Africa Security Brief* (29): 1–8.

Barak, Oren. 2001. "Commemorating Malikiyya: Political Myth, Multiethnic Identity and the Making of the Lebanese Army." *History and Memory* 13 (1): 60–84.

Barak, Oren. 2009. *The Lebanese Army: A National Institution in a Divided Society.* New York: State University of New York Press.

Barak, Oren. 2006. "Towards a Representative Military? The Transformation of the Lebanese Officer Corps since 1945." *The Middle East Journal* 60 (1): 75–93.

Barltrop, Richard. 2008. *The Negotiation of Security Issues in the Burundi Peace Talks.* Centre for Humanitarian Dialogue. https://www.files.ethz.ch/isn/95072/HD%20Centre%20NegDis%20Burundi%20Country%20Study%20PDF.pdf.

Bassuener, Kurt. 2015. *The Armed Forces of Bosnia and Herzegovina: Unfulfilled Promise.* Democratization Policy Council.

Batatu, Hanna. 1979. *The Old Social Classes and the Revolutionary Movements of Iraq.* Princeton: Princeton University Press.

Baylouni, Anne Marie. 2012. "Building an Integrated Military in Post-Conflict Societies: Lebanon." In *The Routledge Handbook of Civil-Military Relations*, by Thomas C. Bruneau and Florina Cristiana Matei, 242–254. London: Routledge.

BBC. 2015. "Burundi Crisis: Military Bases Attacked in Bujumbura." 11 December 2015. https://www.bbc.com/news/world-africa-35070154.

BBC. 2014. "Iraqi Army 'had 50,000 Ghost Troops' on Payroll." 30 November 2014. https://www.bbc.com/news/world-middle-east-30269343.

Benson, Leslie. 2004. *Yugoslavia: A Concise History.* Hampshire: Palgrave Macmillan.

Berdak, Oliwia. 2015. "Reintegrating Veterans in Bosnia and Herzegovina and Croatia: Citizenship and Gender Effects." *Women's Studies International Forum* 49: 48–56.

Berg, Louis-Alexander. 2014. "From Weakness to Strength: The Political Roots of Security Sector Reform in Bosnia and Herzegovina." *International Peacekeeping* 21 (2): 149–164.

BIBLIOGRAPHY

Beshara, Adel. 2013. *Lebanon: the Politics of Frustration – The Failed Coup of 1961*. London: Routledge.

Bieber, Florian. 2007. "The Role of the Yugoslav People's Army in the Dissolution of Yugoslavia: The Army without a State." In *State Collapse in South-Eastern Europe: New Perspectives on Yugoslavia's Disintegration*, by Lenard J. Cohen and Jasna Dragovic-Soso, 301–332. Purdue University Press.

2004. *Bosnia and Herzegovina - State Level Sigma Public Management Profiles*. OECD Publishing.https://www.oecd-ilibrary.org/governance/bosnia-and-herzegovina-state-level_5kmk17zq70r8-en; jsessionid=osANqlzlC-g4X2fv8ofueZra.ip-10-240-5-119.

2010. *Bosnia and Herzegovina: Floods*. International Federation of Red Cross and Red Crescent Societies. https://www.ifrc.org/docs/appeals/10/MDRBA006do.pdf.

2002. *Bosnia and Herzegovina: From Aid Dependency to Fiscal Self-Reliance, A Public Expenditure and Institutional Review*. World Bank. https://documents1.worldbank.org/curated/en/105351468198847162/pdf/multiopage.pdf.

1997. *Bosnia and Herzegovina: Public Expenditure Review*. World Bank. https://documents1.worldbank.org/curated/en/708641468743174371/text/multi-page.txt.

2008. *Bosnia and the European Union Military Force (EUFOR): Post-NATO Peacekeeping*. Congressional Research Service. https://www.everycrsreport.com/files/20080115_RS21774_698f21fa4b2b252e1e95db6fc83a8f4ccobaaacd.pdf.

Bougarel, Xavier. 2006. "The Shadow of Heroes: Former Combatants in post-war Bosnia-Herzegovina." *Internatioanl Social Science Journal* 58 (189): 479–490.

Boyne, Sean. 1995. "Lebanon Rebuilds its Army." *Jane's Intelligence Review* 7 (3): 122–125.

Bremer, Paul. 2006. *My Year in Iraq: The Struggle to Build a Future of Hope*. New York: Simon and Schuster.

Brew, Gregory. 2015. "Our Most Dependable Allies: Iraq, Saudi Arabia, and the Eisenhower Doctrine, 1956–1958." *Mediterranean Quarterly* 26 (4): 89–109.

Broder, John M., and Douglas Jehl. 1990. "Iraqi Army: World's 5th Largest but Full of Vital Weaknesses." *Los Angeles Times*, August 13. https://t.ly/ebyh.

2020. *BTI 2020 Country Report: Burundi*. Bertelsmann Stiftung's Transformation Index. https://www.bti-project.org/content/en/downloads/reports/country_report_2020_BDI.pdf.

Burk, James. 2002. "Theories of Democratic Civil-Military Relations." *Armed Forces and Society* 29 (1): 7–29.

2016. *Burundi Crisis Year One*. Armed Conflict Location and Event Data Project 2016.

2017. *Burundi on the Brink: Looking Back on Two Years of Terror*. International Federation of Human Rights. https://www.fidh.org/IMG/pdf/burundi_jointreport_june2017_eng_final.pdf.

2016. *Burundi: Abductions, Killings, Spread Fear*. Human Rights Watch. https://www.refworld.org/docid/56ceac814.html.

2017. *Burundi: The Army in Crisis*. International Crisis Group. https://www.crisisgroup.org/africa/central-africa/burundi/247-burundi-army-crisis.

2009. *Burundi: To Integrate the FNL Successfully.* International Crisis Group. https://www.crisisgroup.org/africa/central-africa/burundi/burundi-integrate-fnl-successfully.

1995. *Burundi: Targeting Students, Teachers and Clerics in the Fight for Supremacy.* Amnesty International. https://www.amnesty.org/download/Documents/176000/afr160141995en.pdf.

Busterud, Ingrid Olstad. 2015. "Defense Sector Reform in the Western Balkans, - Different Approaches and Different Tools." *European Security* 24 (2): 335–352.

Chandrasekaran, Rajiv. 2003. "Iraq Arms Civilians as Second Line of Defense Against U.S." *The Washington Post*, February 5. https://www.washingtonpost.com/archive/politics/2003/02/05/iraq-arms-civilians-as-second-line-of-defense-against-us/49970c19-5d7a-4ab3-968f-5bac3dc95e04/.

Chretien, Jean-Pierre. 2003. *The Great Lakes of Africa.* New York: Zone Books.

CNN. 2007. "Shadowy Iraq Office Accused of Sectarian Agenda." May 1. https://edition.cnn.com/2007/WORLD/meast/05/01/iraq.office/.

Cordesman, Anthony. 1993. *After the Storm: The Changing Military Balance in the Middle East.* Boulder: Westview Press.

Cordesman, Anthony. 2006. *Iraq Force Development and the Challenge of Civil War.* Center for Strategic and International Studies. https://www.comw.org/warreport/fulltext/0611cordesman.pdf.

Cornwell, Richard, and Hannelie de Beer. 1999. "Burundi: The Politics of Intolerance." *Africa Watch* 8 (6): 84–94.

2018. *Country Report on Human Rights Practices 2018 – Burundi.* US Department of State, document no. 2004140. https://www.ecoi.net/en/document/2004140.html.

Daley, Patricia. 2007. "The Burundi Peace Negotiations: An African Experience of Peace-Making." *Review of African Political Economy* 34 (112): 333–352.

de Taisne, Maxime. 2015. *Resilience of the Lebanese Armed Forces.* MENAS Analysis.

Dean, Robert W. 1976. "Civil-Military Relations in Yugoslavia." *Armed Forces and Society* 3 (1): 17–58.

Deroc, M. 1985. "The Former Yugoslav Army." *East European Quarterly* 19 (3): 363–374.

2019. *"Disarmament, Demobilization and Reintegration: Compendium of Project 2010–2017,".* International Organization for Migration. https://publications.iom.int/system/files/pdf/ddr_compendium.pdf.

Dobbins, James, Seith G. Jones, Benjamin Runkle, and Siddharth Mohandas. 2009. *Occupying Iraq: A History of the Coalition Provisional Authority.* Santa Monica: RAND Corporation. https://www.rand.org/content/dam/rand/pubs/monographs/2009/RAND_MG847.pdf.

Dodge, Toby. 2013. *Iraq: From War to New Authoritarianism.* London: Routledge.

Dodge, Toby, and Becca Wasser. 2014. "The Crisis of the Iraqi State." *Adelphi Series* 54 (447–448): 13–38.

Donabed, Sargon. 2012. "Rethinking Nationalism and an Appellative Conundrum: Historiography and Politics in Iraq." *National Identities* 14 (4): 115–138.

Druzin, Heath. 2014. *Retraining Iraq's Fractured Army: Will it Work this Time?* Stars and Stripes. https://www.stripes.com/news/middle-east/retraining-iraq-s-fractured-army-will-it-work-this-time-1.302407.

Dudley, Danijela. 2016. "Civil-Military Relations in Bosnia and Herzegovina: State Legitimacy and Defense Institutions." *Armed Forces and Society* 42 (1): 119–144.

Duelfer, Charles. 2004. "Comprehensive Report of the Special Adviser to the DCI on Iraq's WMD."

Dulic, Timoslav, and Roland Kustic. 2010. "Yugoslavs in Arms: Guerrilla Tradition, Total Defense and Ethnic Security Dilemma." *Europe-Asia Studies* 62 (7): 1051–1072.

Dury-Agri, Jessa Rose, Omer Kassim, and Patrick Martin. 2017. *Iraqi Security Forces and Popular Mobilization Forces Orders of Battle,*. Institute for the Study of War. http://www.understandingwar.org/sites/default/files/Iraq%20-%20ISF%20PMF%20Orders%20of%20Battle_0_0.pdf.

DW. 2017. "aj-Jaish al-Lubnāni Yabda' 'Amaliyat Fajr al-Jurūd dud Dā'esh" [The Lebanese Army Begins its Operations Against Daesh]." August 19.

Edmonds, Martin, Mills Greg, and Terence McNamee. 2009. "Disarmament, Demobilization, and Reintegration and Local Ownership in the Great Lakes: The Experience of Rwanda, Burundi, and the Democratic Republic of Congo." *African Security* 2 (1): 29–58.

el-Ghobashy, Tamer, and Mustafa Salim. 2019. "As Iraq's Shiite Militias Expand Their Reach, Concerns About an ISIS Revival Grow." *Washington Post,* January 19. https://t.ly/KEnZ.

2020. *Explainer: 10 Things Burundi's New Government can do to Improve Human Rights.* Amnesty International. https://www.amnesty.org/en/latest/news/2020/08/explainer-10-things-burundis-new-government-can-do-to-improve-human-rights/.

n.d. *Fact Sheet: US-Lebanon Military Assistance and Defense Cooperation.* https://lb.usembassy.gov/fact-sheet-u-s-lebanon-military-assistance-and-defense-cooperation/.

Feaver, Peter D. 1999. "Civil-Military Relations." *Annual Review of Political Science* 2: 211–241.

Fitzgerald, Peter. 2001. "The Armed Forces in Bosnia and Herzegovina." *SFOR Informer.* https://www.nato.int/sfor/indexinf/127/p03a/chapter4.htm.

France 24. 2015. "Burundi Army Chief Escapes Assassination Attempt." September 11. https://www.france24.com/en/20150911-burundi-army-chief-assassination-attempt-attack-niyongabo.

Friedman, Francine. 2004. *Bosnia and Herzegovina: A Polity on the Brink.* London: Routledge.

Garamone, Jim. 2018. *Coalition Trainers in Iraq Helping Make a Good Force Better.* Department of Defese. https://www.defense.gov/Explore/News/Article/Article/1528637/coalition-trainers-in-iraq-helping-make-a-good-force-better/.

Gaston, Eric, and Andras Derzsi-Horvath. 2018. *Iraq After ISIL: Sub-State Actors, Local Forces, and the Micro-Politics of Control.* Berlin: Global Public Policy Institute. https://reliefweb.int/sites/reliefweb.int/files/resources/Gaston_Derzsi-Horvath_2018_Iraq_After_ISIL.pdf.

Gaston, Erica, and András Derzsi-Horváth. 2008. *Iraq After ISIL: Sub-State Actors, Local Forces, and the Micro-Politics of Control.* Global Public Policy Institute. https://www.gppi.net/media/Gaston_Derzsi-Horvath_Iraq_After_ISIL.pdf.

Gaub, Florence. 2016. *An Unhappy Marriage: Civil-Military Relations in Post-Saddam Iraq.* Carnegie Endowment for International Peace. https://carnegieendowment.org/2016/01/13/unhappy-marriage-civil-military-relations-in-post-saddam-iraq-pub-61955.

Gaub, Florence. 2011. *Building a New Military? The NATO Training Mission – Iraq.* NATO Defense College. https://www.files.ethz.ch/isn/128709/rp_67.pdf.

Gaub, Florence. 2010. *Military Integration after Civil Wars: Multiethnic Armies, Identity and Post-Conflict Reconstruction.* London: Routledge.

Gaub, Florence. 2007. "Multi-Ethnic Armies in the Aftermath of Civil War: Lessons Learned from Lebanon." *Defence Studies* 7 (1): 5–20.

Gaub, Florence. 2011. *Rebuilding Armed Forces Learning from Iraq and Lebanon.* Strategic Studies Institute. https://www.globalsecurity.org/military/library/report/2011/ssi_gaub.pdf.

Geisser, Vincent. 2017. "The People Want the Army": Is the Lebanese Military an Exception to the Crisis of the State?" In *Lebanon Facing the Arab Uprisings: Constraints and Adaptation,* by Rosita Di Peri and Daniel Meier, 93–113. London: Palgrave Macmillan.

Gleichmann, Colin, Michael Odenwald, Kees Steenken, and Adrian Wilkinson. 2004. *Disarmament, Demobilization and Reintegration: A Practical Field and Classroom Guide.* Frankfurt: Druckerei Hassmüller Graphische Betriebe GmbH & Co. KG. https://www.cimic-coe.org/resources/handbooks/ddr-handbook-eng.pdf.

Gordon, Michael. 2006. "Bush Adviser"s Memo Cites Doubts about Iraqi Leader." *The New York Times,* November 29.

Gow, James, and Ivan Zverzhanovski. 2013. *Security, Democracy and War Crimes: Security Sector Transformation in Serbia.* London: Palgrave Macmillan.

Hackett, James. 2008. *The Military Balance 2008.* London: International Institute for Strategic Studies.

Haddad, George M. 1971. *Revolutions and Military Rule in the Middle East: The Arab States.* New York: Robert Speller and Sons.

Hadzic, Miroslav. 2002. *The Yugoslav People's Agony: The Role of the Yugoslav People's Army.* Farnham: Ashgate Publishing.

Hadzovic, Denis. 2009. *The Office of the High Representative and Security Sector Reform in Bosnia and Herzegovina*. Centre for Security Studies - BH. http://www.css.ba/wp-content/uploads/2011/06/images_docs_ar.pdf.

Hadzovic, Denis, and Mirela Hodvic. 2013. *Draft Report on the Parliamentary Oversight of the Security Sector for BiH for 2012*. Centre for Security Studies. http://css.ba/wp-content/uploads/2011/06/images_docs2_nacrt%20izvjestaaja%20english.pdf.

Hajayandi, Patrick. 2019. *Wounded Memories: Perceptions of Past Violence in Burundi and Perspectives for Reconciliation*. The Institute for Justice and Reconciliation. https://media.africaportal.org/documents/IJR-Burundi_Wounded-memories-WEB.pdf.

Hammes, T.X. 2016. *Raising and Mentoring Security Forces in Iraq and Afghanistan*. Vol. 60, in *Lessons Encountered: Learning from the Long War*, by Richard D. Hooker Jr. and Joseph J. Collins, 277–344. Washington D.C.: National Defense University Press.

Hanf, Theodor. 1995. "Ethnurgy: On the Analytical Use and Normative Abuse of the Concept of 'Ethnic Identity'." In *Nationalism, Ethnicity and Cultural Identity in Europe*, by Kebbet von Benda-Beckmann and Maykel Verkuyten, 41–51. Utrecht: European Research Centre on Migration and Ethnic Studies.

Hartzell, Caroline A. 1999. "Explaining the Stability of Intrastate Wars." *Journal of Conflict Resolution* 43 (1): 3–22.

Hartzell, Caroline A. 2014. "Mixed Motives? Explaining the Decision to Integrate Militaries at Civil War's End." In *New Armies from Old: Merging Competing Military Forces After Civil Wars*, by Roy Licklider, 13–27. Washington D.C: Georgetown University Press.

Hartzell, Caroline A., and Matthew Hoddie. 2007. *Crafting Peace: Power-Sharing Institutions and the Negotiated Settlement of Civil Wars*. Pennsylvania: Pennsylvania State University Press.

Hartzell, Caroline A., and Matthew Hoddie. 2015. "The Art of the Possible: Power Sharing and Post-Civil War." *World Politics* 67 (1): 37–71.

Hartzell, Carloine A., and Matthew Hoddie. 2015. "Institutionalizing Peace: Power Sharing and Post-Civil War Conflict Management," *American Journal of Political Science* 47 (2): 318–332.

Hashim, Ahmed S. 2006. *Insurgency and CounterInsurgency in Iraq*. Ithaca: Cornell University Press.

Hashim, Ahmed S. 2003. "Military Power and State Formation In Modern Iraq." *Middle East Policy Council*. https://mepc.org/journal/military-power-and-state-formation-modern-iraq.

Hashim, Ahmed. 2003. "Saddam Husayn and Civil-Military Relations in Iraq: The Quest for Legitimacy and Power." *The Middle East Journal* 57 (1): 9–41.

Heller, Mark. 1977. "Politics and the Military in Iraq and Jordan, 1921–1958: The British Influence." *Armed Forces and Society* 14 (1): 75–99.

Herd, Graeme P., and Tom Tracy. 2006. "Democratic Civil-Military Relations in Bosnia and Herzegovina: A New Paradigm for Protectorates?" *Armed Forces and Society* 32 (4): 549–565.

Herd, Graeme P., and Tom Tracy. 2006. "Democratic Civil-Military Relations in Bosnia and Herzegovina: A New Paradigm of Protectorates?" *Armed Forces and Society* 32 (4): 549–565.

Hoddie, Matthew, and Caroline A. Hartzell. 2003. "Civil War Settlements and the Implementation of Military Power-Sharing Arrangements." *Journal of Peace Research* 40 (3): 303–320.

Hopkins, Keith. 1966. "Civil-Military Relations in Developing Countries." *The British Journal of Sociology* 17 (2): 165–182.

Horowitz, Donald L. 1985. *Ethnic Groups in Conflict*. Los Angeles: University of California Press.

Hosmer, Stephen T. 2007. *Why the Iraqi Resistance to the Coalition Invasion was so Weak*. Santa Monica: RAND Corporation.

Huggins, William D. 1994. "The Republican Guards and Saddam Husein's Transformation of the Iraqi Army,." *The Arab Studies Journal* 2 (1): 31–35.

Huntington, Samuel P. 1957. *The Soldier and the State: The Theory and Politics of Civil-Military Relations*. Harvard: The Belknap Press of Harvard University Press.

2016. *Iraq: Fallujah Abuses Inquiry Mired in Secrecy*. Human Rights Watch. https://www.hrw.org/news/2016/07/07/iraq-fallujah-abuses-inquiry-mired-secrecy.

2018. *Iraq: Intelligence Agency Admits Holding Hundreds Despite Previous Denials*. Human Rights Watch. https://www.hrw.org/news/2018/07/22/iraq-intelligence-agency-admits-holding-hundreds-despite-previous-denials.

2017. *Iraq: Investigate Abuses in Hawija Operation*. Human Rights Watch. https://www.hrw.org/news/2017/09/28/iraq-investigate-abuses-hawija-operation.

2019. *Iraq: The Protest Movement and Treatment of Protesters and Activists*. European Asylum Support Office EUSO. https://www.easo.europa.eu/sites/default/files/publications/10_2020_EASO_COI_Report_Iraq_The_protest_movement_and_treatment_of_protesters.pdf.

2018. *Iraq's Paramilitary Groups: The Challenge of Rebuilding a Functioning State*. International Crisis Group.

1999. *Is Dayton Failing?: Bosnia Four Years After the Peace Agreement*. International Crisis Group.

Jabar, Faleh A. 2003. "The Iraqi Army and Anti-Army: Some Reflections on the Role of the Military." *The Adelphi Papers* 43 (354): 115–130.

Jackson, Tony. 2000. *Equal Access to Education: A Peace Imperative for Burundi*. International Alert. https://www.international-alert.org/sites/default/files/publications/equal_access_to_education.pdf.

Janowitz, Morris. 1981. "Introduction." In *Civil-Military Relations: Regional Perspectives*, by Morris Janowitz, 9–25. California: Sage Publications.

Janowitz, Morris. 1964. *The Professional Soldier.* New York: The Free Press.

Jarstad, Anna K., and Desiree Nilsson. 2008. "From Words to Deeds: The Implementation of Power-Sharing Pacts in Peace Accords." *Conflict Management and Peace Science* 25 (3): 206–223.

Jeffrey, Alex. 2006. "Building State Capacity in Post-Conflict Bosnia and Herzegovina: The Case of Brcko District." *Political Geography* 25 (2): 203–227.

Johnson, Constance. 2017. *Burundi: Constitutional Referendum Planned.* Global Legal Monitor. https://www.loc.gov/law/foreign-news/article/burundi-constitutional-referendum-planned/.

Jones, James L. 2007. "The Report of the Independent Commission on the Security Forces of Iraq." https://www.files.ethz.ch/isn/129488/2007_09_The_report_of_the_Independent.pdf.

Jones, Seth G., Jeremy M. Wilson, Andrew Rathmell, and K. Jack Riley. 2005. *Establishing Law and Order After Conflict.* Santa Monica: RAND Corporation.

Jorgic, Drazen. 2015. "Gunmen in Uniform Kill Ally of Burundi President Nkurunziza." *Reuters*, August 2. https://www.reuters.com/article/us-burundi-attacks-idUSKCN0Q70AL20150802.

Journal, The Army. n.d. *The Army Journal.* https://www.lebarmy.gov.lb/ar/content/.

Judah, Tim. 2019. *Bosnai Powerless to Halt Demographic Decline.* Balkan Insight. https://balkaninsight.com/2019/11/21/bosnia-powerless-to-halt-demographic-decline/.

Jukic, Elvira M. 2014. "Bosnia Deploys Army to Rescue Flood Victims." *Balkan Insight*, May 15. https://balkaninsight.com/2014/05/15/hundreds-need-evacuation-from-floods-in-bosnia/.

Kaisi, Anwār. 2016. "al-Farīk ar-Rokn Abdul Ghani al-Asadi: at-Tansiq maʿ al-hashd ash-Shaʿbi wasala ila 'Auj 'Athmatihi" [Lieutenant General Abdul Ghani al-Asadi: Cooperation with the Popular Mobilization Forces Reached its Peak]." *al-Mustaqbal al-Iraqi*, October 3. http://almustakbalpaper.net/content.php?id=23048.

Kanso, Wafik. 2007. "Taʿdīl ʿAkidat aj-Jaish Khark li-Wathikat al-Wifāk al-Watani," [Amending the Military Doctrine is a Breach to the Pact of National Reconciliation]." *al-Akhbar*, October 20. https://al-akhbar.com/Archive_Local_News/182600.

Kara, Sohpie. 2017. Lebanon: The Limits of Controlling a National Army in a Sectarian State. In: A. Croissant & D. Kuehn, eds. *Reforming Civil-Military Relations in New Democracies: Democratic Control and Military Effectiveness in Comparative Perspectives.* Gewerbestrasse: Springer, pp. 193–212.

Kechichian, Joseph A. 2008. *A Strong Army for a Stable Lebanon.* Middle East Institute. https://www.mei.edu/publications/strong-army-stable-lebanon.

Kechichian, Joseph A. 1985. "The Lebanese Army: Capabilities and Challenges in the 1980s." *Conflict Quarterly* 5 (1): 15–39.

Kedmey, Dan. 2013. "Iraq is "Run by al-Qaeda": Appalling Carnage Shows Terror Group's Resurgence." *Time*, October 14. http://world.time.com/2013/10/14/this-is-qaedacountry-blasts-and-prison-breakserode-iraqi-sovereignty/.

Khaddouri, Majid. 1960. *Independent Iraqi: A Study in Iraqi Politics Since 1932*. London: Royal Institute of International Affairs.

Khaddouri, Majid. 1948. "The Coup d'État of 1936: A Study in Iraqi Politics." *The Middle East Journal* 2 (3): 270–292.

Kienle, Frederick. 2007. *Creating an Iraqi Army from Scratch: Lessons for the Future*. National Security Outlook. https://www.aei.org/wp-content/uploads/2011/10/20070525_200705NSOg.pdf.

King, Jeremy. 2002. *An Unprecedented Experiment: Security Sector Reform in Bosnia and Herzegovina*. London: Saferworld.

Kingma, Kees. 2001. *Demobilisation and Reintegration of Ex-combatants in Post-war and Transition Countries*. Eschborn: Deutsche Gesellschaft für Technische Zusammenarbeit.

Knight, Andy. 2010. „Linking DDR and SSR in post-conflict Peacebuilding in Africa: An Overview." *African Journal of Political Science and International Relations* 4 (1): 29–54.

Knights, Michael. 2019. *Helping Iraq Take Charge of its Command-and-Control Structure*. The Washington Institute. https://www.washingtoninstitute.org/policy-analysis/view/helping-iraq-take-charge-of-its-command-and-control-structure.

Knudsen, Are, and Tine Gade. 2017. "The Lebanese Armed Forces (LAF): A United Army for a Divided Country?" In *Civil-Military Relations in Lebanon: Conflict, Cohesion and Confessionalism in a Divided Society*, by Are Knudsen and Tine Gade, 1–22. London: Palgrave Macmillan.

Kortam, Marie. 2016. *aj-Jaish wal-Mujtamaʿ: Sharʿiyat aj-Jaish al-Lubnāni fi Daulat wa-Mujtamaʿ al-Tawaʾef* [The army and Society: The Legitimacy of the Lebanese Army in the State and Society of Religious Communities]. Civil Society Knowledge Centre - Lebanon Support.

Krueger, Robert, and Kathleen Tobin Krueger. 2007. *From Bloodshed to Hope in Burundi: Our Embassy Years during Genocide*. Texas: University of Texas Press.

Lakic, Mladen. 2018. "Bosnian Minister Floats Hopes of Progress Towards NATO." *Balkan Insights*, November 14. https://balkaninsight.com/2018/11/14/bosnia-s-fragile-hope-to-activate-map-for-nato-11-13-2018/.

Lamb, Christopher J., Sarah Arkin, and Sally Scudder. 2014. *The Bosnian Train and Equip Program: A Lesson in Interagency Integration of Hard and Soft Power*. Institute for National Strategic Studies.

Lavender, Linda. 2013. *The Re-Awakening of Anbar*. Civil-Military Fusion Centre. https://reliefweb.int/sites/reliefweb.int/files/resources/Anbar_Province_Final%20(1).pdf.

n.d. *Lebanese Armed Forces*. Global Security. https://www.globalsecurity.org/military/world/lebanon/command-structure.htm.

2019. *Lebanese Army Launches Code of Conduct on Human Rights.* January 29. https://unscol.unmissions.org/lebanese-army-launches-code-conduct-human-rights.

2019. *Lebanon: Events in the Year 2018.* Human Rights Watch. https://www.hrw.org/ar/world-report/2019/country-chapters/325424.

Lemarchand, Rene. 1994. *Burundi: Ethnic Conflict and Genocide.* Cambridge: Cambridge University Press.

Lemarchand, Rene. 2007. "Consociationalism and Power Sharing in Africa: Rwanda, Burundi, and the Democratic Republic of the Congo." *African Affairs* 106 (422): 1–20.

Lemarchand, Rene. 1970. *Rwanda and Burundi.* New York: Praeger Publishers.

Lemarchand, Rene. 2008. *The Burundi Killings of 1992.* Mass Violence and Resistance – Research Network. https://www.sciencespo.fr/mass-violence-war-massacre-resistance/en/document/burundi-killings-1972.html.

Lightburn, David. 1998. "NATO Security Cooperation Activities with Bosnia and Herzegovina." *NATO Review.*

Lijphart, Arend. 1977. *Democracy in Plural Societies: A Comparative Exploration.* New Haven: Yale University Press.

Lijphart, Arend. 1977. "Majority Rule Versus Democracy in Deeply Divided Societies." *Politikon: South African Journal of Political Studies* 4 (2): 113–126.

Lijphart, Arend. 1974. *The Politics of Accommodation: Pluralism and Democracy in the Netherlands.* California: University of California.

Longrigg, Stephen Hemsley. 1953. *Iraq, 1900 to 1950: A Political, Social, and Economic History.* Oxford: Oxford University Press.

2010. *Loose Ends: Iraq's Security Forces Between U.S. Drawdown and Withdrawal.* International Crisis Group. Accessed July 12, 2020. https://t.ly/LSdD.

Los Angeles Times. 2008. "Baghdad's Misguided Crackdown on the Sons of Iraq." August 26. https://www.latimes.com/world/middleeast/la-oe-brimley26-2008aug26-story.html.

Luras, Helge. 2014. "Democratic Oversight in Fragile States: The Case of Intelligence Reform in Bosnia and Herzegovina." *Intelligence and National Security* 29 (4): 600–618.

Mansour, Renad. 2020. *The Popularity of the Hashd in Iraq.* Carnegie Middle East Center. https://carnegie-mec.org/diwan/62638?lang=en/.

Mansour, Renad. 2018. "More than Militias: Iraq's Popular Mobilization Forces are Here to Stay." *War on the Rocks*, April 3. https://warontherocks.com/2018/04/more-than-militias-iraqs-popular-mobilization-forces-are-here-to-stay/.

Mansour, Renad, and Faleh A. Jabar. 2017. *The Popular Mobilization Forces and Iraq's Future.* Carnegie Middle East Center. https://carnegie-mec.org/2017/04/28/popular-mobilization-forces-and-iraq-s-future-pub-68810.

McCulloch, Allison. 2014. "Consociational Settlements in Deeply Divided Societies: The Liberal-Corporate Distinction." *Democratization* 21 (3): 501–518.

McEvoy, Joanne. 2014. "The Role of External Actors in Incentivizing Post-Conflict Power-Sharing." *Government and Opposition* 49 (1): 47–69.

McGarry, John, and Brendan O'Leary. 2006. "Consociational Theory, Northern Ireland's Conflict and its Agreement. Part 1: What Consociationalists can Learn from Northern Ireland." *Government and Opposition* 41 (1): 43–63.

McGarry, John, and Brendan O'Leary. 2007. "Iraq's Constitution of 2005: Liberal Consociation as Political Prescription." *International Journal of Constitutional Law* 5 (4): 670–698.

McGarry, John, and Brendan O'Leary. 1999. *Policing Northern Ireland: Proposals for a New Start*. Belfast: The Blackstaff Press.

2006. *Measuring Stability and Security in Iraq, Quarterly Report to Congress.* Department of Defense. https://images.derstandard.at/2008/10/01/Measuring%20Stability%20and%20Security%20in%20Iraq.pdf.

Messara, Antoine Nasri. 2003. *La Gouvernance d'un Système Consensuel: Le Liban après les Amendements Constitutionnels de 1990*. Beirut: Librarie Orientale.

Michaels, Jim. 2009. "Chain of command concerns raised in Iraq." *USA Today*, Feburary 23. http://usatoday30.usatoday.com/news/world/iraq/2009-02-23-maliki_N.htm.

Moore, Molly. 2003. "A Foe That Collapsed from Within." *The Washington Post*, July 20.

Moussa, Nayla. 2016. *Loyalties and Group Formation in the Lebanese Officer Corps*. Carnegie Middle East Center. https://carnegieendowment.org/files/ACMR_Moussa.pdf.

Muggah, Robert. 2004. "The Anatomy of Disarmament, Demobilisation and Reintegration in the Republic of Congo." *Conflict, Security and Development* 4 (1): 21–37.

Muggah, Robert, and Chris ", 4, no. 1 (2015): 4 O'Donnell. 2015. "Next Generation Disarmament, Demobilization and Reintegration." *International Journal of Security and Development* 4 (1): 1–12.

Nantulya, Paul. 2020. *Post-Nkurunziza Burundi: The Rise of the Generals*. Africa Center for Strategic Studies. https://africacenter.org/spotlight/post-nkurunziza-burundi-the-rise-of-the-generals/.

2019. *NATO and Bosnia and Herzegovina Sign Agreement on Protection of Classified Information*. NATO.

Nerguizian, Aram. 2015. "Between Sectarianism and Military Development: The Paradox of the Lebanese Armed Forces." In *The Politics of Sectarianism in Postwar Lebanon*, by Bassel F. Sallouk, 108–135. London: Pluto Press.

Nerguizian, Aram. 2011. *Lebanese Civil Military Dynamics Weathering Regional Storm*. Carnegie Endowment for International Peace. https://carnegieendowment.org/sada/46038.

Nerguizian, Aram. 2017. *The Lebanese Armed Forces, Hezbollah and Military Legitimacy*. Center for Strategic and International Studies.

Nettelfield, Lara J. 2010. "From the Battlefield to the Barracks: The ICTY and the Armed Forces of Bosnia and Herzegovina." *International Journal of Transitional Justice* 4 (1): 87–109.

Nettlefield, Lara J. 2010. "From Battlefield to the Barracks: The ICTY and the Armed Forces of Bosnia and Herzegovina." *International Journal of Transitional Justice* 4 (1): 87–109.

Nielsen, Suzanne C. 2005. "Civil-Military Relations Theory and Military Effectiveness." *Public Administration and Management* 10 (2): 61–84.

Nkurunziza, Janvier, and Floribert Ngaruko. 2004. *"Explaining Growth in Burundi: 1960–2000.* Centre for the Study of African Economies.

Nouredin, Saateh. 2020. "'An ath-Thaurah wa-Maujatuha ath-Thāniyah [On the Revolution and its Second Wave]." *al-Modon*, January 20.

Ntibazonkiza, Raphael. 1993. *Au Royaume des Seigneurs de la Lance : Une Approche Historique de la Question Ethnique au Burundi*. Brussels: Bruxelles droits de l'homme.

Nzohabona, Gerard. 2015. "Burundi Military: 31 Suspected Rebels Killed in Fighting." *Associated Press*, July 13. https://apnews.com/article/3b43504f76aa49f29c484 ac9c0a1dbfd.

Owens, Mackubin Thomas. 2008. "Scholar and Gentleman, Sam Huntington, R.I.P." *National Review*, December 29. https://www.nationalreview.com/2008/12/scholar-gentleman-mackubin-thomas-owens/.

Parasiliti, Andrew. 2001. "Lessons Learned: The Iraqi Military in Politics." In *Iran, Iraq, and the Arab Gulf States*, by Joseph Kechichian, 83–94. New York: Palgrave Macmillan.

Parker, Ned, Isabel Coles, and Raheem, Salman. 2014. "Special Report: How Mosul fell - An Iraqi General Disputes Baghdad's Story." *Reuters*, October 14. https://www.reuters.com/article/us-mideast-crisis-gharawi-special-report/special-report-how-mosul-fell-an-iraqi-general-disputes-baghdads-story-idUSKCN0I30Z820141014.

Partlow, Joshua. 2007. "Maliki's Office Is Seen Behind Purge in Forces." *Washington Post*, April 30. https://www.washingtonpost.com/wp-dyn/content/article/2007/04/29/AR2007042901728_pf.html.

Perito, Robert. 2008. *Iraq's Interior Ministry: Frustrating Reform*. USIPeace Briefing. https://www.usip.org/sites/default/files/PB-Iraq-Interior-5-08.PDF.

Peter D. Feaver, "Civil-Military Relations," Annual Review of Political Science 2, n.d.

Pfiffner, James P. 2010. "US Blunders in Iraq: Debaathification and Disbanding the Army." *Intelligence and National Security* 25 (1): 76–85.

Pietz, Tobias. 2004. "Demobilization and Reintegration of Former Soldiers in Post-War Bosnia and Herzegovina: An Assessment of External Assistance." http://edoc.vifapol.de/opus/volltexte/2008/547/pdf/hb135.pdf.

Piombo, Jessica. 2010. "Peacemaking in Burundi: Conflict Resolution versus Conflict Management Strategies." *African Security* 3 (4): 239–272.

Pollack, Kenneth M. 2015. *Iraq's Mr. Abadi comes to Washington.* Brookings. https://www.brookings.edu/blog/markaz/2015/04/13/iraqs-mr-abadi-comes-to-washington/.

2006. "PSC Demands Total Peace Deal in Burundi." June 29. https://reliefweb.int/report/burundi/psc-demands-total-peace-deal-burundi.

Purdekova, Andrea. 2015. *Making Ubumwe: Power, State and Camps in Rwanda's Unity-Building Project.* New York: Berghahn Books.

Rached, Kardo, and Ahmed Omar Bali. 2019. "Post-ISIS and the Shia Armed Groups." *Central European Journal of International & Security Studies* 13 (1): 122–137.

Raffoul, Alexandre W. 2020. "The Politics of Association: Power Sharing and the De-Politicization of Ethnicity in Post-War Burundi." *Ethnopolitics* 19 (1): 1–18.

Rafizadeh, Majid. 2016. "In First, Hezbollah Confirms all Financial Support Comes from Iran." *al-Arabiya*, June 25. https://english.alarabiya.net/features/2016/06/25/In-first-Hezbollah-s-Nasrallah-confirms-all-financial-support-comes-from-Iran.

Rathmell, Andrew Oliker, Olga, Terrence K. Kelly, David Brannan, and Keith Crane. 2005. *Developing Iraq's Security Sector: The Coalition Provisional Authority's Experience.* Santa Monica: RAND Coporation. https://www.rand.org/content/dam/rand/pubs/monographs/2005/RAND_MG365.pdf.

Rayburn, Joy. 2014. *Iraq After America: Strongmen, Sectarians, Resistance.* Stanford: Hoover Institution Press.

Region Week. 2019. "Burundi MPs Debate on the Re-Organization of the National Intelligence Body." May 29. https://regionweek.com/burundi-mps-debate-on-the-re-organization-of-the-national-intelligence-body/.

2000. *Regroupment Camps in Burundi Condemned: Tens of Thousands of Civilians Still Held in Squalid Conditions.* Human Rights Watch. https://reliefweb.int/report/burundi/regroupment-camps-burundi-condemned-tens-thousands-civilians-still-held-squalid.

2016. *Repression and Genocidal Dynamics in Burundi.* International Federation for Human Rights. https://www.fidh.org/IMG/pdf/burundi_report_english-2.pdf.

Reuters. 2019. "Bosnia Faces Outflow of Military Personnel Over Low Wages." October 29. https://www.reuters.com/article/us-bosnia-army-outflow/bosnia-faces-outflow-of-military-personnel-over-low-wages-parliamentary-commissioner-idUSKBN1X826J.

Reuters. 2016. "Burundi President Condemns Killing of General Amid Rising Violence." April 26. http://mobile.reuters.com/article/idUSKCN0XN0FA.

Reuters. 2016. "Burundi Rebel Group Says Behind Killing of Senior Army Officer." March 26. https://www.reuters.com/article/us-burundi-security-idUSKCN0WS0GB.

Reuters. 2016. "Iraqi Parliament Passes Contested Law on Shi'ite Paramilitaries." November 26. https://www.reuters.com/article/us-mideast-crisis-iraq-military-idUSKBN13L0IE.

Reuters. 2018. "Iraq's Shi'ite Militias Formally Inducted Into Security Forces." March 8. https://www.reuters.com/article/us-mideast-crisis-iraq-militias-idUSKC N1GK354.

Rial, Juan. 2004. *The Question of the Military in Lebanon.* Latin American Security and Defence Network. https://www.resdal.org/ing/assets/Paz_y_Seguridad_01_ing.pdf.

Rihana, Sami. 1984. *Histoire de L'Armée Libanaise Contemporaine: Les Troupes Spéciales du Levant et L'Armée de l'Indépendance 1926–1946.* Vol. I. 11 vols. Beirut: Imprimerie Rahbani.

Riyāshi, Iskandar. 1961. *Ru'asā' Lubnān Kama 'Araftahum [The Lebanese Presidents as I Knew Them].* Beirut: al-Maktab al-Tijāri lil-Tibā'h wat-Tauzī' wal-Nasher.

Roberts, Adam. 1986. *Nations in Arms: The Theory and Practice of Territorial Defence.* New York: St Martin's Press.

Robinson, Linda. 2016. *Assessment of the Politico-Military Campaign to Counter ISIL and Options for Adaptation.* Santa Monica: RAND Corporation.

Rudaw. 2015. "Tashkil Quwa Amniya Jadida li-Mukafaha Irhab fi Baghdad [Forming a New Security Force to Fight Terrorism in Baghdad]." July 5. https://www.rudaw.net /arabic/middleeast/iraq/0507201514.

Rustoom, Asad. 1973. *Lubnan fi 'Ahd al-Mutasarifiyah [Lebanon during the Mutassarifiya].* Beirut: Dar an-Nahar.

Salah Ad-Din As-Sabbagh. 1994. *Fursan al-'Urubah: Muthakkarāt ash-Shahīd Salah ad-Din as-Sabbagh [The Knights of Arabism: The Memoirs of the Martyr Salah Ad-Din As-Sabbagh].* Rabat: Tanit lil Nashr.

Saliba, Amine. 2015. *The Security Sector in Lebanon: Jurisdiction and Organization.* Carnegie Endownment. https://carnegieendowment.org/files/Security_Sector_in _Lebanon2.pdf.

Salibi, Kamal. 1976. *Crossroads to Civil War: Lebanon 1958–1976.* New York: Caravan.

Samii, Cyrus. 2013. "Perils or Promise of Ethnic Integration Evidence from a Hard Case in Burundi." *The American Political Science Review* 107 (3): 558–573.

Schiff, Rebecca L. 1995. "Civil Military Relations Reconsidered: A Theory of Concordance." *Armed Forces and Society* 22 (1): 7–24.

Schiff, Rebecca L. 1996. "Concordance Theory: A Response to Recent Criticism." *Armed Forces and Society* 23 (2): 277–283.

Schiff, Rebecca L. 2009. *The Military and Domestic Politics: A Concordance Theory of Civil-Military Relations.* New York: Routledge.

Schmitt, Eric, and Michael R. Gordon. 2014. "The Iraqi Army Was Crumbling Long Before Its Collapse, U.S. Officials Say." *The New York Times,* June 12. https://www .nytimes.com/2014/06/13/world/middleeast/american-intelligence-officials-said -iraqi-military-had-been-in-decline.html.

Schraml, Carla. 2011. *The Dilemma of Recognition: Experienced Reality of Ethnicised Politics in Rwanda and Burundi.* Marburg: Springer vs.

2010. "Second Generation Disarmament, Demobilization and Reintegration Practices in Peace Operations." United Nations. https://peacekeeping.un.org/sites/default/files/2gddr_eng_with_cover_0.pdf.

Short, Elliot. 2018. "The Orao Affair: The Key to Military Integration in Post-Dayton Bosnia and Herzegovina." *The Journal of Slavic Military Studies* 31 (1): 37–64.

Simon, Reeva. 1986. *Iraq Between the Wars: The Creation and Implementation of a Nationalist Ideology.* New York: Columbia University Press.

Simon, Reeva S. 1986. *Iraq between the Two World Wars: The Creation and Implementation of a Nationalist Ideology.* New York: Columbia University Press.

Slobodan Stankovic. 1980. "Tito and the Army." https://storage.osaarchivum.org/low/2b/11/2b11a530-9551-48e8-a307-b4d2b8d05b3c_l.pdf.

Smith, Crispin. 2021. *Iraq's Legal Responsibility for Militia Attacks on U.S. Forces: Paths Forward.* Just Security. https://www.justsecurity.org/75232/iraqs-legal-responsibility-for-militia-attacks-on-u-s-forces-paths-forward/.

Sorby Jr., Karol R. 2011. "Iraq's First Coup Government (1936–1937)." *Asian and African Studies* 20 (1): 23–45.

Sorby, Karol R. 2010. "The Coup d'état of Bakr Sidqī in Iraq." *Oriental Archive* 78 (1): 35–53.

Spegelj, Martin. 2001. "The First Phase, 1990–1992: The JNA Prepares for Aggression and Croatia for Defense." In *The War in Croatia and Bosnia-Herzegovina, 1991–1995,* by Branka Magas and Ivo Zanic, 14–40. London: Frank Cass.

Stafford, Ronald Sempill. 1935. *The Tragedy of the Assyrians.* London: G. Allen & Unwin.

Stankovic, Slobodan. 1986. *Yugoslav Army Adopts Wait-and-See-Attitude.* RFE Report.

Steenken, Cornelis. 2011. "DDR and SSR Based on UN Integrated DDR Standards Monopoly of Force: The Nexus of DDR and SSR." In *Monopoly of Force: The Nexus of DDR and SSR,* by Melanne A. Civic and Michael Miklaucic, 285–298. Washington D.C: National Defense University Press.

Stojarova, Vera. 2019. "Unifying the Armed Forces of Bosnia and Herzegovina – Mission Competed?" *Vojenské Rozhledy* 28 (4): 71–82.

Sullivan, Marisa. 2013. *Maliki's Authoritarian Regime.* Middle East Security Report.

Sveinsson, Steinar. 2007. *Iraq Podcast.* April 23. https://www.nato.int/docu/speech/2007/s070423c.html.

Tarbush, Mohammad A. 2016. *The Role of the Military in Politics: A Case Study of Iraq to 1941.* New York: Routledge.

2009. *Tārīkh aj-Jaish al-lubnāni: al-Jeze' al-Awal 1920–1945* [*The History of the Lebanese Army: First Part 1920–1945*]. 1st. Yarzeh: Lebanese Army Command – Directorate of Orientation.

BIBLIOGRAPHY

The Daily Star. 2018. "Army Soldier Orders Israelis to Step Back." December 18. https://www.dailystar.com.lb/News/Lebanon-News/2018/Dec-18/472053-army-soldier-orders-israelis-to-step-back.ashx.

n.d. *The Duties of the Army.* https://t.ly/-9f_.

n.d. *The Iraqi Counter Terrorism Service.* Center for Middle East Policy at Brookings. https://www.brookings.edu/wp-content/uploads/2016/06/David-Witty-Paper_Final_Web.pdf.

The New Humanitarian. 2001. "Burundi: IRIN Update on Coup Attempt/Transition Accord." July 24.

2003. *The Path to Partnership for Peace.* Defence Reform Commission. http://richardbainter.com/PDF/Defense_Reform_Commission_2003.pdf.

Tholens, Simone. 2017. "Border Management in an Era of 'Statebuilding lite:' Security Assistance and Lebanon's Hybrid Sovereignty." *International Affairs* 93 (4): 865–882.

Thompson, Mark. 2015. "How Disbanding the Iraqi Army Fueled ISIS." *Time,* May 28. https://time.com/3900753/isis-iraq-syria-army-united-states-military/.

2019. *Timeline: the Rise, Spread, and Fall of the Islamic State.* Wilson Center. https://www.wilsoncenter.org/article/timeline-the-rise-spread-and-fall-the-islamic-state.

2001. *To Protect the People: The Government-Sponsored "Self-Defense" Program in Burundi.* Human Rights Watch. https://www.hrw.org/report/2001/12/14/protect-people/government-sponsored-self-defense-program-burundi.

Turkovic, Bisera. 2005. "Civil-Military Relations in Bosnia and Herzegovina." In *The Evolution of Civil-Military Relations in South East Europe: Continuing Democratic Reform and Adapting to the Needs of Fighting Terrorism,* by Philipp H. Fluri, Gustav E. Gustenau and Plamen I. Pantev, 81–99. Heidelberg: Physica-Verlag.

Uluçakar, Mustafa, and Ali Ali Çağlar. 2017. "An analysis of two Different Models of Civil-Military Relations: The Case of Turkey." *Uluslararası İlişkiler* 14 (55): 41–57.

Uvin, Peter. 2009. *Life After Violence: A People's Story of Burundi.* London: Zed Books in association with International African Institute, Royal African Institute and Social Science Research Council.

Uyar, Mesut. 2013. "Ottoman Arab Officers between Nationalism and Loyalty during the First World War." *War in History* 20 (4): 526–544.

Van Buren, Peter. 2014. "You Too Can Command an Iraqi Division for Only $2 Million." *Reuters,* December 10. http://blogs.reuters.com/great-debate/2014/12/10/you-too-can-com-mand-an-iraqi-army-division-for-only-2-million/.

Van Heuvelen, Ben, and Patrick Osgood. 2013. "Amid Rising Ethnic Tension, Kurdish Brigade Soldiers Stop Taking Orders from Baghdad." *Washington Post,* June 11. https://t.ly/bydQ.

Vandeginste, Stef. 2009. "Power-Sharing, Conflict and Transition in Burundi: Twenty Years of Trial and Error." *Africa Spectrum* 44 (3): 63–86.

Vecernij. 2016. "Rezultati popisa stanovništva: U BiH živi 50,11% Bošnjaka, 15,43% Hrvata te Srba 30,78% [Census results: 50.11% of Bosniaks, 15.43% of Croats and 30.78% of Serbs live in BiH]." June 30. https://www.vecernji.hr/vijesti/cekalo-se-25-godine-na-objavu-rezultata-popisa-stanovnistva-u-bih-ovo-su-prvi-sluzbeni-podaci-nakon-25-godina-1095916.

Vircoulon, Thierry. 2015. *Insights from the Burundian Crisis (I): An Army Divided and Losing its Way.* International Crisis Group. https://www.crisisgroup.org/africa/central-africa/burundi/insights-burundian-crisis-i-army-divided-and-losing-its-way.

Von Dyck, Christopher. 2018. *DDR and SSR in War-to-Peace Transition.* London: Ubiquity Press.

Wantchekon, Leonard. 2000. "Credible Power-Sharing Agreements: Theory with Evidence from South Africa and Lebanon." *Constitutional Political Economy* 11: 339–352.

Washington Post. 2012. "Iraq Confirms Arrest of Minister's Bodyguards." December 21. https://www.washingtonpost.com/world/middle_east/iraq-confirms-arrest-of-ministers-bodyguards/2012/12/21/df60b1c6-4b9f-11e2-9a42-d1ce6d0ed278_story.html.

Watt, Nigel. 2008. *Burundi: The Biography of a Small African Country.* London: Hurst Publishers.

2006. *We Flee When We See them.* Human Rights Watch.

Wilen, Nina. 2016. "From Foe to Friend? Army Integration after War in Burundi, Rwanda and the Congo." *International Peacekeeping* 23 (1): 79–106.

Willy Nindorera, Willy. 2012. "The CNDD-FDD in Burundi: The Path from Armed to Political Struggle." *Berghof Transitions Series* (10): 1–35.

Wittig, Katrin. 2016. "Politics in the Shadow of the Gun: Revisiting the Literature on 'Rebel-to-Party Transformations' through the Case of Burundi." *Civil Wars* 18 (2): 137–159.

Witty, David M. 2018. *Iraq's Post-2014 Counter Terrorism Service.* The Washington Institute for Near East Policy. https://www.washingtoninstitute.org/uploads/Documents/pubs/PolicyFocus157-Witty-3.pdf.

2002. *World Bank Project Appraisal Document for PELRP.* World Bank.

1996. *World Bank Technical Annex EDRP.* World Bank.

2018. *World Report 2018 - Iraq.* Human Rights Watch. https://www.refworld.org/docid/5a61ee64a.html.

Wright, Quincy. 1926. *The American Political Science Review* 20 (4): 743–769.

Yassine-Hamdan, Nahla, and Frederic S. Pearson. 2014. *Arab Approaches to Conflict Resolution: Mediation, Negotiation and Settlement of Political Disputes.* New York: Routledge.

Younis, Nussaibah. 2011. "Set up to Fail: Consociational Political Structures in post-war Iraq." *Contemporary Arab Affairs* 4 (1): 1–18.

Newspapers and Magazines

Al-Akhbar
Al-Hawadith
Al-Jundi al-Lubnani Bulletin
Al-Modon
Annahar
Ash-shira'
Al-Wasat
Majallat al-Jaish [The Army Journal] (Lebanon)
The Army's Magazine (Lebanon)
The Daily Star
Official Gazette of Bosnia and Herzegovina

Websites

https://www.lebarmy.gov.lb
https://lb.usembassy.gov
www.danas.org/programi/haaska
www.balkaninsight.com
www.nato.int
www.ohr.int
http://www.mod.gov.ba
http://mdnac.bi/?q=content/historique-du-mdnac
https://www.un.org/press/en/2004/sc8101.doc.htm,
http://unscr.com/en/resolutions/doc/1719
https://amisom-au.org/burundi/
https://www.unhcr.org/news/briefing/2018/2/5a79676a4/burundi-risks-becoming-forgotten-refugee-crisis-support.html#:~:text=Since%202015%2C%20more%20than%20400%2C000,and%20the%20related%20humanitarian%20crisis.

https://www.ohchr.org/Documents/HRBodies/HRCouncil/CoIBurundi/ReportHRC39/A_HRC_39_63_EN.pdf

https://www.securitycouncilreport.org/atf/cf/%7B65BFCF9B-6D27-4E9C-8CD3-CF6E4FF96FF9%7D/s_2019_837.pdf

Primary Documents

Al-Wathīka ad-Dusturiyah [The Historical Document], 26 July 1941

Arusha Peace and Reconciliation Agreement for Burundi, 28 August 2000

Cairo Agreement, 3 November 1969

Constitution of Burundi

Constitution of Iraq

Constitution of Lebanon

Constitution of the Socialist Federal Republic of Yugoslavia

CPA Order Number 2

CPA Order Number 22

CPA Order Number 28

CPA Order Number 67

CPA Order Number 69

Crosthwaire to F.O., no. 5, 5 January 1962

Dayton Agreement

Department of Defense, "Measuring Stability and Security in Iraq, Quarterly Report to Congress," May 2006

FO 371/20013/E 6797/1419/93, 30 October 1936

FO 371/23217/E 2372/72.93, 28 February 1939

FO 371/40028/E3302/26, 23 May 1944

Kānūn aj-Jaish [The Law of the Army], 10 April 1953 and 19 January 1955

National Defense Law, 16 September 1983 (Lebanon)

Law no. 31, 5 March 2016 (Iraq)

Law no. 1/022 of 31 December 2004 (Burundi)

Law on Defense of Bosnia and Herzegovina

Law on the Intelligence and Security Agency of Bosnia and Herzegovina

Organic law no. 1/04 of 20 February 2017 (Burundi)

Organic law no. 1/17 of 11 July 2019

Slocombe, Walter. "Speech - Foreign Press Center, Washington DC," 17 September 2003

The Bonn Powers of the Office of High Representative in Bosnia-Herzegovina

The Defense Reform Commission, 2003, (BiH)

The Law of the Popular Mobilization Units Commission Number 40 for the Year 2016

The Pretoria Protocol on Outstanding Political, Defense and Security Power Sharing Issues in Burundi

The Taif Accord, 1989

World Bank Project Appraisal Document for PELRP," 2002, (BiH)

World Map Technical Annex EDRP, 1996, (BiH)

Index

Abdel Aziz Ahdab 43, 170
Abdul-Karim Qassim 47, 105–108, 110
Abdul Salam Arif 108–109, 110
Adolphe Nshimirimana 156, 161–162
Amal Movement 44, 48, 55, 183
Armée du Levant 31
Armed Forces of Bosnia-Herzegovina
 (AFBiH) 70, 74, 76, 81–84, 86–89,
 90–97, 174
Army Commander 1, 7, 13, 29, 33–34, 184,
 189, 194
Army of Republika Srpska (VRS) 78
Arusha Protocol/Arusha Agreement/
 Arusha 8, 137, 144–153, 155, 158,
 161, 163–165, 171, 181, 186
Assyrian(s) 101–102

Baabda 44
Baath, Baath Party 7, 98, 106–110, 114–118,
 136, 159, 167, 171, 184
Baghdad 2, 99, 102, 106–107, 111–112, 115,
 123–124, 126–129, 131–132, 134, 169,
 170, 173
Bakir Sidqi 101–103
Bechara al-Khoury 33
Beirut 1, 30, 33, 35–38, 41, 43–44, 47–61,
 67, 103
Belgrade 78–79, 81
Bosnia-Herzegovina (BiH)/Bosnia 2, 4, 7, 9,
 21, 24, 25, 28, 70–71, 74–81, 83–89,
 91–96, 119, 165–168, 173–175, 177, 179,
 188–189
Bosniak 24, 70, 74, 76–80, 84, 91, 93–95, 181
Brigade 43, 47–48, 50–51, 54, 56, 84, 88–89,
 91, 109, 111–112, 119, 124, 127–128,
 133–135, 157, 179, 181, 187
Bshamoun 32
Burundi 137–169, 171–173, 175–178, 180–183,
 186–192
Burundi Democratic Front (Frodebu)
 143–145, 147
Bururi 8, 139, 140, 141, 144, 166

Chain of Command 13–14, 72, 83, 86–88,
 93, 95, 111, 113, 127, 134, 150, 155, 157–158,
 164, 171, 175–176, 180, 186–187

Chief of Staff 41, 47, 49, 95, 120, 150, 156,
 162, 178
Christian 24, 29, 30, 35–39, 42–47, 52, 55–56,
 65, 99, 105, 143, 178, 181
Civil-Military Relations (CMR) 3–6, 8–12, 14,
 16–17, 22, 24–25, 28–29, 37–38, 42,
 51, 56, 64, 70, 73, 77–83, 86–91, 94,
 99–101, 103–104, 109–110, 114–115,
 117, 123, 125–126, 130–132, 150, 161,
 165, 167–168, 171, 173, 175–180, 182,
 187–189
CNDD-FDD 14, 137, 145–149, 152–153, 155–161,
 163–164, 171–173, 180–181, 186–187
Coalition Provisional Authority (CPA)
 115–122, 124, 177, 180
Commander in Chief 22–23, 49, 109, 126–
 128, 130, 132, 150, 168–170, 172, 176, 180
Consociationalism 21, 23, 25, 36, 145, 168, 189
Collective Presidency 24, 79, 83, 85–86,
 88–89, 91, 173–175, 179, 189
Counter Terrorism Service (CTS) 120, 125,
 127–129, 135, 181
Corruption 14, 38, 93, 122–123, 130, 170, 173,
 185
Croat/Croatian 24, 70–81, 84, 85, 91–96, 119,
 166–167, 174, 181
Cyrille Ndayirukiye 155–156

Dayton Accord/Agreement 76–79, 182
De-Baathification 115–117, 131
Deeply Divided/Deeply Divided
 Society(ies) 2, 4, 5, 8–9, 12, 15–17,
 21, 24, 28, 34, 39, 52, 66, 69, 70,
 75, 94, 137, 139, 150, 165, 168–169,
 174–177, 188–191
Defense Reform Commission (DRC) 82
Deuxième bureau 29, 38, 41–42
Disband 94, 101, 104–105, 110, 115, 118–120,
 124, 131–132, 150, 184–185
Disintegration 3–4, 5, 7, 27, 33, 37–38, 42, 67,
 70–71, 74, 95, 97, 124, 136, 169, 173,
 180, 184, 187, 190, 192
Division(s) 4, 8–9, 28–29, 31, 34, 50, 53, 62,
 67, 86, 102–103, 105, 107, 111–114,
 119–121, 124, 126–130, 134, 144, 150,
 161, 183, 188, 190

INDEX
215

Domitien Ndayizeye   147
Druze   1, 30, 35, 40, 43–45, 47, 52, 54, 56, 61,
    65, 181

Egypt/ian   12, 15, 106–108
Emile Lahoud   1, 57, 59, 174
Esprit de corps   3, 7, 123, 190
Ethnurgy   12, 16, 166, 168
ex-FAB   149, 153, 155–157, 171, 180–181, 186

Fouad Shihab   7, 29, 33–38, 40–42, 52, 59, 169
Federation of Bosnia-Herzegovina (FBiH)
    77–79, 81–84, 86–87, 92, 94–95
Female   55, 65–66
Forces Armées du Burundi (FAB)   139–140,
    145, 149, 152–153, 155–157, 163
Force de Défense Nationale (FDN)   149,
    151–153, 163, 177

George Bush   80, 117, 121, 127, 135
Godefroid Niyombare   155–156
Golden Square   104–105

Hutu(s)   23–24, 137–150, 153, 155–157, 161–164,
    166–167, 169, 171, 181, 186–187, 191

Imbonerakure   157–162, 164, 171–172, 183, 186
Institutional reform(s)   6, 45, 48, 67, 80,
    82, 83, 84, 86, 149, 150, 154
Intelligence   19, 22–23, 29, 36, 38, 49, 51,
    55–56, 70–71, 80–81, 84–85, 87–91,
    93, 97, 100, 112–113, 115–118, 121–122,
    125, 132, 150–153, 155–161, 163–164,
    167, 171, 175, 180
Intelligence and Security Agency (OSA)
    84–86, 92
Iraq   2, 4, 5, 7, 8, 9, 13–14, 16, 21–25, 28, 30, 34,
    56, 80, 90, 93, 98–129, 130–135, 159,
    165–173, 175–178, 180–192
Iraqi Armed Forces (IAF)   98, 111, 114–116, 118,
    120, 122–125, 130, 133–136
Iraqi Civil Defense Corps (ICDC)   116, 119,
    121, 123
ISIS   2, 7, 12, 28, 32, 37–38, 43, 61–62, 65, 98,
    123–126, 130–133, 135–136, 170, 172,
    175, 180, 184–185, 190

Jean-Baptiste Bagaza   140–142
Joint Operations Command (JOC)   126, 132
Julius Nyerere   145–146

Kurd(s)/Kurdish   22, 24, 99, 102–103,
    105–106, 108, 110, 114, 117, 120–121,
    124–127, 129, 166–167, 181–182, 185
Kirkuk   103, 108

La Légion d'Orient   30
Law on defense (Bosnia-Herzegovina)
    82–84, 87–88, 93, 179
League of Communists   72–73, 75, 167
Legitimacy   2, 4, 6, 13–14, 16, 20–21, 30, 34,
    38–40, 42–45, 52, 57, 59–60, 63,
    65, 71, 74, 85, 87, 96, 99, 104, 113,
    133, 135–136, 151, 154, 159, 163, 166,
    168–170, 173–174, 182, 187, 190–191
Lebanese Armed Forces (LAF)   29–30,
    33–37, 42–48, 51–69, 175, 177
Lebanon   30–37, 39, 40–48, 51, 52, 53–64,
    66–67, 69, 165, 168–169, 171, 173–175,
    177, 178–184, 186–187, 189, 191, 192
Louis Rwagasore   139, 140, 163

Maronite(s)   13, 23, 35, 36, 46–47, 52, 55, 65,
    169–170, 178
Melchior Ndadaye   140, 143–144
Michel Micombero   140–141, 163
Minister/ry of Defense   22, 39, 41, 48–51,
    65–66, 72–73, 77–79, 82–84, 86–90,
    93–95, 110–111, 115–118, 120–121, 141,
    150–151, 156, 174–175, 177–179
Morris Janowitz/Janowitzian   3, 4, 11–14,
    35, 188
Mosul   2, 99, 122, 124, 126–127, 130–131, 134
Mouvement des Etudiants Progressistes du
    Burundi (MEPROBA)   144
Muramvya   139
Muslim   24, 29, 35–37, 39, 42–47, 52, 55–56,
    74, 168–169, 178, 181

Nasser/ist   106–109
National Defense Law (NDL)   48–49, 51,
    66, 68
National Intelligence Service (SNR)   159–160
National Security Council (NSC)   110, 132
National Service Law   102
NATO   70, 76–82, 92–94, 96–97, 100, 123,
    174, 182
Nelson Mandela   145–146

Office of High Representative (OHR)   77,
    81–82, 95, 179

Office of the Commander–in-Chief 126–127, 132
Officer corps 5, 10–11, 13–14, 17, 35–36, 38, 42, 47, 55–56, 64, 73–75, 98, 103, 105, 107–108, 110, 112, 116, 143, 153, 161, 166–167, 177, 181–182, 187, 191
Orao 78, 80–81, 90, 95

Palipehutu-FNL 144–148, 153
Partnership for Peace (PfP) 80, 82
Paul Bremer 115–117, 120
Peshmerga 108, 124, 135
Pierre Buyoya 140, 143–144, 146–147, 149
Pierre Nkurunziza 141, 148, 155–158, 161–163, 171, 186
Popular Mobilization Forces (PMF) 125, 131–136, 159, 172–173, 183, 185–186
Post–conflict 3–4, 6, 8–9, 15, 17–21, 25–29, 77, 92–93, 149, 165, 176–177, 181–182, 188–190, 192
President 1–3, 7, 14–15, 21–24, 29–33, 35–38, 40–44, 48–52, 57, 59, 66–68, 77, 79, 82, 86, 87, 90, 109, 111, 113, 117, 127, 129, 137, 140–150, 152, 155, 157–164, 168–171, 174–175, 178–180, 186, 188–189
Pretoria Protocol 145, 147–148, 153, 163, 171

Republican Guards 109–111, 113
Republika Srpska (RS) 77–78, 179

Saddam Hussein/Saddam 52, 80, 98–101, 103–104, 109–115, 117–123, 125, 128, 131–132, 136, 159, 167, 182
Samuel Huntington/Huntingtonian 3, 10–12, 14, 188
Security Sector Reform (SSR) 6, 9, 17, 19–21, 25, 28, 70, 77, 82, 84, 91–92, 154, 189–190
Semi–consociationalism 3–10, 21–23, 165, 168–169, 171–173, 175–176, 178, 180, 182, 186–189
Serb/Serbian 2, 5, 7, 13, 24, 70–71, 73–81, 84, 91, 93, 95–97, 166–167, 174, 181

Shiite(s) 22–24, 35, 43–45, 47–48, 55, 57, 65, 99, 102–103, 105, 108, 110, 114, 116–117, 120–121, 123, 125–126, 129, 132–135, 166–167, 169–170, 172–173, 181–185, 187
Sunni(s) 1, 7, 8, 13, 22–23, 35, 37, 43, 45, 47, 52, 55, 61–62, 65, 99, 103–106, 109–110, 114, 116–117, 120–121, 125–127, 129–132, 135–136, 165–167, 170, 172, 175, 180–182, 184–185
Standing Committee on Military Matters (SCMM) 79, 81–82, 84, 89, 179–180
Structural reform(s) 6, 45, 47–48, 81–82, 86, 90–91, 150, 152
Syria 1–2, 4, 6–7, 13, 30–32, 34, 36, 39–40, 44–46, 52–53, 56–63, 68, 98–100, 106, 131

Taif Accord/Agreement 7, 30, 36, 44–45, 48, 52–53, 57–58, 65, 67–68, 165, 169
Teritorijalna Odbrana (TO) 71
Tikrit(is) 110, 112, 124, 131, 167
Troupes Auxiliaires du Levant 31
Troupes Spéciales du Levant 31, 35
Troupes Supplétives du Levant 31
Turkman/Turcoman 105, 122
Tutsi(s) 8, 13, 23, 25, 137, 138–150, 152–153, 155–156, 161–163, 165–166, 171, 181–182, 186
Twa 138

Union Pour le Progrès National (UPRONA) 139, 141–142, 146–148, 163, 166

Vinnel Corporation 119

Walter Slocombe 119–121

Yazidi 105
Yugoslav People's Army (JNA) 71–76, 97, 167
Yugoslavia 2, 5, 7, 13, 70–73, 75, 79, 96, 166–168

www.ingramcontent.com/pod-product-compliance
Lightning Source LLC
Chambersburg PA
CBHW071354290426
44108CB00014B/1542